MY LIFE
HERE AND THERE

From a photograph by Pach Bros.

PRINCESS CANTACUZÈNE, COUNTESS SPÉRANSKY, NÉE GRANT.

MY LIFE
HERE AND THERE

BY

PRINCESS CANTACUZÈNE
COUNTESS SPÉRANSKY
NÉE GRANT

WITH ILLUSTRATIONS

WILDSIDE PRESS

PRINTED AT
THE SCRIBNER PRESS
NEW YORK, U. S. A.

TO

MIKE, BERTHA, AND IDA

THIS TALE OF THEIR MOTHER'S YOUTH
AND OF THEIR OWN
IS OFFERED IN MEMORY OF
THE HAPPY DAYS SPENT TOGETHER

FOREWORD

The amiable reception my readers gave to my articles in the *Saturday Evening Post*, with the encouragement of Mr. Lorimer and Charles Scribner's Sons, has led to my reproducing my story in this form.

It pretends to no value, save as being a sincere first-hand impression of people and events in themselves often important, among whom and through which I lived an interesting life till the period of the World War.

I have written entirely from memory, possessing no documents by which I could verify my recollections, but from the comments of witnesses who have written to me, I believe my assertions will be generally found correct. I therefore venture to present my volume to the public with gratitude for kindness in the past, and a prayer for sympathy and understanding now!

JULIA CANTACUZÈNE SPÉRANSKY,

NÉE GRANT.

NEW YORK, May 1, 1921.

CONTENTS

ILLUSTRATIONS

MY LIFE, HERE AND THERE

CHAPTER I

CHILDHOOD IMPRESSIONS

I READ recently the first chapter of his memoirs, written by a small boy friend of mine. He described with enthusiasm the day he was born; how well he remembered his sister and mother were walking in the garden of his beautiful home when the father came out of the house and announced to them the safe arrival of the new member of the family—himself!

My memory does not run back so far as his, and it is from the many tellings of my favorite story in very early youth that I learned of a brave and handsome boy who when he was twelve or thirteen ran away from school three times. The first time he went to his father on the battle-field. The latter promptly returned him to his teachers; so a second time he joined the soldiers of his father's army and was found among them by a staff officer, who brought him to the general's camp. There the boy was reprimanded and again sent to his studies, only to leave them and reach the army a third time, just before Vicksburg. Finally the father, won by his son's intense sportiness and his adoration for the general himself, kept this young soldier with him, let him fit himself into the stress and strain and hardship of the camp with a commander who lived more uncomfortably than any one about him. A pony was found and an extra cot. At night father and son slept side by side in the general's tent; or the boy lay half-asleep, vaguely conscious of the silent man who walked up and down, pondered over maps, planning coming battles and campaigns, and then sat down to write his orders for the morrow's action.

By day father and son rode forth for inspections, or to some point from which the general was to watch and guide the fighting. Always they were together. Seemingly this big-hearted, devoted boy was never in the way of the commander, and the latter late in life told with delight of the courage under fire and the cheerful acceptance of discomfort shown by his younger partner in the game of war.

"Fred never knew what it was to be afraid," my grandfather would say with a tone of quiet triumph, when he had finished telling some little incident his memory retained of Vicksburg's siege and the months after it. "Fred" didn't like my grandfather's table, though, and he used to go off and mess with the troops by way of variety sometimes. Among these men he gained a popularity which he kept through all his life. On his side he learned to love our soldiers with an affection which never changed.

By his father's side he entered Vicksburg, on the 4th of July, 1863. From then on he remained at the front, and when in 1865 peace came, the boy of fifteen had two years of steady campaigning to his credit, with a fund of experience which aged him, but also was of great service through his later career. After the war followed a year of hard preparatory study, and the young veteran entered West Point. Discipline at the academy was hard, doubtless, on any one who had roamed over battle-fields, and his high spirits kept this particular cadet in hot water; but his excellence at mathematics with a talent for all that concerned horses and drill, shooting, or other military work, helped him to win his pardon always, and he finally came through West Point all right.

As General Sherman's aide-de-camp a trip to Europe gave the full-fledged second lieutenant his first view of foreign lands, and he had the interesting experience of being in France just after the Franco-Prussian War, of visiting the Near East, and from there going into the Caucasus, where he stayed at Tiflis with the then viceroy —the Grand Duke Michael, son of Emperor Nicholas I and younger brother of Alexander II. From Tiflis his host sent my father north with one of his own aides-de-camp, who was to make the trip as a special messenger, carrying reports to the Emperor. Together the two young officers hurried across Russia's vast steppes toward Moscow. My father fell in love with the mysterious beauty of the plains stretching out on each side of his travelling-carriage—plains where the only noises were the beating hoofs of troika horses and the music of their bells. Nights passed when our travellers slept in post-houses by the wayside, or they accepted the gentle hospitality of amiable Russians, anxious to help and welcome strangers. Weeks of ever-changing impressions these, too picturesque to be fatiguing. Then came a stay in Moscow, whence Russia's one and only railroad took them to St. Petersburg.

Here again the good-looking young officer received a warm welcome. Grand Duke Michael had warned his wife, and the Grand Duchess Olga Feodorowna (born a princess of Baden) received the stranger with kindly hospitality, making him at home in her palace on the quay. Her guest never forgot the delight of this visit and the charm of those who were so good to him in his youth.

Returning home in 1872, he actively fought Indians in our Far West, took part in the work of our government's surveying parties in Montana and out in the dry Arizona deserts, where he lived for a time the adventurous poetic life of the opening Far West.

As the next step in his career, my father became attached to the staff of General Sheridan, who was stationed in Chicago. There, in 1874, he met a very pretty young girl, fresh from her graduation at the convent at Georgetown, where she had carried off first honors. Rapidly a romance developed. He was twenty-four, she twenty, when they were married in October, 1874. The country home of Mr. and Mrs. Honoré was the frame of a brilliant scene. The bride's parents were among Chicago's most attractive and constructive people, while the bride and her sister were both of rare individual beauty and charm. General Sheridan and his whole staff in gala uniform were present, and the bridegroom was surrounded by a family group consisting of the President of the United States and many of the latter's distinguished followers and friends, all come to see the happy officer married. The sun shone and music played for the simple ceremony, which was most informal in spite of its brave show of historic names and beautiful faces.

Then the bridal couple went to live at the White House, from where young Colonel Grant made his long expeditions westward as before. In the capital, as in Chicago, the bride was a much-admired favorite. Two winters passed, and in June, 1876, in a quiet room, its windows looking out under the great portico of the President's mansion, a first child was born, an unusually large girl, thirteen pounds of chubby health—myself.

Many years later I returned to the White House for the first time since my babyhood, and President McKinley was kind enough to escort me up-stairs, so I might see the room which had been my first home. I found the simple dignity of undecorated walls and high ceilings attractive, and the view out into the shady garden a delight. I was lucky to start life so well. A first child of much-loved parents, and a first grandchild of such grandparents as were Ulysses S. Grant and his wife, was bound to be much petted. Many were the tales told me of my baptism, when named Julia for my Grant grandmother, and with Mrs. Honoré and the President for godparents, I was christened in the great East Room by Doctor John P. Newman, pastor of the Methodist church which my grandfather Grant attended. A small party— the family, a few intimate friends, and the cabinet stood about. It was my début in official life and it seems I behaved well.

Shortly after this my beautiful maternal grandmother-godmother made me with her own fair hands a soft long dress of mull and old Valenciennes laces, set together in quaint patterns imagined by herself, embroidered and hemstitched in the doing. For gala occasions a pair of bracelets, soft woven ribbons of gold with tiny blue hearts hanging from them, and a wee ring with a diamond like a pin-point, given me by my father's brother, Ulysses Grant, Jr., completed the list of presents which my first Christmas brought me.

I was decked out in these for the event of the season —the President's New Year's reception, 1877. I sat in my nurse's arms and behaved with calm dignity, I heard years afterward, while diplomats and legislative officers with their wives passed by, saluting the President, Mrs. Grant, and then touching gently the White House baby, admiring my rosy cheeks and all my fine clothes. Some of the foreigners even kissed my fat hand in courtly fashion, before they passed on to mix with the other ladies and gentlemen, who completed the family and cabinet circle in the receiving line.

I am sorry not to remember what must have vastly

pleased me—the beauty of the surroundings that day and the soft, glimmering lights, the pretty gowns and jewels, and the uniforms and decorations of that great throng; also the interesting faces of many Civil War heroes, or of men who with my grandfather had done the work of reconstruction in the days following the fight. But I only know all this by hearsay, and the first scenes I remember myself are quite different ones.

My personal recollections begin in a room which I could with effort walk across. It was white with a blue carpet, some vague toys stood around, and a fire burned on the hearth, with a wire screen between it and me, impossible to get through. There was a clock on the chimney-shelf which ticked, and from which others could judge it was my bedtime. On each side of the clock stood a straight turquoise-blue vase, glass or china, shiny, rather broad, and with a pink rose painted on its centre space. It was a matter of supreme interest to me to know what was inside those vases. I always looked up at them from below, and I wanted to look down from above. I think I couldn't clearly explain my desire about them; anyhow, no one ever understood till finally one day my maternal grandfather came to see me. He and I stood in front of the fireplace hand in hand, and I expressed as best I could my urgent curiosity.

With joy I heard him say: "Why, Lord bless me, honey, do you want grandpa to lift you up and let you touch the jars?"

Up I was swung to his shoulder, and there held above the blue vases. I gazed down at last in deep astonishment into their depths, and there was nothing but the flat white bottom to be seen. It was a great disappointment, though I don't know what I had expected to find.

Another important event I recall during that same

period occurred one day when my mother caught her finger in the nursery doorway and gave a little cry. My father came in hurriedly, kissed her and the finger, and helped to put a wet handkerchief on it, while I stood by and watched with interest. I hadn't known before that grown-ups ever hurt themselves.

Later we moved into another house, about which I remember more. First of all, the move itself was of vast interest, and the discussions as to where my bed and where my toys would stand and how the pet canary and my favorite doll would travel across Chicago gave me a feeling of adventure. Soon after this change, came my third birthday, with the first cake I can recall, and a party, consisting of my young uncle—afterward Judge Lockwood Honoré—and my two cousins, Honoré and Potter Palmer. Then memories pile up rapidly. Trips up and down stairs alone gave me opportunities for new discoveries, till one day one of my cousins and I rolled down a flight together. My nose was injured and had to wear splints and plasters for a time, and negotiating stairs without help was forbidden me.

My nursery windows looked into the yard of an orphan asylum, and Nurse Bridget threatened me with bringing in a poor child to replace me, when I was naughty. I went to table soon with my parents and took part in the conversation—and I watched and admired my mother's embroidery and the water-colors which my father painted in the evenings. For many years, till the Russian Revolution brought about its destruction in our home, a little picture of a green field with a brown rock, occupied by three vague white-and-reddish cows, hung on my sitting-room wall, recalling those old days of my childish pleasure in my father's play-hour productions. My contribution to the family circle's life was reciting "Mother

Goose" and kindred poems, and I felt extremely important in the encouragement and praise my efforts drew
from my select audience.

Once my father went away for quite a time, to go
around the world, and mama and I kept house by ourselves, with frequent visits to my cousins or my grandmother. A Christmas-tree, an excursion and picnics on
the sandy beach of Lake Michigan during those months,
stay fast in my mind even now.

Then we left for the West. I recall suddenly being
waked up and dressed in the night on a train which
moved slowly amid shouting crowds. It stopped, and I
was picked up and carried out in some one's arms from
our car to a large open carriage. On the back seat were
already installed Grandfather and Grandmother Grant,
freshly arrived from their journey round the world, and
all about us was a great sea of faces—men's and women's.
Torches, quantities of them, burned, flared up and
smoked, then flickered down, throwing changing lights
on faces which to my child's imagination looked wild
with excitement. As a matter of fact, the owners were
just then receiving a national hero with all the enthusiasm they could display. Every mouth was open, and
hurrah after hurrah filled the air about as completely as
the illuminated faces filled my horizon. "Grant! Grant!
Welcome Grant!" "Hurrah for Grant!" "Hurrah!
Grant! Grant!"

My grandfather sat absolutely quiet in his place, amid
bedlam let loose, but for the first time I remember the
depth and power of his eyes, and how dark they seemed,
though they shone. Grandmama, on the contrary,
waved her hand and bowed and smiled. She was delighted and expressed her delight to her husband, to my
mother, to every one, in fact. Just as I was handed in

to my mother, very frightened by the noise, the vast crowd lurched forward and seemed to be upon us. Hats and hands were waved wildly. If possible, the cheering increased, and shouts of "Move on! Start!" "Unspan those horses! We'll draw the carriage! Wait!" "Hurrah, hurrah for Grant! Grant! Grant!" rent the air again and again. More and more panic-stricken, I hid my head on my mother's lap, and it took some encouragement to make me feel brave again. But I was just regaining my nerve when a sympathetic person in the crowd, which was closer than ever to us, stretched out a hand and touched me. With a shriek I collapsed in my mother's arms, and after that saw nothing more. I was reproached, and my eyes were wiped and my nose blown, and though I hadn't the bravery to look about, by the time we reached our destination I had recovered, and could calmly stand being taken out of the carriage and into the hotel lobby. We had arrived and my torture was over, but for a long time I felt ashamed, and it was a considerable relief to find that most of the grown people did not seem to hold my bad behavior up against me.

Nearly forty years afterward, at the time of the Bolshevik uprisings in Russia, I saw enormous mobs which strained every one's nerves, and I was then as much frightened as anybody; but even in 1917 I was less routed than I felt myself to be when that great hearty American crowd shouted its welcome to my quiet grandfather at Colorado Springs on his return from his triumphant trip around the world.

We stayed there awhile, and in the hotel grown-ups and babies led much the same life. I made friends with these grandparents whom I did not remember, and attached myself to both. Grandmama was delightful; she let me come to see her dress, allowed me to touch all her dainty clothes, and even to try on a ribbon now and then—while in a special corner I found there was a little box or jar kept always half-hidden. Only she and I knew this secret, she said, and somehow the supply of goodies to be found there was inexhaustible and varied—cookies, dried prunes, small apples, peppermints, and so on, followed one another, each better than the last, and always leaving me eager for to-morrow's surprise. Grandmama was gay, knew poetry and stories, and was a human, sunny friend, and a sympathizer to little people about, most of all to her small namesake, the first—and then the only one—of the new generation.

With my grandfather my relations were quite different. He wasn't exactly gay, and I do not remember his laughing ever, but the talk between us was very interesting. He always took me seriously. I felt promoted and inclined to live up to my new position as his companion. Sometimes he would pinch my ear or my cheek and say softly, "Julianna Johnson, don't you cry," and it rather teased me. But generally he held my pudgy dimpled hand on the palm of his, and we learned to count the fingers and dimples together; sometimes I made a mistake and sometimes he did so, letting me correct him. And he taught me "cat-cradle" with a string. We walked together hand in hand, silent, frequently, but at other moments talking of our surroundings, and he called me habitually "my pet" or "my big pet," which made me very proud. I was not at all afraid of him, for he had a charming, gentle way of acting always, and though his face was generally grave, now and then a sudden gleam lighted up the eyes and made them seem to smile in answer to my chatter.

After the little stay at Colorado Springs we all travelled together up to Galena, and I finally overcame my fear of the crowds which were at every station, shouting their welcome to us, hurrahing and waving. The people would surround my window and give me flowers, or ask me for one of those which I had; "for a souvenir," they said. They made me tell them things and then they would laugh and applaud, and I grew to feel I was very important to the party, and that my small private reception was part of the general ovation to Grant. I heard afterward, though I have no memory of the occurrence, that some one asked me if I was a little American or a little foreigner, and I answered emphatically: "I am a Gwant!" I remember being teased about this pretentious remark for many years after it was made.

At Galena we stayed with the grandparents, who returned to their wee cottage there, where they had lived before the outbreak of the war. Grandmama offered me the garden, and I gave up everything else and went in for mud pies, while all the world passed by me in and out of the garden-gate and cottage-door. Handsome big men and many an elegant woman in her best frills came to the modest cottage. After four years on battle-fields and eight in the White House, with their tour of European and Asiatic palaces thrown in, it spoke well for this prominent couple that they contentedly returned to their old place to settle down. We soon left them, and went back to our own house in Chicago.

There I remember many faces vaguely among my mother's friends, but all these were dominated. by the personality most in view, General Philip H. Sheridan. Very different from my grandfather he was, but also with qualities which won and held the devotion of those who served with him, and which made him a social favorite always. I remember him well, for his daughter and I were playmates, and her father would drop in to her nursery, and speak with us on his way in or out. He had a low-pitched but rather loud voice, an easy, merry laugh or chuckle, and a warm, strong way of shaking hands. I believe he was short, but to our small figures he seemed tall enough to be impressive, and he moved rather quickly. He did not have much hair, whether because of baldness or because the head was close-clipped, I don't recall; a round face with fine lines, however, a good nose, and large blue, expressive eyes. These changed constantly in expression—beamed with fun or looked suddenly tender and sad. All warmth and sympathy and Celtic charm as he passed through his children's rooms was the general who led cavalry with such genius.

My father, on this commander's staff, was more in Chicago and less in the Far West, and once he and my mother both went away, leaving me with my lovely aunt—my mother's sister, Mrs. Palmer—during their trip. It was a new experience for me to be visiting and alone, without my own parents, and I had several impressive experiences, one being the family Christmas-tree, the only really large, fine one I had ever seen. Arranged in the evening, it took on great importance in my sight by that fact. Besides, I fancy I was allowed a little more candy, and was given an extra amount of spoiling because I was a visitor. Certainly I enjoyed extremely the excitement of my position in their absence, though I hailed my parents' return with delight. They had been to Mexico, they told me—an official visit which my grandfather made to President Diaz. General Sheridan had accompanied my grandfather, and my father went as aide-de-camp to Sheridan, while there were several important civilians in the party also. Grandmama went, and all the other wives as well—a gay, clever group round the great central figure. They brought back tales which thrilled me for years, and are still told now by my mother to my interested little daughters. The party had had much attention naturally; a splendid ovation was given to my grandfather, and in Mexico City there were fêtes, receptions, and illuminations on the pattern of those Europe and Asia had offered him a few years earlier. I fancy he did not especially enjoy these, but the ladies did. They loved the "daumont" carriages, the parades and pretty clothes, Spanish fans, silver and gold filigree work, willing young Spanish aides-de-camp, and the new and unexpected customs governing life in the large stone palaces where Diaz's will was supreme law. The latter was in the heyday of his power and talent then, and he and my grandfather held many a serious conference which influenced American relations with Mexico through the decades which followed, and helped on friendly understanding and constructive work between the two countries.

All the party shopped, and came home laden with quaint old or modern creations of Spanish hands and brains. Even my grandfather made a purchase; grandmama had a string of quite large pearls, somewhat irregular but of lovely sheen and color, which he had bought her in Mexico City. She was delighted with them and he was pleased, too, I remember. I was deeply impressed with the necklace, because I was taken on her lap and allowed to feel its weight and beauty. She told me that when I should be grown up the pearls would be mine, because I was her namesake; and my grandfather added: "Those are pearls I bought for Julia Grant, and you are Julia Grant, my pet." Through the years thereafter, whenever I was near, I was allowed to fasten the necklace on grandmama, and always as he looked on, smiling, my grandfather would say: "My pet, your grandmama is wearing your pearls again. Do you like her to wear them?" And I did.

When I was five years old a new experience came in my small life. We spent a summer with my mother's sister and my uncle Palmer at their country place just outside of Chicago; and no one who has lived in the country, always taking its pleasures for granted, can realize the joys which a small city girl finds in her first prolonged stay among trees and birds, with a garden-patch to work in for her very own, and lawns to sit and roll on; two boy cousins, also, as daily companions. It seemed a garden of paradise we lived in during the summer of 1881. I had a slight illness, caused perhaps by too many strawberries or cherries, but I was getting well rapidly. I lay in bed still one evening in a little room off my mother's, and was to be allowed up definitely next day when suddenly my lovely aunty came in and took me in her arms, carrying me into her own room, "to pay me a little visit," she said. She tucked me into her own big bed, where I fell asleep.

Early the next morning I was awakened by what I thought was a cat mewing, only it seemed rather loud. Then nurse came in and told me to dress quickly like a good girl, because there was to be a surprise for the two cousins and me as soon as we were ready. I asked about that cat; maybe there was one lost in the house some-where, the nurse said. She was distracted and uncom-municative. She got through with me rapidly and sent me into my aunt's dressing-room, where the latter was doing her hair while talking to my two cousins, who were there before me, and who looked impressed. I joined them with a beating heart, and heard that a brand-new baby boy had arrived in the house, and that because I

COLONEL FREDERICK DENT GRANT AND MRS. GRANT, FATHER AND MOTHER OF PRINCESS CANTACUZÈNE.

had no brother, while the two cousins had one another, this baby was to be mine.

I grew old, with swollen importance, as I listened. It was, indeed, great news! One of the cousins took it quietly, while from the other came a storm of protest and tears. He didn't think it fair; the baby was born in their house and ought to be theirs; I was a girl and always was given everything, anyhow; and, besides, he was the eldest, and this first baby should by right go to him. I trembled with anxiety that my acquisition should slip from me, but I kept a dignified silence while the question was thrashed out. I felt all my cousin's arguments to be both just and good, but, nevertheless, I wanted to keep this exceptional possession which kind fortune had brought me; and in the end I triumphed through my aunt's decision and diplomacy. We had a rapid breakfast, eaten under the strain of intense excitement and impatience. Then we were marshalled into an expectant procession, with my aunt's instructions to walk into my mother's room on tiptoe, sit down in three chairs which we should find there by the door, and await the baby. We might look at him but in silence, and at a signal from our guide we must then march out.

We carried out our orders, and soon after our entrance there appeared from my own old room a nurse holding a bundle. She brought it over, showed a tiny sleeping face first to the eldest, then to my second cousin, who both stared with interest. Finally she came on to me.

"Here is your little brother, dear. Would you like to hold him?" she asked. Nearly exploding with pride and joy, I nodded silently as hard as I could, and she put the bundle into my arms without quite letting it go herself. "In a few days you can help me bathe him," she said, and I felt I had discovered a new heaven and a new earth. Soon my father appeared, and he said: "Well, pet, do you like our baby brother? He is yours, you know."

The poor disappointed cousin was then given a turn at holding the baby, which consoled him a little. I imagine he didn't mind losing him when he saw the new boy was too small to do much playing yet. We were all turned out into the garden shortly after I had been told to kiss my mother quietly, as she had a headache. She smiled and said how nice it was the little brother had come. She looked very pretty but seemed tired, and they told me she wouldn't get up that day.

After that great event I was called a "big girl," and was supposed always to put on and button my own clothes, and do various other small things for myself. Mama was not quite strong for a long time. The baby was named Ulysses, for my grandfather, and I took great delight in helping with his toilet. He wore my White House finery, and he was big for his age, every one said, and very pink and white and strong, and he made a great racket when he cried. My mother was anxious about him often and held him a great deal in her arms, and sometimes when he wouldn't be quiet my father would pick him up, and with the baby's head on his broad shoulder he would croon an Indian refrain learned out on the plains long ago. Apparently it was an irresistible invitation to sleep. I heard it said the baby loved it.

My mother's health continued fragile still, and my father, who had resigned from the army, brought us all on to New York, where we went to a new house, 3 East 66th Street—a very big dark house, it seemed to me. I heard with great interest the grown-ups say it was given my grandfather by the citizens of Philadelphia. Then for a time my life was most exciting. I was very much my own mistress, as our nurse was constantly occupied by the baby, and my mother was not strong enough to do more than attend to him. Various Grant uncles and aunts came to stay in the house, and one aunt I had not known before came from England to visit my grandparents. She was Aunt Nelly—Mrs. Sartoris—and she brought with her three children, who spoke awfully funny English. They had a nurse and a governess who were very severe and almost incomprehensible to me in their talk. I found Aunt Nelly most sympathetic, with lovely eyes and smile and a gentle voice and very caressing manner, and she always wore soft clothes. I never saw much of her through the years which followed, but this impression renewed itself always when we met.

The big new house had many rooms. All the lower floors had very interesting things in them, about which grandmama told stories. For instance, the library's books were a gift to my grandfather from the city of Boston, and the beautiful bindings, richly tooled in gold, were a joy to look upon in their ebony bookcases. A great fire constantly burned in the library grate, and the flames' light played on the black-and-gold brocade of the furniture, which was a gift from the Mikado of Japan. In the front parlor gold, red, orange, green, and white were woven into another brocade from the same source, and a wonderful gold-lacquer cabinet, eleven hundred years old or more, stood as a further testimony of the Mikado's enthusiasm. Some modern lacquer furniture, duplicate of a set used by the Empress in the imperial palace in Tokio, had been given grandmama. Teakwood cabinets stood about, covered with jade or porcelain gifts from the Chinese Emperor and from Li Hung Chang, his wise old adviser. Malachite and enamels there were from Russia, with fine gifts from England and from France. Also precious documents, the freedom of various cities abroad laid in gold-wrought or bejewelled caskets, with medals given by our Congress, swords of honor, and many more souvenirs of a wonderful life filled the large, quiet rooms. Little by little I learned of their meaning, and of that of some of the fine portraits—Sheridan's on his famous ride, and several pictures of my grandfather in one rôle or another. He and my father were now going into a banking business in which one of my uncles was interested; the firm was called Grant & Ward. It was a flourishing concern, and into it my grandfather as well as my father cheerfully put what they had saved, by careful economy from their army pay. In my grandfather's case, even the fund was invested which was given him by New York City to express appreciation of his patriotic service.

My mother was still delicate, and to strengthen her we moved for the winter to a pretty cottage at Morristown, N. J. She and my father were delighted with the place, and I remember very well how interested they were in furnishing their new home, and how attractive they made it, even to my inattentive childish eyes. My mother was looking quite radiant at this time—very young still, she dressed always in charming and becoming clothes. She was much admired and fêted, and my father was enthusiastic in surrounding her with all the luxury his new business profits could offer, thus making a frame for her beauty. Our home was gay with visitors coming and going. My great delight was in our horses, especially one pair, which my father drove himself in a high phaeton, or which my mother drove harnessed to a low trap which he gave her. She had always been an accomplished and graceful horsewoman in her youth, and it was a keen delight to her to handle the ribbons again. There was a wonderful sleigh, too, low, on Russian or Swedish lines, with floating red horsehair plumes and tinkling bells. It had warm, furry robes. Sometimes I was allowed to drive out with my mother, and I was delighted then.

Morristown was a very attractive place to live, and from there occasionally we visited the grandparents again for a few weeks, either in New York or at their seashore cottage at Elberon, N. J. The latter was paradise to us children. On one corner of the large lawn a group of pine-trees sheltered us from the sun and made an ideal playground, and grandmama had had "the woods" fitted up with a swing and other arrangements dear to our hearts. Besides, each child had a tiny garden-patch, where flowers and vegetables were rivals for our care; my brother, grown a healthy toddler, had planted a melon-vine in his patch. Every time he reported, in saying good night to grandmama, that a flower bloomed on his melon-plant, he could be sure, next morning when he ran into the garden, of finding that in the blossom's place lay a ripe watermelon or a canteloupe. He immediately carried the fruit back to the house and sold it to his grandmother for ten cents. His miraculous vine became a family classic! There were big, shady balconies with hammocks at Elberon, and on one of these, just by the stairway leading to our nurseries, stood a small barrel, kept full always of home-made cookies, prepared especially for the benefit of weary, hungry children. Best of all, there was the beach, and the blue ocean to paddle and bathe in. And all these pastimes were allowed us through long, busy, happy days.

Grandmama still let me go in and help her dress. Besides, there was an offer on her part to us children, a secret arrangement which was ideal, according to which if we were any of us in trouble, or were not permitted to do one thing or another as we wanted, we were to come to her, and she would see what she could do to remedy the situation.

My grandfather evidently enjoyed us very much. He continued to call me his pet, also sometimes to sing me the old Julianna Johnson song, and he kept me with him and talked to me a great deal. A wonderful experience was when he let me go out to drive in his buggy with the fast trotters, which were his single luxury. I stood between his knees, which steadied me, and held the reins out in front of his hands, and found skimming over the good hard road as great a joy as he did. He introduced me to his two intimate friends, who spent a great deal of time at the house. One of these was Mr. George W. Childs, the other Mr. Childs's inseparable and devoted comrade, Mr. A. J. Drexel, and both old gentlemen were very nice to me. Mr. Childs often brought me gifts, which I loved. My first gold watch and a little ring which I wore all through my girlhood came from him. We had long talks when he called, and I enjoyed immensely his tales of his early struggle as a poor boy, and how Mr. Drexel and he had built up their great fortunes in Philadelphia, one in the banking business and the other through his newspaper. Both these men spent much time with my grandfather.

A person who at Elberon counted himself almost one of the family was General Horace Porter. He had been on my grandfather's staff, was handsome, dashing, with a charming manner and keen wit, and seemed an acquisition to any group. He was developing rapidly at that time into a fine business man, and making a reputation as a public speaker, also. Another one of my grandfather's circle at Elberon was Mr. George M. Pullman, already at the head of his great business—a strong, grim personality, with a glint of humor sometimes in his eye; a very different type from the gentle one of Mr. Childs, and the artistic, quiet temperament of Mr. Drexel. Often I watched the group gather round grandmama at the corner of the piazza which commanded the best ocean view and breeze. She and my mother talked gaily, and the men joined in. My grandfather would sit quietly, his face relaxed, an amused or interested look in his expressive eyes. He talked little, but now and then he would take the cigar from his lips and place a few words, asking a pointed question, making a comment or even telling some anecdote, always with the simple manner and voice habitual to him. Politics and other serious subjects came up, too, and were fully discussed, but I was too little to care for or understand these.

We had returned to Morristown, and the spring of 1884 was on. One day, when my father had gone as usual to town and my mother drove to meet the train by which he ordinarily returned, he did not arrive. A friend, coming from town, seemed surprised to see her there waiting in her victoria, and approached her, asking if she had not had a telegram. He thought perhaps my father might be kept late, he said, all night even, but he was confused in his explanations—with evident intention. Anxious, my mother returned to our pretty cottage, dined alone and went to bed, after receiving a strange wire which told her almost nothing and only created vague alarm.

The following day passed, and with the evening my father came home looking very weary, pale, and troubled. He hugged me as always, and passed on with my mother to their up-stairs sitting-room. Her cry of surprise and distress rang out, and then loud questions and quiet replies floated to the hall below, where we children sat, frightened. When they came down my mother's eyes were red, and she told me to go to bed quickly—so I went, wondering what had happened.

Next morning I learned. We hadn't any more money at all, and were to go to live at grandmama's, who seemed to have enough, for some unknown reason, to keep her home, while we must give up ours. To me it was compensation enough for any trouble to go and visit grandmama, but as the days passed I grew to feel the drama of the Grant & Ward failure and to see how much my father suffered from it. He went to town earlier and returned later. Our horses and carriages had been driven away the first day and sold. This left the stable empty, and my father drove to and from his trains on the box seat of the village grocer's wagon. To show his sympatHy the kindly man had offered to carry my father. Every day packers came to pack and move some of our furniture. It would have been fun to watch this were it not that my mother spoke so sadly of each thing which went into barrel, crate, or box, and wondered when she would have a home again. Each day my father came back to ask how nearly ready we were. I packed and unpacked my toys and little treasures in a fever of excitement and of desire to help. After a few days, perhaps a week, we had finished.

The house stood empty as we left it, starting to Elberon. It was only years later I realized the heroism of my elders at that time. How on that first dreadful morning when my father and grandfather had reached the city they had been sent for by my uncle, Ulysses, Jr., who was Ward's partner in the bank. How he had told them Ward had run away with all the funds and that the firm had failed. Practically all my father had was in this company, and what little was outside he turned at once into the common till to pay the small investors. My grandfather, in the same position, acted likewise. His house in town, long before this, at his request had been put in grandmama's name by the citizens of Philadelphia, and he had given her the Elberon cottage during his presidency, so he decided she should keep those for the moment and take the whole family in. As a last resort these, too, might be sold, however, to pay the debts of a bank which bore his name, and where poor people had invested savings because of the confidence that name inspired. All his outside funds were placed in the till drawer, and then to make up the rest of what was lacking he set out to sell what he personally possessed.

I have often heard grandmama tell the story through the years which followed, and if I remember it rightly it was this: On the second morning, after their liabilities were ascertained, my grandfather, going down-town as usual, proceeded straight to the office of old Mr. William H. Vanderbilt. There he sat down in the crowded anteroom, awaiting his turn to see the great financier. Some one coming out recognized him, and told the attendant of his presence. The latter went into the private office and warned Mr. Vanderbilt that my grandfather was in the group outside. Instantly the old gentleman came out.

"Why, general, what is this? You waiting here for anything? Come right in with me."

And my grandfather answered, hesitating: "I come with a petition, like the rest."

"Never mind, just come right into my office and tell me what I can do for you."

Once inside, he added that he had heard the bad news, and again asked how he could serve my grandfather, and the latter, greatly touched, was as brief as Mr. Vanderbilt.

"It is true, all that you heard. The firm my boy was in has failed, and though he was not the thief, his and my name were connected with it and perhaps inspired depositors to put in their money. I feel responsible, therefore, and I must pay these debts at once. I have come to you, thinking perhaps you would lend me the necessary sum, and accept the security I can offer—my gifts from various cities and the sovereigns of Europe, my swords and medals, and such other personal property as I own."

Mr. Vanderbilt replied: "I am touched that your good feeling and confidence in me brought you here to-day, General Grant. I shall consider it an honor to lend you this small sum, and I will accept no security whatever—especially not the trophies and honors which mark the record of your life."

But my grandfather was obdurate; he said he knew the security he offered was not intrinsically equal to what he was borrowing, but that as the things had to him a sentimental value, he would feel anxious to redeem them quickly. They argued for some time, till finally the rich creditor gave in to his determined debtor. My grandfather took the check, paid the liabilities of the firm for which he felt responsible, and within a day or two all the treasures from our house cabinets were sent off. Mr. Vanderbilt did not like taking them or keeping them, and he again protested, but in vain. Finally he returned them to grandmama; I think during my grandfather's last illness or just after his death. Grandmama considered she should not keep them, and with the consent of the whole family—and Mr. Vanderbilt also acquiescing, I believe—the things touching my grandfather's public life went to the Smithsonian Institution in Washington, while the swords he had actually used, his shirt-studs, and so on, were kept by the family. The loan was finally repaid from the money my grandfather's memoirs brought in.

I have no documents to go by, and I was very young when all this happened, but I heard the story often told by grandmama, and I repeat it as it returns to my mind after thirty-six years.

It was the Grant & Ward failure which took us definitely into my grandparents' household to live. There we remained inmates during four or five years. My father went on working in New York, and in his spare hours he helped my grandfather in looking up war records or documents among the latter's old papers. These were to be used for some articles my grandfather promised to a magazine, which offered him an unheard-of price, $500, for a series of several. My grandfather was greatly pleased to feel his power to support his home undiminished, in spite of the loss of his small fortune.

So the household, though augmented by additional members, leading a simpler life, perhaps, and run with greater economy, was still a contented one, courageous and busy, each doing some share toward the general comfort. A new and terrible trouble cloud, however, gathered gradually over our heads.

In the spring of 1884 my grandfather, in crossing the sidewalk from his house to his carriage one morning, had slipped on a bit of orange or banana peel, had fallen heavily, and had done his hip and leg an injury. Helped back into the house, a few days of care had prevented any serious developments, but he was left with a slight

limp and a slowness of motion in rising or seating himself, and this trouble caused him always afterward to
use a cane. The loss of his small fortune, with his con-
sequent anxiety as to the obtaining of means to keep his
home and family going, preyed on his mind. The difficulty of paying off personally all the small creditors of
the firm was a still greater problem for his keen sense of
honor to solve, and when the funds were provided by the
loan from Mr. Vanderbilt—he nevertheless continued to
feel he must redeem that obligation immediately.

The hip trouble gave him some pain, and held him to
a sedentary life, barring him practically from all exercise.
This and his weight of care aged him greatly. The
buggy and fast trotters of earlier days became an impossible luxury, and my grandfather grew gray of face as
well as of hair and beard.

When we moved to his house to live, I was for the first
time conscious he was an old man in looks. The hair
was still very thick and it waved, his face was not much
wrinkled, but it showed a few marked lines and a certain
thinness, with less color than before. The strength of
the nose was more apparent than ever; long, aquiline,
well shaped and distinguished, its character emphasized
by the fine brow with rather shaggy eyebrows.

My grandfather often wore a slight frown in those
days, which grandmama would smooth out in passing
with her tiny, beautiful hand. He always gave her a
smile then, and the cloud of trouble for the moment was
raised. I remember his smile as rather out of the ordinary, more in the eyes than in the mouth, for I do not
ever recall seeing much change in the strong, straight
line of the lips and jaw. Only the eyes glowed or grew
deep with humor and intensity. Without analyzing them,
for I was not old enough to do that, the impression

remains with me of immense reserve power for action, for enjoyment, or for suffering—behind a mask which, without being agitated, reflected all sorts of sentiments and responded instantly with sympathetic light to what was going on round him.

He was small, growing old with his lameness and his load of sadness, yet one felt his face and figure to be the centre of decision, of intellect and character, in a group where there were many people out of the ordinary. Simplest of them all, he was their master both in greatness and in perfect command of himself.

He never thought of ordering any one to do anything, never raised his voice or asserted himself; but one saw the respect, almost awe, he inspired, and the devotion given him by all who were near.

I was just eight years old, and my baby brother had grown to be a sturdy toddler of three. He was still with our nurse constantly, and I felt immediately independent by comparison. I had not lost my place with the grandparents by the fact that we had been living away from them in Morristown. While there I had begun to take lessons, including drawing, and once I had made a picture of some fruit in a basket, which I sent my grandfather as a birthday gift. This very bad drawing brought me a delightful letter from him, and I had also previously received another letter. I was so proud of them and read them so often, I think I could almost repeat them by heart, even now after thirty-six overcrowded years have passed. Each covered the whole of a note-paper sheet and began: "My dear big pet."

One was written to ask me how my lessons were getting on and to encourage me at them. "You and grandpa will have to read together when you come here to stay." "Grandpa expects his pet to know how to

read better than any one else after this year's work."
"Have you forgotten with all your lessons how to sing
Julianna Johnson?" "The buggy and fast trotters will
be waiting to take us driving as soon as vacation time
begins." All this in the first letter, which said in its
last paragraph that I must write and tell him what I
thought would be nice for my Christmas presents, "so
grandpa and grandma would have time to shop for
them."

The second letter said at the beginning: "Your mother
and father have come to pay us a visit, and we are very
sorry they didn't bring you. They brought me instead
the beautiful picture you made me for my birthday, and
I hasten to thank my big pet for all the trouble she took
to give her grandpa such a fine surprise. Grandpa hung
the present up where he can see it all the time, and I
hope when next they come to us, your father and mother
will bring you too. Love from grandma and thanks
again from grandpa."

I quote these passages from memory, because the
letters, which had been preserved through years in my
Russian home, stayed in Petrograd, and have doubtless,
with all the other small treasures of family life, fallen
into Bolshevist hands to be destroyed.

So I had kept in touch with the kind grandparents,
and was glad that loss of fortune drew us back into their
home again. We children took up a care-free life on
beach and lawn, and though our food was perhaps ordinary, and various small luxuries were suppressed, I suppose, I remember nothing of privation, save that I wore
my last year's summer gowns—which to me was entirely
satisfactory—and that the fast horses did not exist for
my grandfather to drive, with me between his knees.
These tête-à-tête parties were a feature of our life I did

miss, at any rate in the beginning, but the days were short and full of pleasant games, and we loved the Elberon cottage, anyhow.

All through the early summer my father travelled morning and evening to and from New York, busy with some work for which he was paid enough to make a contribution to the general expenses of the household. But my grandfather no longer went to town. A little room, shady and cool, furnished in simple wicker furniture, which had been called his sitting-room before, was renamed his office now, and we children were told to make our trips upstairs and down by the outside balcony-stairs, "as grandpa was working." Several times grave gentlemen with impressive manners came to the cottage and transacted business with my grandfather. Once or twice they stayed to lunch, and though every one was very polite and talked constantly, I had a feeling that these were solemn parties. However, after each visit grandmama was very cheerful and triumphant, and though I do not remember any expression of opinion from my grandfather, I know now how relieved and satisfied he must have been that his articles were a vast success, were clamored for, and brought him large checks. I heard also he was being begged to write his memoirs in book form, and had received very flattering propositions.

My father, General Porter, Mr. Drexel, and Mr. Childs were always conversing about "the book." It was to be begun at once, and grandpapa was to give his own personal record of the Civil War. It would make him rich, every one said, and they all would help him to look up any data he needed to refresh his memory. My grandfather consented readily, glad to be busy and useful still.

This was the state of things when I remember occasional remarks among various members of the family, or from the old servants, to the effect that he was not feeling quite well. Some one said he had taken cold and had a slight sore throat, and one scrap of gossip told us that he hadn't a cold but had felt his throat hurting when he had swallowed a small bit of peach skin one day; probably something was on the peach skin which scratched the delicate throat tissues. The doctor who was called in said "smoker's throat" and gave a medicine to gargle with. I assisted at the gargling often, and thought the whole thing interesting; only I was sorry my grandfather was not quite well. He was the first grown-up I had heard of as being ill; and as he moved about, always quite dressed, while he kept his usual gentle smile and kindly word for me, I was not anxious. I do not think any others of the family circle were so, at that time.

We children ate at a small table in the corner of the dining-room, an hour or so before our parents had their meals. The nurses served my cousins and me to dishes which were brought us by Charley, a young son of grandmama's old colored butler, Harrison. Charley was a friend and comrade to us, and our meals were very gay; also, we were deeply interested in Charley's future, for if his father and he made enough by the time he was eighteen he was to go to college, "and not just be a-servin' round a house," old Harrison said.

One day the usual conversation was being carried out under the usual conditions—our French Louise urging us to hurry and finish our noon beef and potatoes, "so when all the ladies and gentlemen came to their luncheon we should not be found still sitting there and be ignominiously chased away"; and we children, as usual, were dawdling. Quite suddenly a great rumbling like thunder began, to our amazement, since the weather was clear and fine; then the most curious thing occurred: the whole room—floor, tables, chairs, and cupboards—heaved and rolled. On the table things slid or rocked, and some of the glasses containing our milk were overturned. I recall the swinging chandelier, and that some glasses and plates which stood in a glass-doored cupboard opposite me rang out one against another as they fell. Louise pulled my brother from his high chair.

My mother burst into the room, seized the boy from his nurse's arms, and rushed toward the door, which opened on the balcony, calling me to follow quickly, and to get out of the house before it fell. It was an earthquake! I found my legs easily and at once, and joined my mother. Fright lent wings to my obedience. I had not realized what the matter was, having never known an earthquake before; and as I had never been at sea, either, I had no point of comparison for this queer new sensation of a tottering universe. I had sat petrified, holding my milk glass with both hands to keep it straight, wondering at and scarcely fearing the amazing experience—till my mother's voice gave the enemy a name and told of danger.

On the lawn, where we stepped from the low balcony, we were at first the only members of the household. Just as the moving and rumbling stopped, various people appeared—Louise with our baby's sunbonnet; grandmama with an exclamation that it reminded her of Japan and Mexico, and probably there would immediately be another shock. My grandfather, cane in hand, and my father at his side came from the office, and I remember my father saying laughingly to my mother as she and I turned back toward them: "What were you

going to do about saving me from the earthquake? I
was just as much in danger as the children." And she
answered him he was such a big, strong man she thought
he would be able to take care of himself. Whereupon
the group accused her of having forgotten her husband,
and so on, and I lost track of their conversation. While
they went back to the house we children ran off to see
how angry and choppy the sea had become. It did look
very dark and heavy, with whitecaps all over the surface, which we had left so placid when at noon we had
gone in to our dinner.

It seemed as if my grandfather was ever growing more
quiet, and as autumn came he occasionally mentioned
that his throat was no better, and must be treated after
the family moved to town. Also, now and then, some
member of the family would say to another that my
grandfather had a headache. They attributed it to his
present sedentary life, the trouble to which his hip put
him in walking, or the concentration needed in writing
the book. The talk always ended in remarks about
how fine the book was as an occupation for him—his
deep interest in it, and the satisfaction it would be to
him in his old age to see himself and his family more
comfortably fixed than ever before by the work of his
own brain.

I was allowed once in a while to go into the office. A
large new white deal kitchen-table stood against one
wall, on which lay various books and documents. Several people—my father, General Porter, a secretary, and
my grandfather himself—talked of these and looked at
them from time to time; then they discussed a date or a
movement of troops. Opposite this table was a fireplace, and on one side stood a small sofa, on the other
a wicker armchair. In the latter my grandfather sat

when he did not sit at his large desk, which had its place in the centre of the room. Between the windows stood another smaller desk, where a secretary, a personage new to me, sat always. Sometimes my grandfather was writing, or he would take a pencil and draw a small diagram or make a note. To do this he occupied the middle desk's chair. Sometimes from the deep armchair he would dictate to the secretary instead. One wall of the room was occupied by many books standing in lines on plain pine shelves. A clock and more papers were on the mantel and a white matting covering the floor completed the furnishings, while two windows thrown wide open showed a shady balcony, vine-covered, and a glimpse of Mr. Childs's cottage with the blue sea—a very attractive frame for work hours.

My grandfather would always draw me to him when I went in, with his habitual gentle manner, and would say, "Good morning, my pet. It was nice you thought of paying grandpa a little visit"; and he would add in answer to my question, "Grandpa is well to-day," or "better to-day"; and with a kiss and a quiet stroking of my cheek or hair he would let me go. The secretary was very nice, too, and he showed me how he took down shorthand or typed with a machine, which would probably make a self-respecting stenographer to-day feel discouraged at sight. The secretary and I had several talks, and I gathered he felt it a great honor to be placed with my grandfather, which pleased me very much. I was used to my grandfather's being considered above other men; but because I only knew him personally as so quiet and modest, I was always somewhat dazed by any fuss outsiders made round him. It was difficult to realize at my age much about his being a general or a President.

I remember sitting on the lower step on the stairs one day, near his office entrance from the hall. His door opened, and my grandfather came out, crossed the hall, and took his hat from the table. He saw me and said: "Well, my pet, I'm glad to see you; what are you doing there?" I returned both his compliment and the query, to which he replied: "I'm going out for a little walk." Then I inquired: "Well, have you told grandmama you were thinking of going out, grandpapa?" "Why, no, my pet, I don't really believe I have. Now you mention it, I will, though, at once." He went up the little flight of steps to their bedroom hall, and, knocking on grandmama's door, he went in and shut it. His eyes had their most amused smile as he passed me. Inside the room I heard his gentle, cheerful voice address my grandmother.

"Mrs. G., things have come to a pretty pass; even our little granddaughter seems to have learned who really is the boss, and she has just advised me quite seriously to come and ask your permission to go for a walk." And they both laughed and said other things, farther away from the door, so I could no longer hear. He came out soon, and telling me grandmama allowed him to go, he invited me to accompany him. After that I heard the story of our conversation retailed all over the house, always with more gaiety than I could understand, as I had thought it quite a simple matter.

Soon, for some reason, my father gave up going to town for his work, and he became a constant inmate of my grandfather's office. I did not entirely comprehend why this change occurred, but heard that with his hip injured it was hard for the elderly author to move about after documents, maps, and books, while dictating was fatiguing his voice and throat. The latter, if anything,

GENERAL U. S. GRANT AND FAMILY AT ELBERON, N. J.
Princess Cantacuzène and Colonel U. S. Grant are the two children.

pained him more than ever. Therefore, now, my father, who had lived through those war experiences with the general, was going to take off the latter's hands all the necessary research work and give his entire time to this congenial task of helping the book forward, thus saving his father fatigue and strain, whether in explaining what the latter wanted to a stranger, who knew nothing of the necessary references, or in hunting up each date and map himself.

CHAPTER II

MY GRANDFATHER'S ILLNESS AND DEATH

E ARLY that autumn we all moved up to my grandparents' New York house. My grandfather seemed
to be feeling quite unwell. Either his hip or throat
or headaches were to blame; and because of this a new
arrangement of the second-floor rooms occurred, and an
office was installed up there on the lines of the one at
Elberon, except that a second big desk was added, where
my father was permanently established. The office was
in the smaller of the two front rooms. The larger front
room was made my grandfather's bedroom, instead of
grandmama's, as it had been, while she moved into the
back room, with folding doors open between. The small
room off her bedroom was arranged as a sitting-room for
her.

I remember no parties that winter. At first, every
morning early, my grandfather went down-town to have
his throat treated; then he returned and went to work
on the book, dictating and writing. Late afternoon
found him always for two or three hours in grandmama's
sitting-room, listening to her and those who surrounded
her, all talking gaily. My mother was looking very
pretty, feeling well, and was always well surrounded.
Later in the winter my Aunt Nelly came from England
and stayed in the house. Many great men passed hours
in that up-stairs sitting-room, came in the afternoon and
were kept over for the family dinner, with old-fashioned
informal hospitality. Sometimes several of these would

break away from the group round the fire and go off to
the office to discuss some point on which they differed,
perhaps, as to the hour of a troop movement or something
else concerning some chapter of the book.

General Sherman was a constant guest. He talked a
lot, was tall and vital, with a distinguished face, his
head well poised, and he had a charming, confiding manner. He never forgot he had given my mother her
diploma when she graduated at Georgetown Convent, or
that she had been head of her class there. His special
allegiance went to her always in a pretty compliment,
but he was delightful to all, and a great resource to
grandmama, with whom he chummed admirably, whether
in her serious or lighter moods. Probably he read what
an intense anxiety was beginning to pierce the calm surface of the family circle, and he came and came again.
So did others, with the same feeling of bringing a distraction or a comfort to this vague trouble. Seeing grandmama's worry over my grandfather's silence, which she
attributed to pain, I remember that one day when her
husband having left the room she mentioned this, General Sherman, walking up and down, said to her: "But
the general was always silent, Mrs. Grant. Even at the
worst times of strain, during the war, I used to go to
see him at his headquarters, and he would sit perfectly
still, like he did here to-day. I just walked up and
down and swore then; and I'm sure it did your husband
lots of good, ma'am, and relieved his mind to have me
do it for him." Grandmama laughed and was consoled.
General "Black Jack" Logan came often to sit, too; silent at first sometimes, then breaking into hot eloquence
over some army memory, some occasion where my grandfather's genius had shone.

As the winter advanced, General Buckner, from whom

my grandfather had captured Fort Donelson in 1862, and several other opponents of old war days, took the trouble to show their sympathy by joining the group in grandmama's sitting-room on one occasion or another, for a talk with their conqueror.

My babyhood acquaintance, General Sheridan, reappeared on the scene, stouter and ruddier than I recalled him in the old days, and with rather whiter hair. He had kept his charm of voice and smile, and was intense always in his attitude of devotion. There were others with army titles, but my memory does not retain their names. There were many civilians, too. Handsomest of these was Senator Roscoe Conkling—tall, imposing, with fine gray curls, grizzled beard, and his head thrown well back. He was so distinguished-looking as to hold his companions somewhat in awe. I do not remember what he said—did not understand it very well—but when he talked every one listened, and seemed greatly to enjoy it, and he often talked.

One frequent visitor frightened me dreadfully—Mark Twain, with his shaggy mane of long white hair, waving or carelessly tossed about his low brow, and his protruding eyebrows, which almost hid the deep-set eyes shining beneath them. He seemed long and rather lanky, perhaps because I was still quite small, and he had a vague way of strolling into a room and moving about without seeming to aim for any special spot. Seated, he leaned 'way back, with crossed legs, and his chin thrown up a little; so he looked at one as from a height, his lids half lowered. He shook hands, always rather crushing my small, pudgy paw, and he would eye me with his whimsical expression, probably not even thinking of me as he did so. Then he would slowly drawl out some remark, in a curious, rather bored, monotone voice. Somehow, though I did not dare say it, I got the idea he was a crazy man, and I would draw close to one or another of the grown-ups when he was around. I think I never would have had the courage to be in the same room with Mark Twain alone. I remember once the following summer at Mount McGregor he came upon me in the garden where I was playing, and as he spoke to me I turned, saw him, and fled screaming to the cottage-door, without replying. Since then I have frequently regretted, in reading his great contributions to American literature, that I had behaved so stupidly; for it was a wonderful chance I lost of hearing the best story-teller of our generation tell me a tale, to be repeated with pride to my own child or grandchild later.

A quaint figure was that of Señor Roméro, the Mexican minister to the United States—a tiny thin body with a rather large bald head, a long nose, black eyes, and very small hands and feet. He suffered from dyspepsia, and was very sallow-skinned. His quaint type and the deep gray shadows in his face interested me. He generally said almost nothing, but would draw up a small chair in a modest corner, and would sit watching my grandfather for hours with a face full of sad devotion. Senator Leland Stanford came and talked of things in California, opening up vistas like fairy-tales, with brilliant glimpses of Far Western life, where sun, mountains, great trees, flowers, fruit, and gold disputed first place in the ideas he gave me.

Still others came to my grandparents' house in those days, but somehow these are the only figures which stand out marked in my child's memory as I look back over thirty-five years. One name, that of Jefferson Davis, I remember hearing of as having given my grandfather great pleasure by coming, or by a message sent.

Of the family, I remember my mother was excessively slender and pretty, and my father had grown a beard and seemed older; also, he seemed always very busy. Even when my grandfather was free to come and sit a while, my father generally came in with him, stayed a little, and then went quietly back to the office, where the secretary and also General Badeau were deep in papers.

Somehow—without my child's memory establishing a date, however—there was soon a change in my grandfather and in the family life around him. He was no longer going down-town, or going out at all, in fact; and a good deal of the time he was in a dressing-gown and wore a scarf round his neck, thrown back loosely. Also he came less and less to the sitting-room, and never sat at his desk in the office any more. A big, soft leather armchair appeared in his bedroom, with a pillow in it, and it was said before me that he could not sleep lying down, so that he spent his nights in that great chair sitting upright. He often wore a soft knitted cap when his head ached; and he had, on a small table by him, a bottle or two, a cup of water and a little empty dish, together with a small pad and a well-sharpened pencil.

He did not at all stop work, but always wrote for the usual number of hours each day. Sometimes he would walk about the room and even through the corridor to the sitting-room, generally with his hand on my father's arm. He was quite silent, usually, and wrote on the small pad anything he wanted to say. Now and then, when in the other rooms or without this means of conveying his thought, in a strained voice he would say with effort a word or two; but he enjoyed the family group and would listen with vivid eyes as, for his benefit, added color was infused into the conversation.

I still enjoyed my privileges. If I was in the sitting-
room my little chair was drawn close to my grandfather's
and he would stroke my hair or cheek or hold my hand a
little while. I remember how beautiful his hands were—
large, classic, with long, capable fingers and perfect nails,
to which Nature had left nothing for the manicure to do.
The hands looked strong, and so did the wonderful face
with its quiet, firm expression of mouth and deep eyes,
calm in spite of his constant pain. When he would go
off from the sitting-room some one of the remaining circle always asked how he was, and another would reply
sadly: "No better."

Once a stranger, whom I do not recall by name, said
something about morphine. "He would not take it,"
came the reply. "The only thing he is willing to try is
now and again to have a light exterior application of
cocaine painted over the sore itself. It is especially
hard, because he is forced now to write every scrap of his
memoirs in person; no voice—he cannot dictate."

Then my mother told of the life in the two front
rooms. It seems my father spent twenty-three out of
twenty-four hours there, sleeping on a sofa in the office,
always dressed and ready to spring to his father's side if
the latter woke at night and wanted to write. My
grandfather evidently had to work during what hours
he could, as the pain subsided, permitting him to do so
by chance; and whenever such a period came my father
was there, gentle and smiling, to help look up a date or
to verify a statement, hand a pillow, or do anything
else he could. To sympathize with his father was the
son's one desire, and my mother said it was unhealthy
for my father to be awake and working thus day after
day, keeping himself alive with black coffee; but she
could do nothing with him, she added, and he only

answered her protests by absolutely declaring he meant
to go on aiding his father to the end.

I was allowed to enter the sick-room and stand about
at times. Once I wandered in and stood in a corner
watching, and it appeared to me my father was as strong
and as gentle as any nurse, and that my grandfather
seemed to feel confidence and depend on his big son.

The doctors came to the patient now, and I stood
by once and saw how they examined his throat and
painted it.

The winter wore on and my grandfather grew worse
steadily. He remained constantly in his room. With
strict orders given me to make no noise, not even to
talk, and to come right out again, occasionally I was
allowed in. One noticed a great change; the face was
pale and drawn and the fine hands were very thin.
When he was not writing they lay open on the arms of
his chair, extremely still; or else with a slow, quiet
movement he would open and close his hands, rubbing
the thumb over the closed fingers backward and forward.
It was never a jerky motion, but one as if he were thinking, much as a well man walks quietly up and down
while he thinks. Never did any one mention an impatient word or gesture on his part, and his two doctors—
one of whom, Doctor Shrady, I liked very much—were
always saying it was wonderful how he stood the days
of agony and the long sleepless nights. He would never
take anything to give him respite, as they had often
begged him to do. Also, every one spoke of the wonderful work he was still doing, and of his chapters, which
were piling up, and how his strength held out.

Two or three times there were sinking spells, and a
frightened family gathered about him, fearing the end;
but he rallied, and even occasionally seemed for a few

days to show an appreciable improvement. I remember on the 27th of April there was a birthday dinner for him; all the family were gathered and a few friends besides. I was allowed to sit up for the grown-ups' meal, and to have some of their ice-cream—a rare treat which impressed me more than did the few guests, among whom I seem to recall the faces of General Sherman and Mark Twain again, with my grandmother's delight that some unexpected remark of the latter had created a general laugh in which my grandfather had joined. I may be confusing this with another dinner earlier that season, however, as there were two or three such.

Again, an incident which stands out in my memory is that one evening before dinner a frightful series of howls was heard in the hall outside grandmama's door. She, who always asserted we children were much too suppressed by our parents and nurses, rushed out from her room in a dressing-gown, my mother appearing in the same array on the staircase above, while even my grandfather, cane in hand, opened his door, and my father came from the office, having dropped his work in haste at the evident agony in his small son's voice. I sat on the steps, since, when the racket began, we were following our nurse up to our rooms from our own early dinner. With the crowd assembled and with grandmama imploringly begging the three-year-old to dry his tears and confide his trouble to her, young Ulysses straightened out his wrinkled face, opened his eyes, and, looking straight at her, answered: "Want an appul!"

It seemed grandma had secretly instructed him to "shout and make a noise" when he wanted anything, so she proceeded to make good by sending for the apple; but my mother's indignation and humiliation were very great! My grandfather had watched the scene with delight, and referred to it several times, saying, "That boy knows how to manage women"; and finally, "I'm afraid Ida will have to spank that youngster of hers"; but he liked both the vigor and the wit of the sturdy little grandson who bore his name, and my father was not displeased with anything which brought a ray of light to the invalid's tired eyes.

Toward spring all sorts of things which interested us children began to happen outside the house. An army of reporters camped on our sidewalk, watching the windows of the second-floor front. Incidentally, they questioned every one who came out of the front door, and we children received a large share of attention whenever we appeared bound for our daily walks. We were mentioned frequently in the papers, and my mother disliked this, and gave us strict instructions not to talk to the reporters as we went by them. One day when she had been out for luncheon and during the whole afternoon, and had missed a playroom riot of which Nurse Louise told her, she sent for us, and looking at my brother, she said with sorrow in her voice: "I hear you have been dreadfully naughty to-day. Now isn't that terrible?" Ignoring the latter question, the culprit replied, with gay interest: "Now, how did you hear that, mama? In the newspapers?"—and brought down the house.

There was a great procession that spring, too, I remember—a beautiful parade, which marched up past our house to salute the old commander. He stood in the bay window of his sick-room, looking down on the veterans he had commanded long ago, with their following of younger men and boys; and as they went by, in spite of military discipline, all eyes turned upward, and they gazed at the fine strength of that face, still fighting and unconquered. From two windows over his we children enjoyed the fine sight, feeling the parade was all for our benefit and pleasure, understanding nothing of the tragedy of this last review.

Partly unconscious of the full significance of the drama in our home, we spent a happy winter, with lessons, walks, and games following one another in monotonous succession. Toward the end of spring we were scarcely ever allowed in the sick-room, and, if at all, my father would carry little Ulysses in his arms, saying, "Sh!"— then would take me in for a moment, leading me by the hand gently, and would stand with me a few seconds by the side of the great chair. My grandfather's head was bent usually and he appeared very ill, but always there was a look and a smile in my direction; and then, "Come, sweetheart," my father would whisper, "dear grandpapa is tired now." He would lead me back to the lighted hall. But I heard them all talk of how the book was still progressing, how each day at the hours of least suffering some pages were added to it, and one person would say, "The book is killing him," and another would reply: "No, the book is keeping him alive; without it he would already be dead."

Then came talk of summer plans. The doctors thought Elberon too damp and too low, and real mountains too far, with air too rarefied. Some one suggested Mount McGregor, in the foot-hills of the Adirondacks—accessible, dry, invigorating, cool, all that was wanted—a small hotel where one took one's meals was there, it seemed, with a wee cottage, just large enough to hold the family; woods of oak and pine; a great, sweeping view out over the valley far away. The question was decided; moving the invalid frightened every one, but the journey came off all right.

My grandfather, with doctors and nurse, made one

group; and my father, invariably at his side and in charge,
was always able to understand his parent's least gesture
or see what was needed quicker and better than others;
grandmama, with Aunt Nelly and my mother, formed
another group under the leadership of my uncle, U. S.
Grant; then we children followed, with our French
Louise; while, finally, various servants with baggage and
wraps made a cavalcade which crowded the special car
offered our party by the railroad. An all-day trip it
was. I think we arrived in time for a light supper, and
were put at once to bed; and we slept with light hearts,
for in telling us good night some one had said: "Isn't it
nice, dear grandpapa has stood the trip so well? And
the doctor says he will soon be all right in this fine air."

It seemed really true. The air was cool and clear,
while our tiny cottage was most conveniently arranged
for the invalid's comfort. On the ground floor there was
a little room—supposedly a dining-room—with a smaller
parlor off it; then a large room called the office, and a
pleasant, sunny, quiet, corner room, with a cot for the
attendant, and two big chairs, like those in New York;
or perhaps the same ones transported. These two rooms
opened one into the other, and had their own door out
to the broad porch, where the invalid could sit or be
wheeled about or even walk a little, sure of an even
surface for his feet.

For a time the effect of the change and air was wonderful, though the pain and difficulty in swallowing were
as before, of course. An augmentation of strength came
within a day or two, and my grandfather was able to be
out a great deal, to wear his clothes, and stand the
fatigue of dressing and undressing; he again took a large
part in the family's life, which was arranged around him
so he should have as much company and talk as would

amuse and distract him. He was wheeled down to the summer-house on the cliff frequently, and looked contentedly out over the great valley spread beyond. If I was playing in the garden when he started I was called; and, delighted to be with him, feeling very maternal and important, I trotted alongside the wheeled chair, chattering incessantly, and now or then tucking in the corner of his scarf or lap-robe. I loved that view myself, and always felt the silent man was in sympathy, for when I would exclaim my pleasure at its splendor and turn to him with a "Don't you like it, too, grandpapa?" he would nod, and smile with his eyes, quite in the old way; and I forgot, childlike, how ill he really was.

Through June and part of July we lived like this, and crowds came and looked and went away. On Sunday vast concourses of people, respectful and quiet, arrived by train on the mountain top, gazed at the view and wandered round the cottage, in the hope of catching a glimpse of "the general." Children were brought, to be held up to look, and shrubs were broken and carried off, with any other odds and ends within reach, to be kept as souvenirs.

So many came and stood about that one day a group of soldiers appeared on the scene and set up a tent or two, proceeding to establish sentinels, who marched up and down a few feet beyond the balcony and permitted no one without a pass or a real mission to come beyond their chosen line. We children grew very intimate with vague, friendly people in these multitudes, and we had a great many compliments and questions put to us. No doubt we were very indiscreet, though I do not remember any trouble coming from it.

We led an outdoor life, and as we took our meals with Nurse Louise over at the hotel, we saw very little of the grown-ups in the family circle, who spent their time sitting near my grandfather or with his doctors in consultation. We enjoyed ourselves immensely. There were rocks and big trees; a small, still, shimmering lake behind the cottage; and out in front a tiny garden, with beyond it an open space and the few trees which were grouped about the summer-house, whence was the lookout. Enough for a children's paradise this was, and I loved it all, having been used only till then to the open sea, sky, sand, and lawns at Elberon. These surroundings seemed mysterious, with something of fairy or of goblin charm about them. I liked the sunlight coming through high oaks with their moving leaves; and I spent much leisure looking up into them as they whispered among themselves. It is the first time I remember feeling any appreciation of Nature.

One day there was a thunder-storm, so sudden and violent that it frightened us children very much as we undressed. The cottage was struck by lightning, which ran down a defective lightning-rod and branched off from it through the window of our nursery. Louise sat at the window, and was for a moment transfixed by the shock, though, as it passed, the only real harm done was to her apron, which bore traces of burning. I saw a line or ball of flame pass and go to an upper corner of the room, and there disappear. It went by my little brother, who was standing in his crib and who fell over backward with a squeal, saying some one had hurt his face. We were easily consoled, though, for our small troubles, and liked being the centre of attention and telling our story as often as chance offered an audience, but the distressing thing was that though the damage in our room consisted of a scorched apron and a small hole in the wall, outside the house one of the sentinels had been thrown down and killed. His dramatic end was for a long time a deep sorrow to us children, for we had known him well and were growing fond of him.

I became conscious one day that the grown-ups on the balcony near which I was playing were worried. Grandmama was saying something in an anxious voice, Aunt Nelly was silent, looking far away, and my mother was arguing against grandmama in her most contagiously cheerful tone—the tone a child recognizes as the one used to persuade one that having a tooth pulled or an arm vaccinated is going to be a pleasant experience. "Now, Mrs. Grant, you mustn't talk that way; General Grant has been so much better you are used to it, and this setback makes you nervous. You will see it is just the fatigue of writing, and he is free at last and can rest. You'll see"; and so on, or words to that effect. I did not then understand and cannot now recall the whole conversation as I overheard it, but evidently the speakers were worried about my grandfather; he had finally ended his book, and was not so well as before. It was true he had not come out-of-doors that day, nor dressed as usual. I felt queer. As the French say, "My heart tightened itself," and I wondered what was happening or impending. I realized I was small and left out. For two or three days my grandfather stayed in his room, and I was not allowed in. The only news I had was when I asked it of my mother or Aunt Nelly. They would say in passing, "No, grandpapa isn't quite so well, dear," and then hurry on. Grandmama and my father scarcely ever came out of the sick-room, while the nurse or our old butler, Harrison—who had been helping as my grandfather's body-servant—would give us no satisfaction either if we met them. Once old Harrison shook his head and said: "I'm afraid the general is very bad."

Once, also, I heard the doctor and my father, who had come into the little dining-room, talking: something about other doctors to come for a consultation. And then the house doctor said: "Isn't there something we can give the general to write, Colonel Grant? It might make his interest and spirits rally; make him want to live."

And my father replied, "We can certainly invent something to propose to father, if you think writing will help him to rally again"—and they went away.

Soon—it may have been a day later, or two, or three— my mother came out on the balcony and called us children. "Quick, papa wants you to come and see dear grandpapa," she said.

We joined her, and she took us into the room where my grandfather was more or less reclining in his great chair. Grandmama was crying quietly, and was seated by his side. She had in her hands a handkerchief and a small bottle, perhaps of cologne, and was dampening my grandfather's brow. His hair was longer, and seemed to me more curled, while his eyes were closed in a face more drawn than usual and much whiter. Beads of perspiration stood on the broad forehead, and as I came forward old Harrison gently wiped similar drops from the back of the hand which was lying quietly on the chair-arm. My father sat at the opposite side from grandmama, and the doctor and nurse stood at the head, behind the invalid. Old Harrison had been kneeling near my father, but rose, and I took his place. My mother came behind me. "Kiss grandpapa," she said, but I could not reach over and up to his cheek. I noticed once more how beautiful the hand was. I looked at my father, who nodded, and who put his arm about me. Then I stood for a moment or two, steadied by him, when my mother whispered: "We must go now." With a lump in my throat I leaned down and kissed the beautiful hand, and was led out of the room.

When Nurse Louise waked us and dressed us early next morning she told us about how "le général" had had a bad night; and that all the family had been down with him till two or three hours ago; so we must be very quiet and creep out of the house to our breakfast without any noise, as now "le général" was sleeping well, and so were the others.

As we opened our nursery door and stepped into the hall Harrison rushed across it from my parents' to my grandmother's door and knocked there, having left the first door thrown wide open. We reached the stairs and I saw my father throw on his jacket—probably he had been asleep in shirt and trousers, ready for any emergency. He rushed out of his bedroom and passed us without seeing us at all, taking the staircase faster than I could imagine his doing. My mother was moving about rapidly, putting on her things, also, and across the hall from grandmama came a sob, and "I'm coming," in reply to Harrison's quick knock.

What happened further I do not know, for Nurse Louise was very energetic and got us out rapidly; but as we were leaving we heard grandmama's voice saying, with the sob again: "Ida, do you think it's true? I can't believe it! I can't!"

We children were taken over to the hotel. I was put in my chair and told as usual to eat all the things before me; but I couldn't. I was too frightened by what I had heard. Other nurses and children appeared and asked news of the cottage; and Louise would shake her head, shrug her shoulders, and indicate she couldn't talk openly because of us children. Breakfast dragged; then one of those serving it suddenly said: "It is all finished over there at the cottage." And when Louise contradicted, the servant continued: "Yes, yes, a telegram has just been brought over to forward from the hotel office, and the messenger said General Grant had just died."

I felt stunned, could not swallow another mouthful, and would have cried out then and there, had it not been that Nurse Louise, with good-hearted tact, undid the small brother's bib and said: "Come." So we got out into the air, and I was better at once. We returned to our cottage much later, though, for Louise's common sense had suggested a long walk as an excellent method of keeping us out of the way, and we had gone round the lake before reaching home.

It was a sad household. My father was with the undertaker down-stairs; mama was busy in her room and couldn't see us. Grandmama was wailing and sobbing behind her own closed doors. There was not anything we could do, and we wandered away to the garden. Against all rules, when nurse and my brother settled down to rest, I went slowly off by myself further on into the woods. I think this was the first time in my life I had felt heavy with sorrow. I did not go far—discipline forbade it—but once out of sight I sat down to digest the great trouble. It was not just a relative who had passed away out of my small world, but a friend and comrade from whom I had always had both understanding and sympathy, together with a strong, gentle, protective affection, which I was too young to analyze yet old enough to appreciate deeply. I had at times realized his suffering and patience, so admiration and pity mixed with the other sentiments which overcame me finally when I broke down. The storm passed. I dried my tears and thought; was there nothing I could do to help my father, who was in the cottage "attending to every-thing," it had been said.

I seemed without resources for usefulness. Then I remembered one made wreaths for dead people. . . . Perhaps I could make a wreath. Often we had done so in play, with nurse's help.

Uncertain whether I could succeed alone, I looked for flowers, but there were none in sight there in the woods. Discouraged and tired, I gazed about me, when suddenly it occurred to me that the prettiest wreath I had ever made was a flat one of oak-leaves. There were enough of these at hand. I was at once aflame with importance in my effort and enthusiasm. I picked a quantity of leaves from the low sprouts of some fine trees, ran over them to see they were all perfect, and sat down to work. It went quickly, and in a half-hour or so the wreath of broad, shining leaves was finished, and looked well, as it lay spread on a flat-rock table at hand.

The next thing was to get it to my grandfather. I knew my father was in those closed rooms, and thinking to find him, I ran back to the house, approaching from the rear, so the garden and nurse should both be avoided. Once on the balcony I went and looked in the window of the death-chamber. My father was not there, but in the centre of the room stood a coffin, a thing I had never seen before; and moving about, two men, strangers to me, were setting out a few chairs, probably for use at the service soon to be held. I was recognized at once by the elder of the two men, who came to the door and inquired what I wanted.

"I've brought grandpapa a wreath; I thought my papa was here," I replied. He said, after a little hesita-tion: "Sure, miss, and your papa is just after going up to snatch a little sleep, and I wouldn't dishturb him if I was you. Suppose ye give me the wreath to lay on the gineral. It's a mighty fine wreath; and I think there's no harm in your coming in to help me yourself."

In I went with the undertaker, and he laid the wreath carefully in a circle on the casket. Then he left me standing there, gazing down at the familiar face under the glass, while he went off about his business of tidying up. It seemed heartbreaking that my grandfather should be so still, and dead.

I could not struggle against the queer feeling assailing me, and I lost track of things for a time, till I remember being carried in someone's arms up to my mother's room, and laid on the big bed there, and she was reproaching me for being disobedient and having run away from nurse.

However, later I was very proud, because with carloads of flowers coming by every train, and florists bringing special great set pieces which filled the house with their beauty and fragrance, my wreath was the only one on the casket. Finally it began to fade and the leaves to curl a little; but my father reassured me: "Never mind, pet, my little girl's wreath is going to be varnished so it will keep, and then it shall be buried with grandpapa. I know he would have liked to keep it with him always."

And I was glad to have it so. Somehow my deepest sentiment had gone into the little, silly contribution to the offerings brought him.

Impossible to describe in detail what our family life was from July 23d to August 8th. I remember vast crowds of men's hatless heads, and of women in black. The flowers piled up, and the resolutions of sympathy, engraved and framed, piled up, too. Letters were coming in by the basket-load. Yet there was no confusion or talk. The maximum result was obtained always by my father's power of organization, his patience and self-control. Devoted as he was to his wonderful parent, and consequently doubly hurt by his sad death, my father never let a complaint escape him, and he did without the privacy he must have longed for. He saw to every detail, answered questions from all over the country. He decided everything connected with the funeral trip, and attended with much care to details. This was not easy, with all the veiled rivalries among those who had united to honor Grant and mourn his loss.

My father went down to New York with the body on the special train, draped with black, which carried the casket. My uncle Ulysses came on to stay with and look after the family, taking us down to New York in a special car. Once in town we were all lodged at the old Fifth Avenue Hotel. Tremendous crowds circulated in the streets below our windows, and I was deeply interested in watching the people. Clothes, all black, were brought in, and each member of our party bought something which was necessary to complete wardrobes in need of deep crêpe weeds. Flags everywhere hung at half-mast, and a long continuous procession passed through the doors of New York's City Hall, to pay respect to my grandfather. For days his remains lay in state, and the crowds went solemnly by; men, women, and children, slowly moving on weary feet, waiting, looking, straining for a last glimpse at the well-known face.

The morning of August 8th came, and early our family took up its stand in the funeral carriages, ready to swing into line as soon as the great hearse should pass. Even my childish brain was awed by the immensity of the demonstration. From 23d Street to 116th Street a five-mile stretch of sympathetic people covered sidewalks and fences, windows and doors, and every face was sad; some were even weeping. Except the crowd, I recall little of those hours spent in the funeral carriage. With both my parents and my Aunt Nelly we were shut into intense heat and semi-darkness. Some sandwiches, the long silences, and now and then a question asked and answered; my weary body and my own wet eyes I only felt occasionally, but I remember well my father's white, set face and his strained, hoarse voice. My young brother gave my mother some difficulty, for his movements and talk were not always easy to control. I think she must have had great trouble keeping both of us children in order.

At last we arrived at Riverside, and the afternoon sun shone brightly down on the tiny temporary brick tomb. The services, simple and beautiful, were carried out rapidly, without a hitch, and ended with "taps." Then we drove back to our hotel with a feeling of unutterable weariness and loss.

From that time till the spring of 1889 we lived with my grandmother Grant. All the first part of those years my father worked at the book, which my grandfather had left in manuscript to his heirs. It had to be gone over still and the proofs corrected, while endless detail work was also involved getting maps and illustrations carefully prepared. Instead of the little office in the second-floor front, this room was switched back to its old employ of my grandmother's boudoir, and she moved again into what had been recently my grandfather's bedroom. The plain work furniture went up to the third floor, and there, in a room just over the earlier office, my father carried through his daily task—saw publishers, arranged their terms, and carried out in detail the instructions of the dead author. As the money came in after the first edition of the memoirs was sold, he handled all his mother's business in addition.

It was a great gratification to have the two volumes, written with such courage, while fighting death and enduring a martyrdom of suffering, fully appreciated by the public, and attaining the results for which they were written.

The first check sent in by the publishers beat all records for size. It was for over three hundred thousand dollars!

CHAPTER III

IN VIENNA

ONE day, in the spring of 1889, when I was nearly thirteen years old—a quiet, overgrown girl with long, heavy hair, but otherwise with no distinctive trait—my mother called us down to her room at supper-time, and announced that she had a great surprise to impart. We were all going to Vienna, to live there a long time! President Harrison had named my father "Envoy Extraordinary and Minister Plenipotentiary" to Austria, and we must prepare to be off very soon. My interest and excitement were intense. I wrote the new title over and over, till I knew how to spell and say it by heart. What I had heard of Austria was limited and vague, but I asked more, until I was informed that Vienna was considered one of Europe's brilliant capitals, that there were great families living there whose names were known in history back through the centuries, as those of robber barons and Holy Roman emperors. Also there were art, music, fine clothes, court functions, fancy leather goods, galleries of treasures, palaces. All these words figured in our table conversation now, and I followed their trails, varied as they were, to dictionaries, and drew my own conclusions.

Our sailing date was soon announced. We were going to land at Southampton, be in London a short time, and then go straight to Vienna, either through France or Germany, as my parents should decide at the last moment. Anyhow, we would have quite a trip, and I was elated by this prospect. I had always been told we were too poor to go abroad, and I had so far learned as much as I ever hoped to know of foreign lands through albums others brought home. I had been quite resigned to this privation, but was delighted by the sudden turning in our path and the new prospect of adventure and discovery.

We sailed early in March. Grandmama, with a companion, decided to come, too, and spend the summer months abroad; so our party made six. The night before our embarkation we all dined with my father's brother, and lost in that large family company we children, unnoticed, ate of every dish, from oysters to marrons glacés. Our ordinary simple diet had not prepared us for digesting such a banquet, especially on the eve of a trip at sea, and the results of our orgy were frightful! For several days we tossed on a stormy ocean, unable to touch food or even to sleep much—helpless victims of our gluttony. My small brother had high fever, and my mother felt his life was really in danger, for the ship's doctor could do nothing, he said, and merely recommended fresh air when we could go on deck, and quiet till then. Mine was a healthy case, as I was much stronger always than the boy.

About the third day out my father carried my limp brother up on deck, and I was able to go that far on my own feet. Then we stretched out and wistfully watched a sullen, lead-colored, hideous sky, and a rough sheet of water equally ugly. The boat still rolled and tumbled. Young Ulysses was himself by and by, however, and he explored the wonders of the ship with interest. In more recent times the luxury of steamers makes one forget the uncomfortable life habitual on them during my childhood. Food then was always indifferent and frequently

wretched. In those days what dainties our friends sent
us were really precious, and I remember especially the
pleasure we took in a barrel of oysters and some oranges,
which were gifts at parting. Our steamer-chairs also had
been given us. But in spite of this my first impressions
of my journey out into the world were horrid!

At last, with the help of several books, the long, dull
trip, which lasted about ten days, ended. We entered,
after the trip by boat-train to London, a huge caravansary where one got lost. Bad food, rooms that did not
remember being cleaned, mud, drizzle, darkness—all contributed to our doleful feeling, as we did our round of
sightseeing. The Tower of London I liked very much,
however; more than anything else I remember.

My father and mother were "commanded" to a
drawing-room and went, both looking very fine. I was
allowed to help my mother dress. She was quite radiant
in orange brocade embroidered with silver beads, and
she wore a becoming touch of brown and white at her
shoulders and on her head.

That day Queen Victoria was holding court, and was
gracious enough to remember my grandfather had visited
her at Windsor Castle years before. The Prince of
Wales, Albert Edward, mama said looked desperately
bored, while the Princess was smiling and gracious. Distinguished men, statesmen of various countries, asked to
meet my father, and talked with him about the different
interests of America and the currents of European politics—all of which gave my parents rather an unusual
first reception in these official circles they were just
entering.

It seemed curious to me to be abroad, where everything was so different from the frame I was used to.
The English country from Southampton to London had

appeared very beautiful to my eyes—greener, richer vegetation and bigger trees than at home, with here and there a castle or a manor-house almost hidden away. At that time it was beyond my powers to define the feeling I had, but in the light of later knowledge I think it must have been the dignity and growth of these traditional homes with a history which appealed to me. Attaching the past to the present, they gave promise of strength and a continuous long future. Even a child is sensitive to such things as atmosphere, and realizes differences, and, though London suffered from smoke and noise, though our hotel was a hideous place, with much gilt and dirt and uncomprehending German waiters, and though we were very uncomfortable, I liked the streets and buildings immensely.

After our short stay in London we left for Vienna, direct by way of Belgium and Germany. My father was anxious to reach his post and take over the work given him to do, and his sense of duty suppressed all further stops on the way. He was sorry to disappoint us, he said, and promised to bring us back some day to see these lands we were skimming through. My mother gave me a blank book and pencil, with which I was "to keep a diary about Europe." Luckily this document was lost not long after it was written, but I remember with warm affection the little black oilcloth book and my pencil. They kept me busy and amused, from our arrival at Ostend, or whatever was the port, all through the long journey south to the Austrian capital.

In Vienna the legation carriage and footman were awaiting us, and we fell in love at first sight with the place. There was a long drive from the train to our hotel, which stood in the heart of the old city. The quarter first traversed had broad, open streets and stuccoed houses, large but quite uninteresting. Then we reached the "Ring," with its rich public buildings and its parks, covering the space of what had been the fortified walls of old Vienna. Suddenly we turned short at right angles and plunged into a tiny street, so narrow that it was almost possible to shake hands from one side to the other. And such sidewalks! Two people abreast was their utmost capacity; a third person had to walk in the street itself. It was crowded with a gay, well-dressed, talkative mass of people rushing both ways, getting tangled up and untangling themselves. Now and then a "fiacre" passed, the driver cracking his whip and shouting to make way. Then came some lumbering family carriage with big colored crests on the side-doors, or a push-cart would pass, with vegetables and fruits piled high on it, or with fragrant violets and daffodils. Before each vehicle there was a scramble to the sidewalk and a flattening out of pedestrians against walls, amid laughter and shouts.

The shop-windows looked most attractive on this smart street, which was the famous Kärntnerstrasse. I liked it and the people. Suddenly we stopped. Our footman, whose name was Franz, and who at once announced he had been with the legation many years and spoke "Engleesh easee," got down and opened the door. We all alighted before what looked a very unpromising place, and went in. Franz explained that there was a newer hotel, but not so elegant, and that it was "not for Excellenz to live in." It was on the Ring and was quite modern, while this, the Munsch, was where kings and princes and Excellenzen always stayed; and "You will very much like eet, Excellenz."

Inside a clean, low hall, painted white and with marble floor. There was no lift, but a wide staircase walled

on each side, white, with a thick red carpet. One flight
up, there were a dark landing, heavy red velvet curtains,
and a door of white painted wood. This flew open, both
panels, and we stood on the threshold of the apartment
of kings, princes, and Excellenzen!

Enormous rooms, two of them, one in brown-and-blue
brocade of large design, the other furnished in red damask; lots of gold everywhere, on frames, mirrors, and
carved backs of chairs. There were great chandeliers of
gilt, bronze, or Bohemian glass—candelabra, clocks, and
vases of elaborately worked metal stood on high mantels.
A hundred people in each room would not have made a
crowd. One room had five windows, the other more,
perhaps. Tables and chairs stood about in formal style.
Perhaps to kings, princes, and Excellenzen this might be
a normal habitation; to a simple little American girl it
looked like a palace, vast beyond belief. Our bedrooms
were in proportion, but there were no baths at all, nor
even toilet-rooms. My father asked the price, and was
told a figure which proved that in Vienna space was a
drug on the market. So we took the rooms.

We children had one with the funniest beds—head and
foot boards equally high, heavy quilts with sheets buttoned back on them, and a soft down cushion as large
square as the bed's width, to use as an extra comforter.
The walls were so thick and the window spaces consequently so deep that these made attractive alcoves for
use. I had in mine a desk and chair, while my brother
used another as his playroom.

We all decidedly liked the place as soon as we got used
to its queerness, and it was pleasant to have excellent
food well served in our rooms by a friendly, smiling
waiter, who spoke all sorts of languages, though he was
not particularly comprehensible in any.

With the memory of the Kärntnerstrasse in my mind I did not think of a possible view from our windows, and it was only after a long time that I went where the desk stood and glanced out. An enchanting scene was below —a large cobblestone-paved square, and in the centre a fountain with simple, perfect lines, quite an early and a very good creation. About this was grouped a motley throng in bright peasant costumes, most decorative. Then radiating out from the centre were quantities of push-carts covered with fresh flowers—piles of them— and any you wanted, and as many as you could carry, I found cost really a very small sum. The edges of the square were vacant and the whole space was surrounded by façades of lovely old houses, while just opposite our hotel the Capuchin church stood, where all the Haps-burgs have been buried these many centuries. It was a simple structure.

The Viennese seemed a charming, happy-go-lucky peo-ple, with a love of finery, a childish gaiety, and a desire to help everyone about them.

That first morning I did not gain any further knowl-edge, but I already had the feeling I was very much at home in this new place. Breakfast was brought up soon, and all the grown-ups exclaimed over their delicious coffee. By the end of the meal bathrooms had become a matter of indifference to all of us, and we were com-pletely under the spell of Vienna. We unpacked our trunks, glad to think we were to stay on for some time in the transformed old palace, for that was the real origin of our hotel.

My father made his first call on Count Kalnóky at once. The latter attracted him, as he did every one else. I heard afterward that Kalnóky had been consid-ered one of the most delightful men of his epoch, and that much of his success in handling the delicate mechanism of Austria-Hungary's foreign policy had been because he was such a personal favorite with all who negotiated with him. At that time we knew nothing of him, save that he presided at the Foreign Office, and that a first call was due him. When he returned my father's visit and spent a half-hour with my mother, the gay connoisseur was quite evidently taken with her beauty, and made himself so agreeable that a warm friendship was at once established between the American Legation and the Ballplatz.

At the end of his visit we were sent for, as the Minister said he was keen to meet a pair of children who came to Austria from so far. I was very much interested to see this first native who crossed my path. He made us some simple, cordial speech; asked if we had seen the pretty Würstel-Prater, how we liked the country, and he made his way straight to our small hearts by his warmth and sympathy. Of medium height and fairly heavy build, he had thin hair, a round face, and somewhat prominent eyes. He possessed, also, a guileless expression, a very pleasant voice, a good-natured laugh, and, without any familiarity, seemed at once to be on rather intimate terms with those he met. He inspired confidence in my father from the first, and they remained firm friends throughout the remaining time Kalnöky was in office. Though there were various delicate and difficult negotiations carried on between their respective governments, more and more my father grew to trust the man who on that first day had given us a welcome which seemed sincere.

I had never been out of the Anglo-Saxon circle at home, and I was struck by the fact that the Minister of Foreign Affairs bowed low over my mother's hand and kissed it in adieu, and that at the door he stopped, clicked his heels together, and made a general bow to our family group. I think, also, he wore a monocle, which amused me. He was an old bachelor, I learned, and poor, and he had, though he was of noble birth, made his own career. At the Ballplatz—where he occasionally gave an official party, opening up the palatial rooms and doing everything with great dignity and splendor—he lived habitually in one of the smallest apartments and kept very quiet socially. He always used a smart fiacre instead of a private carriage, and one saw him sometimes flying along at breakneck speed such as only the typical Viennese cabbies dared to adopt.

In fact, "Wiener chic" ordained that any man with pretensions to success should make a point of using a very fast fiacre, except when on gala occasions of ceremony it was replaced by court carriage or family-crested clumsy vehicle.

Later I met Kalnöky often, and watched and listened always with great interest as he talked. He was vivacious, talented, cultivated, yet always with a shrewd sense of values and a judgment which made him one of his Emperor's most valued servitors. Of different quality and race from the Aehrenthals, Berchtolds, and others who brought Austria to the brink of the precipice in 1914, Kalnöky was a patriot, statesman, and a gentleman as well.

Our first month we spent at the quaint Munsch Hotel. We grew to be comfortable and to like more and more the view of the square and the luxury of meals served in the huge salon. We even got used to the lack of baths, and a tub in our rooms seemed quite satisfactory.

Court mourning was deep, for Rudolf, the Crown Prince, had died just a few weeks before our arrival.

How this dreadful loss had come on them few Austrians knew. "The Vetčera" was at the bottom of the trouble, of course. With him on the last fatal party had been, besides herself, Prince Philip of Coburg, and one other man whose name I have forgotten. Among the groups far from court, gossip over Rudolf was rife and every sort of scandal was passed about. The Emperor was deeply affected and people were received by him only on state business. The Empress had retired in her grief to some far-away palace and stayed there. We were told that, when questioned, various members of the court had replied: "Our Emperor, whom we love dearly, is suffering a great loss, and he does not wish it discussed. We know nothing." Evidently the diplomat whose curiosity had led him to ask indiscreet questions was not an example to follow, but the colleagues whispered, and, naturally, the nobility must have done likewise, even while toward foreigners loyalty to the bereaved sovereigns was maintained.

The Emperor was adored by his subjects in the gay capital, who showed affection and admiration, also, for the dead Crown Prince, and sympathized even with the latter's follies. Both men had had a simple charm and real love of the city's life, in which they had always taken part unofficially. The Crown Prince, like his father, was known as a wonderful shot and horseman. He had a quick wit and a bright smile, and had spent much time in the theatres and cafés, or in the Prater, rubbing elbows with the crowd. He had used a fiacre, like all the *jeunesse dorée*, and spoke the Viennese patois to perfection.

His people were inclined to sympathize with his various peccadilloes, on the score that he did not care for the Belgian princess he had been obliged to marry, and who, they said, had made scenes and misunderstood him always. "The Vetcĕra" was one of Vienna's own daughters, a great beauty, though her bringing Rudolf to the point where suicide or murder must end their romance was really exaggerating matters. The easy-going mentality and invariable weakness for the romantic made the people say this gently: "They were very much in love and very handsome, and the Stéphanie was not adroit." Then the gossips sighed. . . .

Whether the death of the Crown Prince at his Meyerling shooting-lodge was accident, suicide, or murder; whether the party was sober or intoxicated, there is no doubt that Prince Philip of Coburg—who was married to another Belgian princess and, consequently, Rudolf's brother-in-law as well as friend—acted with tact and promptitude when the tragedy occurred. Before any one was up next morning the Empress had been awakened at the Hofburg palace and informed. She had been vastly brave, and had faced the situation with the pride which always characterized her. After a moment to steady herself, she had said she would in person tell the Emperor, and had gone about her errand at once. He was more bowed than she by Fate's blow, but together they had traversed the ordeal of the funeral ceremonies, hushed discussion to what extent they could, and at the time of our arrival in Austria were more than dignified in their mourning—she in her retreat, he with courage facing his duties.

Because of this my parents had little social life at the beginning of our Austrian experience. After meeting Kalnŏky, a few calls and presentations followed, and they saw colleagues who were of superior or equal official rank, ambassadors and ministers, but that was all.

Spring grew into summer. My father had taken hold

of the legation work, and was handling it so that the clerks and secretaries were amazed at how much they could accomplish, and how alive they were.

An apartment had been found for us, with another in the same building for the legation offices, and we were to take possession early in the autumn. Meanwhile my parents' furniture had been cabled for. Unused since the Morristown cottage days, we all rejoiced over the arrival of the pretty things of which we were so fond. It was decided that we should move out for the summer to a quiet little country hotel situated on a beautiful hillside, near Vienna, where a valley spread with cyclamen-blossoms, pink and white, stretched at our feet. The summer at Baden promised to be very agreeable.

Before we went to the country the subtle charm of the Kaiserstadt (Emperor's city) was at work making us welcome. Soon we really thought the people most lovable and their background as entrancing as themselves. It pleased us to think we were to live in this frame for a time; four years, perhaps, if all went well? Life took on a new interest, even to a little girl.

That first summer in Austria was quite different from anything I had ever lived through. Baden, and beyond it, Bad-Vöslau, where we went for the month of August, were both small and not particularly fashionable resorts, but had the great advantage of being near town, so my father could spend his office hours at the Embassy. Yet they were really countrified as far as our life went, and entirely quiet socially. My mother found them restful. From Vöslau the view out over the valley was beautiful, on the order of that over Paris from St. Germain, but greener and with a greater sweep of valley. The vegetation along drives and walks through the country was rich and varied, there were large swimming-baths in

pretty surroundings, which, being supplied with continuously running water from naturally warm sulphur springs,
offered us children much pleasure. The largest pool
seemed almost a lake, and there were excellent swimming-
masters. We took swimming-lessons, and progressed
rapidly. I found afterward, however, it was much easier
to swim in sulphur-charged than in ordinary water, and
that I was far from seeming proficient elsewhere.

Somehow time passed very quickly in these surroundings. We were the only foreigners in either Baden
or Bad-Vöslau, and we knew none of the Austrians about
us. One could not, however, but admire and like them
as one looked on. Gay and sunny, they sang and
laughed, and never quarrelled nor wore discontented faces.
In the mornings at the pool they shouted with one
another, and if I found myself in deep water a friendly
pair of eyes seemed always watching me, and a friendly
hand was outstretched to hold my chin, with a cheering
word about how well my swimming was going. In the
afternoon one saw groups in pretty clothes wandering
over roads or fields, the girls' arms full of poppies and
corn-flowers, daisies and buttercups. Along the roadside
were scattered farmhouses with vine-clad arbors, and
there were always little family parties seated in the green
shade, drinking milk or beer or the light local wines.

It was on Sundays or in the evenings, though, that
spirits were highest. No matter how small the place,
one always found a restaurant or two with tables in the
open, and with really good music played by a more or
less important orchestra. All the population turned out
to sit in the cool air for hours, eat their light supper and
listen to their national operas or operettas, or·dance to
the inimitable Strauss waltzes, as only young, light-
hearted Austrians can. The elders, sipping their beer or

wine, gently, placidly nodded in time to the music, with
an amiable expression on their fat faces. Nearly all the
older people had grown heavy with comfortable living,
while the youngsters moved gracefully and were usually
slim. Later, as I grew to know society better in Vienna,
I noticed that among the nobility only the women put
on flesh with years, evidently from their sedentary lives
and large families, while riding, shooting, mountain-
climbing, and immense activity, both in their civilian
lives and their military profession, as well as in the super-
intending of the work on their estates, kept Austrian men
thin as well as immensely alive and interested.

Not so the bourgeois class we saw at Baden or Bad-
Vöslau. Apparently "business" meant to them opening
offices or shops slowly and late, carrying on the day's
work in a spirit of contentment, and closing up as early
as possible to return to their ham-and-salad supper and
the endless glasses of beer *en famille* afterward. I am
sure no two middle-aged business men ever talked shop
after office hours in old Austria, and, though they could
scarcely be called "live wires," they gave the impression
of making a solid, reliable class for the foundation of a
political state. Such peasants as we saw were dull-
looking and never seemed able to digest what one said
sufficiently to give a straight reply; but they partook of
the general amiability and struck one as rather helpless
children, content with their lot, devoted to their Emperor, and without the slightest ambition to move on in
the world.

This stability in the Austrians' lot had a very marked
effect on the people of all classes. The nobility were
born where they were, to stay there. They had inter-
married for generations and everything was laid out for
them from birth. They must be agreeable, unpreten-

tious, truthful, fine sportsmen and accomplished socially, but no one asked them to be intense or intellectual or ambitious; and they never were. They lived in their châteaux in summer and looked after their people, of whom they did take care in the most paternal way. They lived in dignity and state in winter in their great palaces, where, except for an occasional ball, they entertained only a few people, and those quite informally. Rarely they went abroad. One or two sporty couples went to England each year, where the men hunted and the women shopped. This was especially the case in such families as had English traditions or blood. A few of the men took long shooting trips to India, Africa, Russia, or the Rockies; also they went to Paris and Monte Carlo or Biarritz for a few weeks' change and gaiety. But in general they lived at home, where their own court society, the races in the spring, the country in summer, and their shooting in autumn and early winter made an agreeable routine programme, each year like the other. They were all handsome, high-bred, and extremely winning, but not much varied in type, and perhaps giving one the idea that they had mentally stood still for a long time with no desire to grow in any way. Their constant intermarriages made them so interrelated that one was always surprised things went as well as they did with these aristocratic brains and bodies.

In the middle class, tradition seemed as powerful as with the aristocracy. One had a feeling the bourgeois also lived and provided for his family on the same plan his ancestors always had. They kept their banks, offices, and shops, their hotels or apartments in certain quarters of the city, distinctly theirs, and they had their villas out of town, with fine carriages and horses. In high-finance circles society was gay, extravagant, and showy, and in the shopkeepers' group more modest but equally typical.

Beneath these three classes were the peasants. None of the groups intermingled their lives except inasmuch as their necessities of mutual requirements overlapped. At church the nobles sat in their loges, high finance and the bourgeois in places apart, while the peasants filled the body of the church; but all stood under one roof and apparently had kindly, tolerant smiles for one another. At a religious or patriotic festival the peasant on the sidewalk, the bourgeois in the window, and the noble in the procession were all warmly devoted to church and sovereign. There was no competition, no disdain, none of the ill feeling brought about by our fight for existence or our ambition to shine. Each, no matter what he did, would always stay in the station to which he was born, and he seemed to like that station and make the most of it, without desire to climb.

"Noblesse oblige" made the aristocrat busy himself with his duties toward the state and the peasant, whom he helped and took care of. He left business to the bourgeois. The latter handled it well, and the peasant did his work, which was rarely too hard, and took his amusements in off hours, depending on his landed proprietor for much that elsewhere he would have had to think of himself—such as supplies in a bad year, care in illness, or a decision as to the settlement of his possible difficulty with a brother peasant. Un-American all these arrangements were, but with certain advantages, for each class had its happiness and pleasures at their appointed times, and on the whole the state was kept and well served, and the people looked content.

Provincial and narrow and in some ways antiquated in their methods, also much more Oriental than ourselves, they lacked the intense push we prize; but the Austrians used up less strength, had to stand less wear and tear, and lived longer. One saw quite old couples in every walk of life sitting about, resting after their work years. On the whole, marriages seemed happy, also, and masses of children crowded about parents who treated them well and cared for them lovingly, even if rather casually because of their numbers.

Spending three or four months in the country gave us an opportunity to look closely at the people, not of the capital and the court but those who composed the mass of the Austrian nation, and one could not be near them without recognizing their qualities. Soft voices, gay spirits, warm hearts—they radiated kindness. Never pushing, not caring for foreigners at all, they yet were invariably courteous and ready to serve us to the best of their ability. A sunny, happy, kindly, innocent, attractive crowd always—who when the Emperor's birthday, with its celebration of music and song, occurred put all their devotion for him into their expressions of enthusiasm. They would say with affectionate tones: "Unser Franzerl, naturally we love him, for he is so echt Wiener." Calling him "our little Francis" and saying he was a "real Viennese" seemed to bring the man close to them, not as the great ruler but as one of themselves; and truly, later, as I knew him, he seemed to deserve their sentiment and to return it quite sincerely.

We heard from many, stories of his fondness for his people; how in his youth he adored Vienna and its citizens, wanting them to enjoy their lives; how he had helped with all the charities and amusements for the poor of the city; how he always circulated freely and informally among them, and was seen on the Ring constantly; how there was none so humble that he might not go direct to Francis Joseph and tell his trouble, sure of a hearing and sympathy, and often also having justice or assistance given him by the Emperor's personal order. The ruler's simple life was well known, and tales of his unspoiled ways were told; how he slept in a camp-bed in a whitewashed room with no carpet, in the midst of his fine palaces; how he rose daily at 4.30 A. M. and began his work, afterward eating only the lightest of breakfasts; how he attended mass daily. So it was, His Majesty gave the example of frugality and industry to his people and thought of them while his empire still slept, not even disturbing his old valet, who posed to the outside world as the master's friend and confidant, and undoubtedly was the source of a good many of the stories which circulated and everywhere created a pleasant impression of the sovereign.

After the Crown Prince's death the Emperor buried himself for the first period of deep mourning at the palace of Schönbrunn, alone with his sad thoughts and bitter disappointment, while his people waited in hushed sympathy outside his gates. When he drove out they stood along the road to town in bareheaded respect, peering anxiously into his face for signs of recognition, and looking for the old smile they had grown used to. Soon it came back, at least for those whom he passed thus, or those who immediately surrounded him in his household. Then he took up the burden of his duties; but after his son's disappearance the Emperor gave up everything but these duties of his great position. One exception he made: the shooting in season on his various estates.

My father had come home extremely pleased with the sovereign, when at his first reception by the latter he had presented his credentials. His Majesty had shown infinite cordiality; had said he was immensely glad to have my father represent the United States in Austria; had told how well he remembered receiving my grandfather at Schönbrunn many years before, when during his trip around the world the latter stopped for a while in Vienna. The Emperor asked my father about the last years of President Grant; asked news of grandmama, whom he also remembered. He said he was pleased she liked his home well enough to return again now on a pleasure trip. Then he inquired if my father were married and had children, and their ages, and did he shoot? On the affirmative reply to this, he went on to say he hoped they would shoot together some day, and that he also trusted we would like our life in Vienna and be happy there. He was all smiles and amiability, very magnetic—an example of what a man in his situation should be to win the hearts of those who approach him. He spoke no English and my father no French, but each had some knowledge of the language which the other used, so though an interpreter was present there was little translating to do.

Several times I saw the Emperor in the streets of his capital during the first winter we spent in Vienna. Occasionally he passed in a closed carriage, but generally he drove in a victoria, rather an informal-looking small one, where the back of his seat and the hood were low behind him, exposing him more fully to view than seemed usual in such vehicles. He seemed to show himself purposely to the passers-by, and he looked about with interest while the coachman, in rather plain livery, drove two fine horses rapidly. I do not remember a footman always being on the box, nor an aide-de-camp in the trap, though there may have been. The Emperor habitually wore the uniform of an Austrian general—or perhaps a field-marshal—with a full, large emerald-green plume; and I recall how the latter floated out backward from the rapidity of motion; also how he not only seriously saluted when people bowed or curtseyed at the roadside, but how he would smile genially and give a friendly little nod frequently, while he watched humble groups pass. Each person attributed this apparent recognition at once, to himself or herself, as a mark of favor.

Francis Joseph was very erect and had a slender figure for his age—fifty-nine or sixty, I think—with the healthy, ruddy skin of one who spends much time in the open air. He was rather bald, with white hair on the temples and at the back of his head. All the hair was clipped very short, but he wore fairly long, snow-white whiskers, and had a shaved chin, well modelled; thick lips, but his mouth seemed mobile, and his smile was agreeable. His nose was heavy and a little too short to be called aquiline, though it seemed that shape in profile. His eyes, I think, were gray. One remembered them less for their color than for the light in them—of intense sympathy and interest in whomsoever he talked—and for the amusement which often suddenly gleamed in them. Altogether a magnetic, dignified personality, without evidence of effort to draw one to him, and certainly without pose, was the Austrian Emperor in 1889.

He had done his best through many troubles and failures in war and peace, had fought intrigue abroad and at home, and had suffered keenly; yet he held his people's love, respect, and admiration, kept all the various nations of his empire attached to himself, however they might feel toward one another, and in many ways had managed to make good. At last, by his son's death, he stood on the threshold of old age without a natural heir prepared to follow him. One of a group of nephews would inherit his throne. He knew them to be unpopular, yet fate had thrust them now into the place of his own brilliant Rudolf, and Francis Joseph, the first shock over, turned patiently again to his duties as a ruler, and to the more delicate task of educating Francis Ferdinand, the son of his brother, for the succession; an effort, nobly faced without complaint.

We got back to town early in the autumn. The legation moved into its new quarters and we into the big apartment over it, amid the American furniture, which had arrived. There was much joy and excitement in unpacking our things and installing them in our foreign home, where there was plenty of room to spread out. As they were made habitable the great spaces looked very well indeed. Our entrance and marble stairs were quite imposing, and the apartments opened up nicely, from a very light large front hall, where were grouped many typical souvenirs of America.

Among these hung a number of rare and beautiful red Indian head-dresses, of feathers, beads, and leather, given to my father, or captured by him in the Far Western fights in which he had spent his early years of service. There was one whole dress of wonderful bead embroidery, bright blue in tone and so heavy I could not lift it, which had belonged to a red chief's daughter. There were, besides, various arms—spears or guns father had captured, as well as his own guns, with which Indians in battle, or buffalo for food and robes, had been killed. All through the years we spent in old Vienna this collection of trophies was slowly augmented. One after another heads, antlers, and stuffed birds arrived, marked with dates and the names of the estates on which they had been killed, and many sportsmen wandered out into that hall after dinner or tea to examine and compare these with some they had heard of elsewhere.

My father was in his element among these first-class sportsmen, some of whom had world-wide records. His own included grizzly bear and buffalo, as well as deer and smaller game in the United States, tiger and elephant in India, and various animals on the African continent; all that had been within his reach anywhere he had travelled.

The Emperor, remembering their conversation, "commanded" my father to an early shooting party of the court, a formal affair. On that first day he beat the other guns and established his reputation. He returned home somewhat weary from the effort of walking and sport after years when he had not held a gun, but delighted with the perfection of organization and the quantity of the game. He had been congratulated and praised by all the other sportsmen, the Emperor included, who had said to him, "if he shot like that he must come again, and often!" It was the custom that each chief of mission who could handle a gun was invited once every autumn to a day of imperial sport. One or two exceptions, men really fond of it, were asked to shoot several times. My father was one of these fortunate sportsmen at once, and after the second season we spent in Austria he was, I believe, included in every shooting party near Vienna which the Emperor gave; much to his own delight, for my father loved the long days in the open, the congenial companions, and the fine opportunity to use his own skill. He also valued the relations so established, which gave him opportunity to place a word now and again to the great advantage of the work he was in Austria to do.

An Emperor in shooting garb, or a Minister of Foreign Affairs over a hunt picnic luncheon, must necessarily be in less formal and less defensive mood to handle business; and they soon learned to trust and like the unpretentious, honest, and very capable representative of America's interests.

Franz, the legation footman who had met us at the station on that morning of our arrival, was much honored that my father, finding on inquiry he knew all about firearms, had promoted him to be "huntsman" instead of looking farther afield for some one to fill this place. With happiness the man would lay aside his livery and don homespun and leather clothes, and if my mother chanced to make some plan for the shooting days he would reproachfully say to her: "Excellenz forget; Excellenz and me, we go to shoot mit Majestät to-morrow—we make no calls." Franz was devoted to the Emperor and glad to be in the latter's neighborhood where he could see him; also he snobbishly enjoyed his rank of huntsman; but most of all he was intensely proud of my father's enormous bags, and he counted the pheasants, hares, or other animals which were put out of commission with a feeling of glory. Always on their return he would announce with grave triumph, "To-day Excellenz kill most hares," or "To-day Excellenz get next most hares. One other have much better luck, more hare run to him—Excellenz not miss!" But Franz liked the shorter announcement best, and generally was lucky in being satisfied that his candidate had carried off the honors.

Besides these big shoots on the imperial estates, my father had opportunities, always seized, of getting chamois or capercailzie on the mountainous estates of various huntsmen he had met before. Among these were Prince Henry Liechtenstein and Prince Montenuevo. The latter was head of the house descended from Napoleon's Austrian Empress and her second husband, married when she returned to her home country after the Res-

toration in France. Liechtenstein and Montenuevo had
been in the United States on a shooting trip to the
Rockies in my father's young days, and the latter had
been a member of their party, so that they had chummed
during weeks of rough frontier life.

When we reached Vienna these sportsmen came to call
at once and Prince and Princess Montenuevo were most
friendly and charming, and invited my parents to their
home. Afterward my father and Montenuevo did much
shooting together. Liechtenstein had not married. He
was one of the handsomest men in Austria, and one of
the greatest sportsmen. A younger son of the reigning
house whose name he bore, he used his income wandering, and when at home lived quietly in a small flat at his
brother's palace. He rarely went about in society,
though when he did go he dwarfed every one by his
size, looks, and wit. A most cultured cosmopolitan, at
home in Paris and London as well as in Vienna, he was
content to live for books and sport, with an occasional
romance, which he managed to handle adroitly enough
to avoid both scandal and broken hearts. He and my
father had much in common in politics, their military
life, books, and travel, as well as sport. They also had
many friends in common scattered about the world, and
Liechtenstein made himself delightful to my mother and
became a frequenter of her salon in an informal way.
He had been initiated into the Order of Malta or of St.
John of Jerusalem, and could not marry, he said; and he
would laugh and exclaim: "Why should I, Mrs. Grant?
I am old, and my brother is married. He has five sons
or more; surely that is enough!" But rumor had it that
Henry Liechtenstein wandered and was a knight because
of some fair lady whom he could not marry, but to whom
for years he had given his allegiance.

If he wore such chains they must have weighed on him lightly, for he was cheerful company, and in the years I knew him I never saw him refuse to smile on any attractive woman. He made himself so agreeable that many a feminine sigh went up to heaven over his travelling propensities, which savored of a desire for escape. He was one of the most interesting and splendid figures in all my impressions of Vienna, and my father and he were warm friends again in their prime, as they had been in youth. Prince Liechtenstein introduced my parents to his family. We found the members of it knew almost no foreigners and realized not at all what was going on in the great world outside their frame. With a quaint expression of despair when my mother would say, "How can you go away and leave such charming surroundings for long, wild trips?" Liechtenstein would reply: "Yes, of course you are right, they are charming, but they are all my family here, and I must take the air sometimes and see those who are not my family. Here in Vienna I get into a cab on the Ring and say 'Take me home,' and the fiacre looks at me and drives to my door. It is not interesting to be only with those who have known you since you were born, so though I like to be here I also must go away sometimes to breathe."

Years after we left Vienna I met Henry Liechtenstein in Paris, in the salon of a great beauty. He was a star still in a most distinguished constellation, and had kept his active brain and handsome figure, though his hair was grown white. We met as old friends, and I enjoyed his quaint conversation, which carried me back to my early youth. He showed real enthusiasm in asking for my parents, and he came to see me once or twice, before I left Paris, to talk of them and of old times.

Later, on another trip, I saw his towering figure in the

crowd on the Rue de la Paix—handsome still, but his face much aged. He recognized me and stopped to make the usual friendly inquiries. I told him I was departing that day for Russia. He said: "I am sorry, but give my friends there my remembrances and also messages to your dear parents, when you write to them." Then we passed on our several ways, to meet no more, for shortly afterward I heard that Liechtenstein had died in Vienna. Since the war I have been glad he did not live to see the misery in his own country, his family scattered and sacrificed, and all his friends in the Allied nations grown to be the enemies of what he represented. To me Liechtenstein stood for all that was best in Austria, under the old régime and traditions.

I remember once some one spoke before me of a trait Austrian servants showed of agreeing with their masters, even to the point of asserting things of which they knew nothing or which they knew to be untrue, rather than to contradict or tell an unpleasant bit of news. Liechtenstein showed great tolerance of what some other person present had dubbed the "Austrian people's tendency to lie." My father said, smiling: "But you yourself and your class never would lie. Why do you defend it in your people?" "Well," said Liechtenstein slowly, as if for the first time this point was brought up in his mind, "we of the nobility can't lie. We have the obligation to be different from our people and more carefully realize values—to be gentlemen—while our people are like children—they have many good traits and impulses, but not the obligation to be responsible or entirely truthful. Yet it is not wickedness when they do not tell the exact facts; it is more a desire to please or to be polite and amiable. Sometimes, also, it is due to fear, a luxury the aristocrat cannot permit himself."

I began to understand that in Austria nobility was not a matter of mere palaces and jewels, riches and power, but also a matter of bravery, honesty, and loyal protection to those who had been confided to the aristocrats as "their people." The latter gave work and faithful devotion in exchange for protection and care to them and theirs, in hard times or illness, and it might be that, though their ideals were not ours, a good deal was to be said for the beauty of lives and traditions under such a monarchy.

So I discovered little by little that ancient lands have qualities as well as our homeland for which we claim such high ideals. Both suffer by the fact that in reducing theory to practice individual men contaminate ideals by casual interpretations; but even if one loves the new world better, it is no reason to accuse the old of all the vices. As I grew to know Austria and the Austrians, I grew also to love them and our life there. They seemed all to dislike the Germans, took great pains to use with affectation their own Viennese patois, which had a much softer sound than the language of the northern Teutons. The Viennese dialect was used in the small theatres both at Baden and Bad-Vöslau, where, by the way, the performances were varied and very first class. It was used also in the operettas, the imperial theatre, and even the opera, where altogether classic programmes were given by companies of the best talent in Europe. The Emperor and his court spoke entirely in the same language used by the cabmen and market-women, who had coined this soft, pretty idiom. Nothing pleased people more than for strangers to affect their way of slurring and swallowing words and softening consonants or dropping them, or changing terminations of the harsh German diminutives, and saying Mäderl for Mädchen, or Lämperl for Lämpchen.

We children took to the ways of the Austrians quickly, and had an Austrian Fräulein Mitzi to teach us through the summer. In the autumn my brother entered the Thérésianum, the great school founded by Maria Theresa for her nobility. It was difficult to enter and stay there because, firstly, the Austrian of rank only was acceptable, and, secondly, the course was difficult for any outsider to follow. But a few exceptions had been made, and at the time my brother entered, the young Egyptian who afterward became Khedive was the only other foreigner in the Thérésianum. He was in a class a year or two ahead of my brother. Aged eight, the latter was taken by us all one morning to begin his new life in the great building. Leaving him there to fight out his destiny among strange boys and teachers nearly broke my mother's heart, and she always regarded the years he spent in the Thérésianum as a terrible experience in her child's life, I think.

Really, it was difficult to fit oneself into new ideas and use a new language. The course was a more serious one than that into which small boys in America plunge when they first go to school, but on the whole, after a few weeks, my brother liked his companions and teachers. At any rate, for four years he did well and seemed to have an excellent feeling for those with whom he associated.

In the Legation offices all went smoothly. My father liked his staff, especially his naval and military attachés (the latter was an old comrade of his West Point days), and both had charming wives; so his official family was a gay and happy group.

CHAPTER IV

VIENNA SILHOUETTES

AT the head of the corps of diplomatic representatives stood the magnificent figure of Monsignor Galimberti, soon afterward Cardinal, and the intimate friend of His Holiness. Galimberti was considered one of the handsomest, cleverest, most cultivated, and affable men in Europe, and wielded immense power with His Apostolic Majesty, the Austrian Emperor, first son of the Church of Rome. Galimberti enjoyed society immensely, and always played a great rôle, with his rank and brains and beauty of robes and feature. A man somewhat over fifty, high-bred, and with quick, clear eyes, he led the conversation and captivated those who surrounded him, whether in his capacity of prelate, man of the world, statesman, or merely a human being. He was seemingly very unpretentious, with a kindly word for the footman who took his cloak or the child who was presented to him. Italian by birth and traditions, he was cosmopolitan by education, and quite unbiassed, and he made himself sincerely admired. He found time often to stop in at my mother's for a chat, and the success of the Protestant American couple in winning and holding his interest caused much talk, we heard, among their Catholic rivals for the prelate's attentions.

Next came the Italian Ambassador, who in looks, charm, intellect, and dignity was a social rival of the papal nuncio. The two men, of course, politically belonged to different factions, though Count Nigra was a Catholic. But he represented the King, who in United Italy was the usurper of the Vatican's temporal power,

according to the Pontiff. The Holy Father did not receive King Humbert or the beautiful Queen Margherita,
and could not himself move beyond the gardens of the
Vatican. Austria's Emperor, I think, was in a difficult
position, for his title of Apostolic Majesty had been
given by the Roman popes centuries ago, and the Haps-
burgs had always been the most enthusiastic supporters
and the "eldest children" of the Vatican, while, since
the Triple Alliance had been inaugurated, the King of
Italy, like the German Emperor, was Francis Joseph's
friend and ally. Within the century and his own reign,
Germany had captured Austrian provinces in the north,
while Italy had seized Tuscan and Venetian lands, and
the old Grand Duke of Tuscany lived in exile in Vienna
under the protection of his Hapsburg cousin.

Count Nigra was just the man to ease a strained
situation. Of international reputation for his suave and
supple qualities of brain and manner, a man of wealth
and culture, he made the Italian Embassy the scene of
constant and most agreeable small parties. Bores were
not admitted except at a few big official parties, and then
they were so overbalanced by wits and beauties that they
seemed unable to tarnish their surroundings, as elsewhere
they might. Nigra, himself a delightful conversation-
alist, led off in the gaiety of his feasts, and his *cordon bleu*
was one of the best chefs in a capital famous for its
admirable food. A series of official dinners occurred
each year at the Italian Embassy, where the court and
diplomatic corps were agreeably mixed, and at these presided in turn, once each, the wives of the host's colleagues. The wife of an ambassador or minister was
glad always to mention she was to play hostess at the
banquet of such a date. Therefore there was considerable conversation, some of it a little acid, when it was

discovered by close observers that there had been three
or four dinners in one season at which my mother had
done the honors, and that by degrees Count Nigra more
and more frequently invited the pretty American lady to
sit at the head of his great board.

Both my mother and father enjoyed the Italian's parties extremely, for they were soon favored by the friendship of those men and women Nigra frequented. Consequently my parents felt at home at these gatherings,
which were as informal as possible, in spite of their elegance, the beautiful appointments of flowers and silver,
and the damasks and art collections with which the
talented old bachelor surrounded himself.

It was amusing to notice how pleased people were by
an invitation from him, and how the women prepared
and reserved their best gowns for the frame of the Italian
Embassy, while men would speak of the good dinner to
come, and the probably interesting talk. To Count
Nigra's credit it must be said that in four seasons I never
heard of any one who was disillusioned by what he offered
them in the way of entertainment. Aside from his
superficial gifts, he was admired and beloved. I saw him
often after I made my début, and was really touched
when months after I returned to America the mail one
morning brought me a New Year's greeting with the
best of wishes for my success in America, signed "Nigra."

After his signal services at the Hapsburg court, where
he had established the best of relations between old and
hereditary enemies, this distinguished diplomat received
the recompense he merited at his King's hands, and was
recalled to Rome to take over the Ministry of Foreign
Affairs. Some years later he died, mourned by a host of
friends the world over. Constantly in my later life I
found a bond with some stranger through our mutual
admiration and fondness for Count Nigra.

GENERAL FREDERICK DENT GRANT AT THE TIME OF THE
SPANISH-AMERICAN WAR.

Germany, the third member of the "Triplice," was represented at Vienna by the best they could send, Prince Henry of Reuss, a cultivated and agreeable aristocrat, elderly and dignified. His Embassy palace was in the new part of town and seemed showy, large, imposing, uninteresting, and somewhat arrogant in its nouveauriche gilding and its modern portraits of equally modern emperors. Prince Reuss and his wife were not themselves so new as their surroundings, however. She, of Saxe-Weimar blood, though heavy, red-faced, and typically German in looks and dress, had brains far beyond the recipe of the young Emperor William for the women of his empire, when he said they should be exclusively interested in their "Kirche, Kinder, und Küche " (church, children, and kitchens). Princess Reuss's ancestors had been among the small German sovereigns who cultivated the arts, and Goethe at Weimar had lived all the latter part of his life as their protégé. Her father was own brother to Augusta, old Emperor William's wife. Emperor Frederick was therefore Princess Reuss's first cousin, and William II was her second cousin. She had apparently no particular scruple in showing that she did not agree with various parts of her young sovereign's policy. She frankly said his attitude toward his parents and toward Bismarck was all that was arrogant and lacking in the respect due them.

Finally, when Bismarck was summarily dismissed by William II, the ex-Chancellor passed through Vienna on his way for a cure, and Princess Reuss chose the moment to make a conspicuous demonstration by going to call on him. She announced to all her friends she did so because she had been brought up to see in Bismarck the genius who built Germany, for which good Germans should not be ungrateful. She added further spicy remarks, suggesting that in her opinion the German Em-

peror was ignorant and young, and should be shown how
to behave. I fancy William II was already far beyond
learning from any one, least of all from his cousin. Reuss
himself made no sign, and one could only wonder how
far his silence was official, and whether he approved or
disagreed with his wife. He let her talk without pro-
testing, however, and she went to call on Bismarck while
her husband stayed shut up in the Embassy.

Vienna discussed and enjoyed the situation very much
indeed, for I think honestly the gentle Austrians cared
little for their northern allies. Doubtless Berlin echoed
this, and the upshot was that after a few months Prince
Reuss, who was older than his wife by nearly twenty
years, retired from the diplomatic service. They returned to Germany to educate their children shortly
before my father took us home to the United States.

Princess Reuss had the qualities of her race, for she
was a fine musician, a serious reader and thinker, with
an admirable practical mind and sincere convictions.
My father enjoyed conversing with her, as did other
brainy men, who were always interested in her conclusions
on the political questions of the day. She was a student
of art and history, and could be very amiable and altogether simple, but she was immensely direct, thought it
not worth while to make an effort when there was no
feeling of sympathy behind it, and, consequently, ignored
a good many smaller people, when her smiling on them
might have contributed to her general popularity or made
the fêtes at the German Embassy more brilliant than they
ever appeared to be in Vienna's season. She seemed a
very devoted but somewhat severe mother, with three
nice children, two sons and a daughter.

Twenty or more years after all this, in Russia, I met
the latter again, a typical, gentle, round-faced girl, get-

ting on in life, still unmarried, and with a subdued look. I no longer felt I knew her well enough to ask what her life had been, but I fancied it was not a gay one.

Outside the "Triplice" ambassadors, there were their rivals, though so excellent were social relations that no friction ever occurred. As an individual, first among these stood Prince Lobanoff, the Russian Ambassador, a bachelor, a student of people, history, and politics, a man of immense distinction and charm of mind and manner. Rich, with collections of books, furniture, and works of art, he represented the best Russia could produce. A Slav, artistic, supple, strong, amiable, simple, a delightful companion and a warm friend, he was a most able representative of his Emperor. Both the latter's noble, splendid nature and his strength were felt; for Alexander III, the home-loving autocrat, was reigning then in St. Petersburg and made his power for good realized, in wholesome fashion, all over Europe. The Ambassador was well surrounded by able men and attractive women, and the latter received with him to perfection. We grew unaccountably intimate with them, as one does with Russians, who are always natural and charming. For many years afterward we kept up the warm relations formed.

My father and Lobanoff corresponded after we left Vienna until the latter died. He had, like Nigra, been recalled to his own land to a high post under Nicholas II. At the time of his death he still filled this post. Among his papers was found an analysis of his sovereign's character, judging the latter most exactly both in his good qualities and his weaknesses, a portrait which afterward our Emperor unconsciously lived up to in every detail, proving what an admirable psychologist Prince Lobanoff was.

Very shortly before his death Lobanoff sent my father a fine photogravure of a painting of him which had just been completed. Then we heard of his death and thought the thread was broken, but years later my Russian brother-in-law married the distinguished old man's grand-niece, and I found myself surrounded in the latter's salon with Lobanoff souvenirs, some of which were gathered in Austria in those old days, when I had known him.

Prince Lobanoff's Embassy counsellor was Prince Gregory Cantacuzène, a relative of my own future husband, and I knew his daughter well and was very fond of her in our youth, little dreaming we should be connected some day, or that our boys would be classmates in the Russian Imperial Lyceum. There were several other members of the Russian Embassy in Vienna whom I met again in my adopted home and with whom the relations established long before were later taken up with pleasure.

The British Ambassador was a sunny, agreeable, good-natured sportsman — Sir Augustus Paget — handsome, friends with every one, very keen about shooting and the races, which were so good in Austria. He was well over sixty years old, but was learning to skate with enthusiasm and vigor, genially admitting he had had small pads put into the elbows of his skating-jacket and into various other vulnerable spots as well, where experience had taught him it was wise to protect himself. Lady Paget had been, and was still, at fifty or more, a great beauty, with enchanting clothes and distinguished manners and conversation, and she made the Embassy an attractive, homelike meeting-place to all Anglo-Saxons. She and my mother liked one another extremely.

The French Embassy was in a class by itself. Occupying the ancient and historic palace of the Lobkowitz family, its official parties were always well done and gay, with good music and fine silver from the French Government's garde-meuble. Also there was a daughter in the house who dressed smartly, and, known as the possessor of a comfortable dot, she was sufficiently surrounded by the youthful diplomats, especially her father's various young secretaries. But there were very few informal parties at the French Embassy. Albert Decrais, Ambassador, a short, thick-set wine-merchant of Bordeaux, might be a good man over his desk, but his lack of social talents prevented him from taking a place of importance among his colleagues, once the official bow and smile were accomplished. His wife was like himself, and remained mainly occupied by her homesickness for Bordeaux!

There was an old Turk, too, who after some years of ambassadorship committed suicide one day. Every one expressed official regrets and really felt rather sorry for his two sons, nice boys, who had been brought up in Europe and were pleasant members of our small dancing-class.

Among the ministers heading legations, old Count Bray, from Bavaria, eighty-four and an admirable shot as well as a cultivated, charming man of the world, had an agreeable position, since he represented the Austrian Empress's native country. Also Mr. de Lövenorn, the Danish Minister, had a brilliant wit with a sharp tongue, and was much invited. He had a particularly warm welcome in the agreeable small circle of which the Duke and Duchess of Cumberland were the centre, the latter being the youngest daughter of the King of Denmark and sister to the then Empress of Russia and the Princess Alexandra of Wales. Lövenorn was therefore received at first on this account by the Russians and British, too, and afterward by his own accomplishments and conversational talents he held his place. He and my father became excellent comrades, and when later I found him representing his country at the court of St. Petersburg he brought up pleasant memories of the days when so often they had talked and smoked or played whist together in Vienna. The various Belgians were agreeable and, representing the father of the widowed Crown Princess Stéphanie, they were welcome everywhere. Otherwise the diplomatic corps was composed of more or less average personalities, who made a neutral background for these particular stars in our firmament.

We seemed to have many attractive people constantly at our house, and by the time I was old enough to be presented at court, I had a number of well-disposed friends among my father's and mother's colleagues and among the *jeunesse dorée* which composed the groups of secretaries. I also had a lot of intimates among the young Austrian girls, usually so shy with foreigners that I apparently was the only non-Austrian in their midst; but their typical ways were half their charm to me, and their simple natures and manners led me to feel at ease.

Those early years in Vienna were spent very quietly, though the legation almost always contained a number of interesting people to whom I was allowed to listen, when I was at liberty. But for three winters I had mainly to study and was rarely in company.

We were a great deal with our parents, for through the spring and autumn their evenings were free, except when their informal dinners to travelling compatriots filled the legation salons. During the height of the winter season we usually went for an hour or two with them in the late afternoon to skate. My parents had both been very good at this sport in their youth, and they took it up again with much enjoyment as a change from office work or housekeeping cares. My brother and I were both learning, though I never managed to compare with my elders. However, I liked extremely both the gay crowd on the ice and the exercise in the cold air.

One year I studied dancing with some little girls at the palace of the Hungarian representative to the Austrian court. Hungary underscored its independence of the sister empire by sending this representative to live in state in Vienna. The palace was vast, dark, ancient, and splendid. The representative of the King of Hungary to the Austrian Emperor as a personage was equally magnificent. Mr. Sögueny, whose family had been too proud to accept a title from any modern sovereign's hands, made just claim, I was told, to one of the oldest and greatest names in Hungary. Sögueny was agreeable and distinguished in brain, manner, and looks, apparently also possessing the fire typical of his race. He impressed me very much with his swift and elegant movements, his swarthy skin, and intense blue-gray eyes, and though his black hair stood up straight in cultivated disorder on top of his head, giving him a ferocious look, he seemed the quintessence of perfection in his dress, and was a most affectionate and gentle father to his three daughters, Camilla, Maria, and Lili, who were my friends.

A year later, as I was going on sixteen, my mother arranged a larger class of boys and girls of the diplomatic corps, to dance at the legation on Saturday evenings. Young Dutch, Turks, Russians, English, French, and Spaniards came with their mothers and fathers to these early parties, and by degrees a number of secretaries and attachés won their way into being included, till the group grew far beyond the original intention of the organizer. However, we had delightful gatherings, and they helped me to know the young colleagues who would number among my partners when I was old enough to make my bow at court.

By this time my parents, and I also, were feeling very much at home in the beautiful Austrian capital. I had learned to speak German almost as did the natives, also I liked the whole atmosphere of our life, and I never had a feeling that any of the old customs were disagreeably strange. They had too much of historic interest and artistic value.

Especially two great ceremonies which occurred yearly made a strong impression on me. I grew to appreciate their religious meanings as well as their grandeur. One was a pageant through the streets of the old capital, and was called the "Corpus Christi Procession." It occurred a few days before or after Trinity Sunday, and in the soft June heat the ancient city looked its best. At a certain point on the route in one of the squares, where the architecture of the façades and a perfect gem of a fountain made exactly the background required, a stand was erected for such diplomats and foreigners as cared to view the scene.

Early in the morning we took our seats there and waited. Opposite our stand was placed a small temporary chapel, very handsome with its canopy of crimson velvet, embroidered and fringed in gold and fitted with an altar, with the flowers and vessels, missals and crucifix necessary to a service, which would break the progress of the solemn march. Soon—for all functions in Vienna were very prompt—a hush fell over the company assembled in the square, and one looked about at this picture of the Middle Ages, which really it was in all respects save our own incongruous clothes: the perfect blue against which roof lines of red or green or brown tiles silhouetted themselves made a delightful effect, as did the balconies and windows in which women and girls in bright gowns were seated, the gentle murmur of the fountain, the gay velvet of the chapel, and our own red stand, together with a strip of carpet in the same rich color rolled out over sand which was spread to soften the cobblestones along the route. On the sand and over the carpet were scattered twigs and green leaves, symbolic of the holiday and adding their note of color.

A procession approached solemnly through the sunshine, and it was quite impossible even to name all the participants in this magnificent throng, more mediæval even than its frame. There were choir-boys and incensebearers in scarlet with white lace, prelates in robes of black and gold and purple, bishops and archbishops in full regalia, the first among them marching in state under a red-and-gold canopy, and carrying high the Host on a covered tray, so all might see and cross themselves devoutly as the Holy of Holies passed them by. There was no music but the slow, lovely chant of the young choristers. With dignity the lines came to a standstill in front of the wee chapel, where a short service was held; then the march was resumed and went on through the winding streets, till it ended in one of the churches.

As the procession halted, and the personages in it took their places, it was to be seen that behind the prelates, following the canopy, his bared head bowed in the hot sun, walked His Majesty the Emperor. None was a more attentive son of the church than he, and his simple sincerity and faith were evident in the example he set the archdukes and the members of his court. He was in full uniform and carried a great candle in one hand, together with his headgear. With his other hand he devoutly made the sign of the cross at proper intervals.

In a body the archdukes were a fine-looking group. Old Charles Louis, the Emperor's brother, looked older and less vigorous than the sovereign, whose junior he really was by several years; he moved slowly and without Francis Joseph's quick compactness. His three sons came next in line. Francis Ferdinand, the new heir since Rudolf's death, was tightly buttoned in an unbecoming uniform, seemed large and heavy, with sandy hair and mustache, and dull eyes. No wonder the people felt less enthusiasm for him than for his brilliant cousin, who had been an heir after their own hearts, in spite of all his failings. The handsome reprobate, Otto, came next. His conduct was the town's talk, and he was to die from dissipation. In this group was a third brother, an overgrown youth with amiable expression, called Ferdinand.

Then there was old Archduke Albert, a hero of several wars, his body slightly bent by age, but with a spirit which still carried him through long ceremonies. He was pointed out to me by my father as the most distinguished in reputation of the imperial family, and later at court I met him, when he seemed very amiable and told me how he had known my grandfather during the latter's visit to Austria. He had white hair, closely clipped, a closely clipped white beard and mustache as well; he was frailer and more shrivelled than the Emperor, and his eyes behind his spectacles looked old and strained though not dull.

Albert was rich and had a palace, one of the handsomest in Vienna, which stood up well above the surrounding buildings on an eminence, and there he and the charming old Archduchess Elisabeth, mother of the then Queen Regent of Spain, had their apartments. Surrounded by many souvenirs of their past, this old fraternal pair led a contented life. They enjoyed doing good to their people, and fulfilled their round of duties, both religious and civic. The Emperor was fond of both and they had a unique position at court, whenever they chose to appear, which was very rarely. Generally they saw a variety of people within the walls of their own palace, where their dinners brought together many choice spirits, the light repast of perfect food and rare vintages, followed by fine music, providing an excuse for meetings well worth while.

There were several more male members of the Hapsburg family in the procession of the Corpus Christi feast-day, but only one other person attracted notice—that was the Archduke Eugene. He was admittedly the most picturesque person at the Austrian court, towering by nearly a head in height above the tall men of the aristocracy, and bearing his well-proportioned figure finely. His beauty was, however, even more a matter of expression and high breeding than of feature. The color of his eyes or the shape of his nose was of no consequence, but one kept the remembrance of his ability to represent a thousand years or more of imperial traditions, and in spite of comparative youth his dignity was as great as his simplicity. To meet him was the ambition of almost all the women, but when the introduction was over and a few polite sentences had been exchanged, the incident was closed once and for all. Eugene's occupations were of a serious nature, and he gave himself up to them completely. He had joined the Order of St. John, and I never saw him appear at any but religious or state ceremonies—and then in the full robes of his order. The sweeping plumed hat of Rubens's time, made in black, became his small head, with its short cropped curls, while his long white cloth cape with its black Maltese cross over the heart, together with the boots, gauntlets, and other garments of the same period, seemed most effective. This costume stood out in the mass of bright colors at court, yet all theatrical effect was counteracted by the earnestness of eyes and unconsciousness of carriage. Those belonged to some knight of the Round Table, and held even strangers in respect.

I do not remember seeing the Archduke Eugene at a court ball. He never danced, and at these functions my interest was centred completely in the young officers or diplomats who best understood Strauss's rhythm; but in the "Corpus Christi Procession" the religious uniform of St. John's and its wearer caught and held one's attention. It was so at the "Foot-Washing Ceremony," too, where somehow he seemed to be the central figure in a group of picked men.

This quaint ceremony, with its lovely tradition of the humility of power and riches toward poverty, occurred for many centuries in the beautiful frame of the old Hofburg palace quite regularly Thursday morning in Holy Week. A small gallery was erected for the diplomatic corps, whose members came at an early hour, the men in uniform, the women all in black. The great room, softly lighted, was very impressive. Finely proportioned, decorated as in old days only it could be done, when real artists made a life-work of such ornamentation, its carvings and gilt, touched lovingly by time, made the background seem worthy of the ceremony which soon was to take place there. In front of our gallery stood a raised dais, knee-high, and on this twelve seats with a long table just found room. Only a few chamberlains were about. They made us welcome and showed us to our places, then resumed their whispering among themselves.

In the distance we heard vague chants from the imperial chapel, where mass was being celebrated. The service finished, voices approached us from a distance through the halls. Then, as usual, handsome Count Hunyady, grand marshal of the court, appeared and stood in an imposing position before the double door at the extreme end of the room exactly opposite to us. From a side entrance a strange group appeared: twelve old men—the "oldest and poorest beggars" in Vienna—were brought in. They were white-haired and childish of face, and looked just right in the costumes they wore, cut on long, straight lines in some dark, soft material. Quaint capes covered their shoulders, and broad-brimmed soft hats were on their heads. Linen collars, startlingly white, were turned down about their necks.

I am sure Rubens or Vandyke must have designed those clothes for the beggars of a Holy Roman Emperor! As they were helped up the two or three steps of their platform and seated themselves painfully, it was easy to see the old fellows were pleased with their finery. They smoothed it or the table-cloth with satisfied looks, and nodded and signed to one another. They probably were all over eighty and some looked much more. Finally they gazed in silent admiration at the room, which doubtless to them was the realization of a fairy-tale oft told, and they leaned back in their seats, then finally concentrated their attention on the door dominated by Count Hunyady's person.

Indeed, the old count was well worth looking at. He was a very gay gentleman in his off hours, 'twas whispered, well known for his successes and his escapades. Though he still kept his beautiful figure—shown now to full advantage in his tight Hungarian uniform of scarlet and gold and white, with the sable-trimmed dolman hanging from his shoulders—the early good looks of his face were somewhat dimmed by years. White curling hair gathered thick enough to show the care given it, and admirable features were a marked advantage in spite of wrinkles in the olive skin. His expression was one of acute boredom, which occasionally lighted up to a smile at some witticism or became quite winning if an attractive woman turned her glance on him. Habitually at court functions he floated through his round of duties with a perfect knowledge which translated itself into negligent elegance. Hunyady was much admired by certain ladies at court, who watched his every motion, while others had a way of speaking of him with a show of disapproval. I think the Emperor thought him excellent in his rôle, and knew he was entirely reliable in handling the most complicated ceremonies. His Majesty occasionally glanced at the brilliant functionary with amused amiability, as he might at a pretty woman's play of vanity. The two men were old comrades, and, to do the count justice, I heard he was as good with horse and gun as he was perfect at the court.

As sounds of the chant approached, Hunyady's face kept its mask of indifference, but he glanced about the room with a quick eye guaranteed to take in any detail which might be wrong. Then he shrugged his shoulders, shaking his becoming dolman, and straightening up to his full height he struck the floor sharply three times with a long cane which was the badge of his office. Every one instantly turned toward the door and gave the grand marshal complete attention. Affecting still his expression of calm, Hunyady again struck the floor three times, and as he did so the two doors swung open slowly behind him, disclosing the room beyond. Half-way across what seemed an immense stretch of polished inlaid floor advanced the Emperor at the head of his court. Hunyady moved then with continued comprehension of his rôle, clearing the way for the sovereign to the centre of our hall. Right opposite the semicircle of old men he stopped, turned and bowed low and gracefully to His Majesty, who was crossing the threshold of the doorway where a moment ago the grand marshal had stood.

As the Emperor entered every one rose, bowing or curtseying to His Majesty. The latter returned the salutations, looking to left and right with his usual gentle expression, and then he advanced to the point indicated by the grand marshal. Hunyady, straightening again, moved aside to give various further directions, if necessary, but all the actors were so used to their parts that no coaching was required. Passing his plumed headgear and gloves to the person indicated for that service, Francis Joseph, in all simplicity, stepped up to the beggars' table, and immediately twelve of the royal Hungarian body-guard appeared, each carrying a tray heavily laden with a meal prepared and served, ready to be heated. These trays the guardsmen held at a distance of about two feet from the table's edge, while the Emperor, passing down this open passage, transferred all the dishes, from the first to the latter, so that the dinner of each guest was placed before him by his imperial host. Naturally the old men needed time and help to eat, so the food was not eaten there. I was afraid they were losing their dinners, but I was told not, and that the trays, dishes, and food would be snugly packed in twelve baskets and put into the twelve court carriages which, after the ceremony, would convey the quaint members of the feast to their several homes. Also I heard that enough food was given to each to feed a family party of six people for supper that evening.

The splendid Hungarians gathered up and bore off all their trays of food, then instantly another row of huge men in court livery stepped forward, to carry away the whole of the semicircular table in one movement. Without a hitch they picked it up in sections, one from in front of each old man. The Emperor came forward again, and three members of the court fell in line near him, one carrying a basin, another a tall jug (both of which may have been ordered by Maximilian from some Renaissance artist, to judge by their lovely workmanship), while the third official carried a beautiful towel. Two pages or chamberlains preceded the Emperor and rapidly removed one shoe and sock from each old man. Then the sovereign passed slowly down the line, and each naked foot in turn was held over the basin while the ewer-carrier poured on water and Francis Joseph splashed and rubbed a little, afterward taking the towel to wipe the foot dry.

He did this whole job with his usual earnest good-will, much more carefully than those who were helping would have done it, for they looked decidedly bored as they moved from one to another of the mendicants, while His Majesty never lost interest for a moment, and seemed to finish the drying thoroughly. Following Francis Joseph came two more officials, who put on all the footgear and fastened it, the old men still keeping their seats.

All this had taken some time, but as a finale to the feast the Emperor passed down the whole row once more. One of the Hungarian guardsmen carried on a tray twelve small but heavy bags, which we were told contained gold pieces. Each hung like a locket on a long ribbon or string, and to one after another of the guests of honor Francis Joseph spoke in a kindly tone, as he put in each case a ribbon over the head. The impression of his sunny smile was the last to light the memories of this day of days for the pensioners.

No Christian could have been more sincere in the performance of a religious duty, and as one watched him in the midst of his power humbling himself to wash the feet of his poorest and oldest subjects, one realized fully why it was that outside the palace his people loved Francis Joseph.

While the long and complicated function lasted, archdukes and members of the court stood about in uniforms of red and blue and green with gold or silver trimming glistening as it caught the light—a perfect riot of color, in which Eugene's white-and-black figure stood near a column, immobile as a statue.

I was told these functions had lost much of their effect by the absence of the empress and her following of women. This might be, for certainly the balls where the women took a part were very fine; but the Corpus Christi Procession and the Foot-Washing Ceremony as pictures seemed to me complete; and the life and color of these scenes burned themselves into my memory, as well as the religious spirit of the Emperor and the example he set his subjects.

A uniform almost barbaric in its splendor was that worn by the Hungarian guards—scarlet it was, with gold embroideries and trappings. The boots, knee-high, of pale-yellow leather, were skilfully embroidered around their tops, and to finish off this magnificence a leopard's skin was fastened over one arm and under the other, with a huge buckle on the chest which seemed to suggest the workmanship of Oriental hands. The men, both in this regiment and that of the Austrian imperial guards (who were scarcely less handsome, though more modern as to uniform), were all picked for size and looks, I think. They were young and measured over six feet. At that time I had seen nothing more grand than they were when they appeared on duty, whether to line up round the walls of the old ballrooms or to fetch and carry for their sovereign when he was serving twelve beggars.

In the year before I went to court I had another very interesting experience, which was a visit I made with my parents to the castle of Prince and Princess Alfred Liechtenstein. A long time back the Liechtensteins had asked us, and I was included in the invitation in spite of my youth, because the host and hostess had a daughter who was also to make her début during the following season. I had already met her and her older sister and liked both of them extremely.

Prince Alfred Liechtenstein was head of the younger branch of his house, but his first cousin, the reigning Prince of Liechtenstein, had neither son nor brother, so Alfred and his eldest born were heirs to the principality. Incidentally, he had four other sons and two daughters —Fanny, who was a most cultivated person, and Thérèse, who promised to be a beauty, as her mother was. Even years and flesh had not spoiled the classic face and the fair skin of Princess Liechtenstein, while the serenity of her expression bore witness to the sheltered, happy life she led. She and her husband, who openly adored her and who was her first cousin—for she was a sister of the reigning prince—had divided their lives between the family principality where she was reared, the gay Austrian capital, where they used the second-best palace of her brother, and old Hollenegg Castle, which was built by their ancestors some time in the tenth century. In a gentle way they took immense pride in Hollenegg's beauty and historic value, as in the traditions of great deeds done and positions well filled by many Liechtensteins since the beginning of the Austrian Empire. Hollenegg, with its courtyard of stone and beautiful wrought-iron well, with the colonnaded galleries one floor above another, with its ancient chapel built within the court, was full of poetic sentiment to the owners of the place. Outside it had been originally the most forbidding of fortresses, with several towers, that still stood grimly above the main walls, their narrow windows scarce allowing light to enter such rooms as were at all habitable. A fine moat, deep and wide, had once surrounded the vast pile, and this was in part left in its old proportions for its decorative quality, while in other spots it was filled in to allow the lawns to run up to the bastions.

The rough stone's severity was now draped in the richest of flowering rose-vines, white and pink, which decked the old walls with wreaths worthy of their victorious traditions. Trees had had time to grow up to large proportions, and spread out on the lawn, where a tea-table near a bowling-green made a tempting, home-like note. In the courtyard peacocks trailed or spread their tails, and within this square, with its grass and gardens, the roses also climbed over all balustrades and balconies. The courtyard architecture was varied in epoch, as generation after generation had improved the place or built new features in the style of their own times. One long gallery was colonnaded in a way recalling northern Italy, and probably was the result of the proprietor's visit to Sforza villas. Elsewhere a suggestion of the architecture of Byzantium made one ask if a crusader or some traveller of the family had been there. There were various pointed arches or doorways, too, taken from Gothic models, with graceful light decorations. The mellow light and the uniform material of pale stone lent themselves to a general effect of rich harmony, and the gentle touch of seasons which had passed, covered faulty seams with vines.

The inside of the castle was equally interesting, for who could resist its legends or the state apartments' dignity and the dark mystery of the rooms of older date? Walls of stone, of silk embroidery, of marble or of chintz made the castle a series of surprising contrasts as one walked through. There was a dungeon with a secret passage from its gloomy depths up into the guard-room in the tower. Still farther up in this same part Prince Alfred slept, in a room which by its furnishings recalled robber-baron days. The prince said he liked to sleep among the ghosts of struggling times, and to look at him, with his six feet two and more of fine manhood, kept fit with exercise, and at the eagle nose and the proud head, one could not but admit his nobility of type fitted well into this frame of his rugged ancestors.

Meals at Hollenegg Castle were rather informal as to the family's attitude toward them, but with a service which was perfection and table and liveries keeping up great state. Huge and very magnificent pieces of silver stood about on sideboards or were arranged to decorate the table. The knives and forks were heavy and of ancient models, as were the glass and china. There were flowers and fruits in great profusion, splendid in variety and beauty—a pride with the prince, for all were produced on the estate. The menu was long, complicated, and excellent, but we sat a minimum time at table, because of the number of servants.

A head butler stood in one place and directed the proceedings by a glance or gesture, watching for the earliest moment when plates might be changed; and at one meal I took time to count sixteen men in livery under him. One had to live in feudal style to keep an army of retainers trained from generation to generation in that manner. Not to step on one another, they must have space.

This they certainly had, for the great banquet-hall at Hollenegg Castle, with its marbles and stuccoes, and soft lights, looked sixty by seventy feet or more. The table, with monumental silver, with eighteen people seated and sixteen more waiting on us, made a mere island on the floor's centre.

It would be difficult to enumerate the rooms through which one passed in going to meals from the well-lighted library, in which we gathered. Huge, dim halls, lighted by vague lamps or candles, only suggested their perfect proportions. In one I saw panels of beautiful Renaissance carving, while another had some quite lovely jade-green flowered silk covering its walls. At our exclamation of delight in this color scheme, the old prince looked pleased and said: "Yes, it is pretty. I am glad you like it. But it is very old—my ancestor received the silk as a gift when he went on a special mission to Louis XIV, and it has hung here since his return."

Scattered about on tables and in glass cabinets were family souvenirs brought back from foreign countries by many Liechtensteins from crusader days down. It would take a volume to describe them all. Things seem to me more attractive for living with them, and not merely walking past them in a museum—so I enjoyed these treasures vastly.

It was with real regret I left Hollenegg Castle, and I had no words to express to our host and hostess my delight in the visit. At their recommendation we stopped in Gratz on our way back to Vienna. Besides being a quaint city with old façades and squares well worth a passing look, it offered to our interested explorations the large ruins of its old walls and castle dating back to feudal times and famous for their extent and historic value.

CHAPTER V

MY DÉBUT AT COURT

AFTER Hollenegg our Vienna apartment seemed frightfully new for a time, till we became accustomed again to things made within our century which were meant to fit themselves into our quite modern lives. Naturally we soon settled back into our own ways, and finally we thought of the days at the castle as of a tale of old chivalry; now, alas, completely swept away by war and revolution.

There was much simplicity among the Austrians as well as grandeur, and many of the aristocrats went for some part of the year to tiny shooting-lodges or cottages, where they would live in rough clothes, looked after by a maid, a cook, and a huntsman or two. They seemed always to look and feel at home, and in this to me was the height of their civilization and distinction. Even the Emperor took himself off from his finery at Schönbrunn to a small villa he owned at Ischl. There he spent his time dressed in homespun, walking in mountain paths with his daughters and their children, who came to visit him, or talking with the peasant, the woodsman, or the traveller whom he chanced to pass seated by the roadside. The Emperor was on excellent terms with all these his people, and many were the stories of what he had said or done at Ischl among these humble subjects. One could not hear so much of the sovereign without affectionate interest springing up in one's heart, and I looked forward to being presented to the fine old man. Whenever I could I went where he was to be seen.

So it chanced that I caught a first and only glimpse of

the German Emperor, too, when the latter came to visit
his ally, Francis Joseph, and was received with the honors due his rank. From the train to the Hofburg the
court carriages drove with impressive array of archdukes,
ministers, courtiers, and aides-de-camp. Francis Joseph
sat with the visiting Emperor in a large victoria, in which
he did not look so much at home as in his own usual
small carriage. He was dressed in a German uniform
and he seemed unnatural to me; but William II was
thoroughly enjoying his position, and I think he liked
the gay Austrian uniform he wore.

The people on the street applauded and cheered—not
so much as they usually did their own Emperor, but
enough to show good breeding and hospitality toward
their sovereign's guest—and William, sitting very
straight, saluted to left and right, while his old host sat
back and watched the people with his tolerant smile.
Now and then, when he picked out a familiar face in
the crowd, he directed toward it a friendly glance, accompanied as always by a quick smile. William II looked
pretentious, still, and unhealthy. His drawn white face
seemed most unattractive, and I understood fully the
Austrians' feelings when they thought him an unsympathetic ally. Never at any point did his affected pose
relax or did he have a smile to accompany his salutes.
The rumors from court said he had not made a favorable
impression there either; in fact, casual remarks led one
to feel that he had played his rôle wrongly and had not
acted in a sincere manner, so that his departure was
hailed with satisfaction by both the city and the palace.

I was only a little over sixteen when Mr. Cleveland
was elected President, in November, 1892. Soon after
this he honored my father with a charming personal letter telling the young American Minister of the pleasure

he had in learning of his fine work during the past four years to cement good relations between Austria and our country, and saying he would be glad if my father would remain on at his post under his own Democratic administration. My father was greatly flattered by Mr. Cleveland's offer, and wrote at once to express his appreciation of the praise of the future President, but he declined the honor of continuing as Minister at Vienna, since he felt the position should go to a representative of the President's party. He told Mr. Cleveland, however, he would be only too glad to remain on until such time as the latter selected his successor, so that the new man would have no difficulties at the début.

It meant that we should be in Vienna until the late spring, and my parents decided (as possibly this would be my one and only opportunity to see a court), in spite of my extreme youth I should go into society, or at least to the great court ball, where a "circle" reception of the diplomats was held, and where I would consequently have an occasion to be presented to the sovereign.

Since Rudolf's death there had been no dancing at court, but this year the Emperor's two granddaughters, aged about sixteen, were to come to Vienna for part of the season. The old sovereign was anxious to give them a good time, delighting in the pleasure he could furnish, and to have their sunny presence and that of his daughter, Princess Gisela, of Bavaria, near him. He had borne the loss of his son so bravely that he had won every sympathy. He was alone, for the empress was still buried in her melancholy, and either travelled or stayed hidden in one of her distant châteaux in Hungary. She loved these better than any in Austria. The Austrians spoke of their empress in a different tone from the one they used for Francis Joseph, and it was whispered about by the people that she was mad. If you asked how they knew, they would suggest she was a Wittelsbach, and these were all mad—and "See how she travels" was added by way of proof positive. She, on the other hand, it seems, said the Hungarians understood her, and that she must keep away yet for a time from the gay functions which were considered part of her duties as empress of the dual monarchy.

Late one winter while we were in Vienna, the empress had once returned to the capital, and a state dinner or two had been given for the heads of foreign missions where ladies were "commanded" to attend with their husbands, since Her Majesty would preside with the Emperor. My parents were at one of these feasts, which, by the way, occurred at five in the afternoon. The meal itself was as short in service as possible. This was usual, and many of the guests at court dinners complained, that as a lackey stood behind each place and removed the plates as quickly as the sovereign finished with each course, and as Francis Joseph was the most abstemious of men and was served first, they had the feeling their food was merely passed before them on a plate, which the arbitrary footman put in from the left and withdrew at once from the right side.

This evening, with the empress present and the ladies of her court, it was a longer party. She ate more slowly, and talked more to her neighbors, and then after dinner she went down the line of foreign ambassadors and ministers, always making a few amiable remarks and entering with some into lengthy conversation.

Reaching my father, she said to him in admirable English as he bent to kiss her hand: "The Emperor has told me a great deal about you and about your wonderful shooting, Colonel Grant, and I have spent much time of late years reading of your country with its marvellous scenery and people. I have long wanted to go there, and I have a trip all planned. You must help me persuade the Emperor to allow me to take the journey and see all I have read about."

At my father's question as to what she had read she plunged into a discussion of the books, naming nearly all the good authors of typical American tales—Cooper, Irving, and so on. Then she went on to tell that she had read also my grandfather's *Memoirs*, which she praised, repeating how much interest and pleasure she took in America, its ideal development and great men. Finally she mentioned some of her past travels and spoke of her love for the change these gave her, especially of the charming palace of Achilleion, on the island of Corfu, which she owned and wanted to sell now, because she was too old to go and live there. And would my father, if he had occasion among his compatriots, speak of this fact? She would like to sell the place to an American, and would send an album of photos of it to my father. She seemed much younger than her age in her enthusiasm, and the dialogue was of unusual duration.

All the guests were greatly delighted with the variety and animation of her conversation, and quite completely under the spell of her beauty, though she was approaching sixty at that time. Not a gray hair was visible in the piles of braids and curls famous in all Europe, and the luminous dark eyes had kept their fire in spite of many tears. Her features were admittedly perfect, and her figure, tall, still slim and willowy, was handled with perfect ease and unconscious pride. Her robes were of long, sweeping, unrelieved black, made not in the momentary fashion but on lines of special grace, and her gentle way of talking and apparent pleasure in it won

every one completely. She had lingered over the long
row of gentlemen, while the Emperor had finished the
whole number of their guests, and then she smilingly said
she had forgotten time and must hurry. Down the line
of ladies she passed, with but a pleasant word or an interested question to each. At the door she turned to
give the assembled company a sweeping look and bow.
Apparently each individual felt it to be for him, and
afterward from their conversation about her it was easy
to see she had captivated all the group, to whom she had
deigned that evening to show herself.

My début was a matter of intense excitement to me.
I was so young that my parents' decision to let me go
out interested all their friends. In my life it meant that
changes, which a young girl accomplishes usually by degrees were made at one sweep. I continued my lessons
until the New Year of 1893, and wore short skirts and
my hair in a pigtail, and then magically I was grown, and
my hair went up, while my gowns touched the ground.
The sudden transition in my exterior life was reflected in
my mentality, also. I was old at once—much older than
ever again I expect to be—and felt that the dolls which
had collected about me during my Vienna life must disappear. Their presence seemed a humiliation, and over-
night I found I no longer cared for them. Also, I had a
solemnly grand time putting my study-books away, tear-
ing up the copy-books, disposing of all the signs of childhood and education.

I did not in the least fear any of the new experiences I
was to have, but felt quite confident that being grown
was very wonderful and very well worth while. I do not
believe it occurred to me that making one's début meant
fun or anything else very light. It was too important
an event, and I rearranged the little frame to which I

was accustomed with somewhat the same attitude of mind in which a man makes his will—I must be renovated completely, and give my whole mind up, as I would my time, to new ideas and new habits. I expected to write a few letters and do a little sewing, read a book or make conversation like the majority of grown-up women whom I knew, and for the rest of my days, to be entirely taken with the business of society.

I was too young to realize how foolish was my theory of what was to come—too young to have had any previous experience to measure by; and it was no wonder that very many of the men who talked to me during the next few months were amused. I had lived away from girls of my own age, and had been so entirely dependent on my parents for companionship that I was peculiarly simple and unpretentious, sure everything old with the sanction of custom must be right, and that all the world was like my own home circle. I had never even been allowed to read the newspapers, and in the family—with no sister and no girl cousin near my age—I had been alone of my kind, absorbed in the interests my parents had chosen for me, which were quite childish as to pleasures and quite elderly as to duties. In the light of present-day young girls' bringing up, and even compared with that of others in those days, my education was out of the common, and as I made my appearance in the great world, to play my small part in its life, I must have been a rather quaint little figure.

At just sixteen and a half, I was taller than the average, and slim, and from much training I held myself very straight. My hair was not put up on my head, for my mother thought me too young, but my braid, which was heavy and shiny, was twisted by myself, and fastened in a great bundle low on the nape of my neck. I was

very much pleased when the dressmakers tried on my
ball gowns, with their ugly rounded queer decolleté cut
straight across the front and back and down off the
shoulders, as prescribed by court tradition. They said
it was a blessing mademoiselle had such charming shoulders! It had never occurred to me that shoulders differed
one pair from another, nor had I looked at mine; and my
mother, the only person who had ever probably been
interested, had not spoken of their existence save to tell
me to keep them straight.

The dresses, three in number, made for me by the
great Drécoll himself, fitted and hung beautifully. I
regretted that as a young girl I was not allowed to wear
a train, but my skirts nearly touched the ground, which
was a consolation. I had nothing to say about their
choosing. My mother had excellent taste and I was delighted with the fine feathers which were to be mine.

At that time Drécoll was reviving crinoline lines, and
all my splendor swung out from my small waist to the
whalebone which held the skirt bottom stiffly, giving
almost the amusing silhouette of 1830. One dress had
soft white ruffles of transparent gauze, and its stiff satin
waist was covered with clear crystal beads strung like
a chandelier. I had never seen anything prettier, never
dreamed such a lovely dress would be mine, and to cap
the climax I had white satin slippers and long gloves for
the first time. The second gown was of Nile-green gauze
ruffled over silver cloth from top to toe, and seemed extremely grand to me; while the third was of coral-pink
tulle, with ribbons of different widths sewed horizontally
round its skirt—a tiny one at the hips and a broad one
at the lower edge. I found myself losing a good deal of
my solemnity, as I whirled about in the privacy of my
own room, to see how the airy skirts would swing. I had

tried on the dresses after they came home, and as I
stopped and looked into the mirror, I saw I was all rosy
from the exercise and my pleasure in it.

For some days I went about with my mother and
father, calling. In the legation's large, deep landau, and
at the various embassies and palaces, this going out
and being presented took on a serious aspect. Each
of my mother's acquaintances said the same things,
when my mother would announce that she had brought
her little girl to introduce her, as "We are taking her to
the coming court ball"; and I made my curtseys and
answered always how interesting it would be, when I
was asked if I was glad. Most of the women patted me
on the cheek or the shoulder, and said I was a *gentille
fillette*, and wished me great success; and my mother impressed upon me that I must enjoy all this; that I was
getting it, because it was the only time I would ever see
anything so picturesque and historically interesting, and
that I must carry the memory of it with me always.
My father would pat my cheek and say he wanted me
to see what the old court life was like before he carried
me off home, and he always added: "I want my little girl
to have a good time." I must admit these dull visits
did not seem to me agreeable or impressive, and it was
with keen impatience that I awaited the great evening
of my first court ball.

I had several advantages over other débutantes of the
season. Firstly, I had very young parents, and until
that moment my mother had been an enthusiastic dancer
and a belle at all the balls. Though only thirty-eight
and looking ten years younger, she decided she and I
could not dance at the same parties, so she stopped, and
thus swung her numerous partners among the diplomats
over to my use. Secondly, I spoke the Viennese patois

as well as French with ease, and felt, in fact, rather more at home in those two languages than in my native tongue. Thirdly, I was too young to have any thought in going about, beyond the sheer joy of a healthy young animal in living, and I was too unspoiled not to admire and fully appreciate all the beautiful and picturesque sides of every entertainment, while every fibre in me responded to the rhythm of a good Strauss waltz.

I had been to a number of small *Contessen soirées*, a kind of gathering which I believe was known only to Viennese society—real evening parties in semiball array, with refreshments, music, cards, or conversation, lasting from nine o'clock until about midnight, with no chaperons and no men. No married women came to these fêtes; they were entirely made up of young girls, and with liberty complete those present indulged in the gaiety, laughter, and song their bubbling spirits craved, and time flew. I enjoyed myself vastly. It was the first time I had ever been anywhere alone, and I liked all these girls extremely. They asked me to a great many reunions. Each one called every one else by her first name and used the familiar "thou," making for intimacy at once. The girls I had known before, like Fanny and Thérèse Liechtenstein, saw to it that I should meet thus the large circle of their cousins.

There was another kind friend who helped me much in this way, too—Countess Louise Taaffe, whose father was in the cabinet. He adored his daughter and did all he could to distract her from her fragile health and much suffering caused by a deformed spine. Lovely eyes and hair accentuated the pallor of her interesting face, and she wore simple, dark, loose gowns, old laces, and a few fine jewels. In her father's ministerial palace she was established in the largest and most pleasant rooms,

and she filled these with beautiful things, with flowers
and with music. "I spend so much time here I try to
tempt my friends to join me," was her smiling reply to
compliments on the apartment's attractiveness. But she
rarely invited men, though she could do so without a
thought of impropriety or the necessity of a chaperon,
as she had been made a canoness of one of the established
religious orders, and this rank conferred upon her the
privileges of a married woman. She loved the gay laughter of her girl friends, and often gave *Contessen soirées*,
to which I went. I thought her very pretty, in spite
of her deformity. Her culture and intelligence and her
readiness to be cheerful were quite charming, and I formed
for the first time a warm friendship with a person of my
own sex and somewhere near my years.

Besides pleasure in her company she gave me much
help, for I discovered that to the men she knew, she had
spoken of me and told them to be kind and give the little
stranger a good time. Also hers and other such parties,
made me at home among the girls, and they in their
kindly feeling introduced to me many of their partners
at the first big function.

Never once was I made a victim of any of the small
mean pin-pricks of which one usually hears girls complain on entering society. All these comrades, from first
to last, gave me the warmest welcome and the best feeling they could, and I felt sincerely I was one of themselves. Some were very pretty, all wore their clothes
well, were extremely graceful and smart, and had a fair,
soft look. Invariably they had nice manners. Young
Countess Hunyady was a beauty, with all the elegance
of her handsome father, grand marshal of the court. She
and Countess Mitzi Harrach were the best dancers by
general admission, and were both rich and very gay,

much surrounded by young officers of the guard regiments; Countess Clotilde Mensdorff had a charm and distinction all her own, and the older men who looked for conversation gathered about her always. The rest were a joyous group, typical of their country in the sparkling spirits and the warm hearts, which composed old Viennese society.

I was reacting to all these influences as I dressed for the great ball, and I thought it showed only in slightly heightened color or in a faster measure to my beating pulses. I had not thought at all about whether I would have success and partners. No one had spoken of that to me and I had forgotten about it, in the general effect that the anticipation of going out had on me. So I was quite lacking in anxiety and only glad to don my finery and to go to see the court.

My toilet finished, I went to show myself to my parents, and with a lock of hair changed here and there or a pin added to my dress my mother gave me a last careful inspection. Then she put on my throat a beautiful old necklace of Mexican filigree. I had never worn anything so grand before, and it went admirably with the silver and crystal on my gown. I think, when my mother told me, I would do if I only held up straight and tried to have good manners, that I was quite the happiest person who started for the old Hofburg that night.

My father saw me all decked out and pretended not to know me. Then he said: "My little girl is looking terribly fine to-night. It is all very pretty, sweetheart, but you must not go and really grow up, as I don't want to lose my little girl"; and then for a tonic my mother told me in a good-natured tone: "Well, no one will notice such a young girl, but you must just stand about and look on, and answer if you are spoken to, and in case any one does look toward you, that gown is really very handsome. So don't think about yourself now, but take in all the picturesque customs and the great people, whom later you will be glad to remember." Whereupon her evening cloak was put over her own slim figure in radiant rose brocade, and she led the way down to the waiting carriage.

A little drive through the dark and cold of a winter's night, and we found ourselves in the line of diplomatic carriages, moving slowly up in single file to the great palace doors. There, on alighting, one lost one's identity in the feeling of general excitement and tense expectation. At the bottom of the long, high staircase Franz took our wraps and we glanced in a mirror as we passed. There were no cloak-rooms, or dressing-rooms, for a last prink, but my mother gave my ruffles a little fluffing up with her fan and straightened my silver belt; then she whispered: "Now you must do all the things indicated, at once and without asking questions, and if no one invites you to dance, never mind, but just stand and look on. If any one does ask you, then accept and look pleased, and when the Emperor speaks to you remember to reply in whatever language he uses, and speak clearly—you don't have to be at all shy."

Just then a very nice and very clever secretary of the Dutch Legation came up and joined us. He had previously asked me to dance the cotillion with him, and now he said with smiling amiability, after the exchange of good evenings: "I see it is a most beautiful vision you are to-night, mademoiselle, and I am happy to think I am so fortunate as to be the partner of such a dancer. You will be the belle of the ball!"

My mother answered for me: "Baron, how kind! But you must not spoil my daughter. She is only sixteen and came just like a little girl to look on at this wonderful fête. She does not expect many invitations to dance."

And the kindly man returned quite positively: "Well, perhaps, madam, you are right; but unless my judgment is much at fault, I fear I shall have few opportunities to dance with my own partner. Shall we go up to the hall? There are several young colleagues, who made me promise I would present them to mademoiselle before the circle, if you consent?"

One of the ambassadors came in with his wife and we all wandered up the great stairs lined with sentinels and flunkies, and at the top were received by an officer of the court, who directed us to the hall where the Emperor was to make his official round of the diplomatic circle.

I trod on air. Though I did not believe the amiable baron's words, he had offered me the first compliment I had ever had, and this was my first ball. My dress was pretty, and I began to think there was a very pleasant time ahead, though I was vague as to what form it would take. Anyhow, as I followed my parents into the beautiful white room, I trod on air.

The scene of my presentation at the Austrian court was a handsome room in the more modern part of the palace, and its decorations in white-and-gold wood panelling, with brilliant brocade, were Empire, or later, in style. The fine proportions and lighting by many wax candles made an appropriate setting for diplomats, who were all decked out in their best finery. My father and his secretaries were the only men in simple evening dress and stood out, marked by this, in the throng, where most of the masculine portion rivalled the ladies in wearing splendid gold and silver lace and multicolored clothes— red, blue, green, and white. The American naval and military attachés were well qualified to hold their own,

for, though less trimmed, their full-dress uniforms were
well cut, and both Captain Hein and Lieutenant Sar-
geant were magnificent specimens of our national manhood.

By degrees as various groups came, the chamberlain in
charge sorted out the component elements and arranged
them according to the rank of each mission's chief, this
point being decided by the length of time since each
ambassador or minister had presented his credentials to
the sovereign. It caused much comment always that
the United States should not send an Ambassador instead of a Minister, and should, in spite of her importance in the world, by her own choice take a second
place at court. It was as if the country did not feel its
real value. This and dressing her envoy in a swallow-
tail coat at court functions, whether they occurred at
10 A. M. or were gala evening parties (thus putting the
American Minister on a par with the hired waiters),
seemed to us, as it has to many a representative, somewhat unfair. Both these old customs have now been
changed, and the ambassadors of the United States at
present rank with those of other first-class nations, wearing a dignified uniform, quieter than those of Europe,
but, like our military and naval dress, showing good
taste, material, and cut.

Shortly after our entrance, several men were introduced
to me, and each paid me the banal little compliment the
occasion demanded. All the younger ones asked me not
to forget them in the ballroom later. I was also presented by my mother to such of her women colleagues as
I had not met before. There were very few who were
handsome among them. Lady Paget was altogether
regal, while my mother's dark beauty was at its best.

Suddenly we were all silent, and the three raps on the
floor had just been heard, announcing the solemn entry

of the Emperor and his court, when a little frightened exclamation at our left attracted attention. My mother turned, as I did, only to hear Madam G——, the wife of one of the ministers, say: "What shall I do? If I could only get behind you all, and not have to stand out here in the first line, where every one can see!" She was looking down at her feet, and seemed ready to cry; and naturally our eyes followed hers to her slippers. The poor little woman, through absence of mind, had changed her stockings to go with her white gown, and then, perhaps meaning to change later, or simply from inattention, had slipped on her bedroom slippers. They were small and of some bright color, much betrimmed, but they did not go with her gown.

To me it seemed the woman's situation was as painful as she found it herself, but my mother was not so disturbed and said coolly enough: "It doesn't at all matter. Those look very pretty; any one who notices will think you are trying to start a new fashion in wearing a contrast, and once the circle is over, our feet won't be in view. Anyhow, there is nothing to do, for here comes the Emperor."

Then we, as well as the victim of the strange mistake and all others in the room, turned toward the door, where the Emperor stood bowing and smiling genially, with the Duchess of Cumberland on his arm. We all curtseyed and the long procession advanced into the room. It broke up into informal groups to chat and wait, while the Emperor and the Archduchess Maria Theresa, representing the empress, went round the long semicircle of diplomats, speaking to the chief of each mission and his wife, as well as to any new members of the various embassies and legations, who had not as yet been introduced at court.

The Emperor began with the senior ambassador and

moved on rather rapidly down the line, without, however, any signs of being bored or hurried. He also left
all the men and women convinced it was a pleasure for
him, the Emperor, to have those few words with his
guests. It was all the effect of a rather intimate simplicity of manner, which was the sovereign's marked char-
acteristic in society, for he rarely talked lengthily or
seriously to any one. He approached my father and
mother and said in French, with a warm handshake:
"How are you, Colonel Grant? Good evening, madam!
I hear your little girl is here to-night and that she is very
gentille. I must meet her."

Immediately my parents separated a little, and as I
stepped forward and curtseyed low, His Majesty held out
a cordial hand, which grasped mine hard for a moment.
He looked at me with a quick, pleasant glance which took
in everything. In French he spoke again: "I'm glad you
came to my ball, Mademoiselle, and I hope you will find
it pretty and will enjoy yourself. You will, if you speak
German; our people love those who speak their language and are at home among them. You have been
years here with your father—have you learned to speak?"

I answered in German: "Ja, Majestät! I do speak
German rather better than English, and I am quite at
home in Vienna. One could not dislike such a beautiful
place."

The Emperor threw his head back and laughed with
real amusement. "But you speak Viennese—it is quite
charming! Where did you learn our patois?" And I
said I had picked it up, because I found it so much
prettier than North German. Whereupon His Majesty
looked exceedingly pleased and amused, and went on to
ask me a number of questions in quick succession.

Finally he said, "I am sure you will have great success, and I shall watch it with pleasure!"—and with a supple bow to me and saying to my mother, "I congratulate you, Madam Grant," he passed on to the neighboring group and spoke to the wearer of the bedroom slippers.

I did not have time to see whether he noticed these, as the archduchess was upon us, and after she had exchanged a few words with my mother and father, whom she already knew well, I was presented to Her Imperial Highness. Maria Theresa was a most lovely apparition that night, in soft white with splendid diamonds on her dress and neck, a spreading brilliant diadem in the heavy curls and braids of her remarkably fine hair. She had a delicate, high-bred face, large luminous brown eyes and a slim figure, which she carried with much pride. Her expression was very sympathetic and her voice gentle and low, and though she said but a few words to me before she passed on, she made those pleasant, and with an attractive smile wished me success. She was the wife of Archduke Charles Louis, the Emperor's brother, but she was scarcely older than her senior stepson, Francis Ferdinand, heir apparent to the throne. It was said she suffered greatly from being transported into the Vienna wintry weather, that she had lung trouble, and was very fragile and sad; but she showed none of this at a court ball, and filled her rôle with distinguished certainty of gesture and action, which made every one present keep the memory of her grace.

As the circle finished, the procession reformed and the Emperor led the way, offering his arm again to the Duchess of Cumberland. They were followed by the Duke of Cumberland and the Archduchess Maria Theresa, then the rest of the imperial family, and after them we all fell into line, embassies first and legations following these, each according to the rank of its chief.

Our march was a long one, through the halls of the new
portion of the Hofburg, then into the older portion,
where some of the rooms were smaller, but where the
materials and decorations used on floors and walls were
much rarer and finer. The furniture also was more
beautiful, and valuable collections and objects of art
stood about: Italian Renaissance work, rare bronze and
amber objects, Gobelin tapestries and Louis XV furniture and silks, beautiful carvings, glass from Venice and
Bohemia, and lacquer or porcelains from the Orient—too
much to do more than notice as we went by.

My excitement had been mounting ever since the
first door opened early in the evening, when I had stepped
into the palace, and by this time I was keyed to a much
higher pitch. Finally we moved through an archway and
found ourselves in the immense ballroom of the Haps-
burgs, where for centuries back they had held their court.
No wonder it had attained a splendid reputation! To my
inexperience the space seemed vast, and the crowd impossible to count. There were men in uniform, civil and
military, and in wonderful Hungarian national or family
costumes, with jewelled swords, buckles, and buttons on
their velvets—dark, swarthy types, who wore their splendor so it seemed part of themselves. The women had
to do their best to keep pace with these men, whether in
Hungarian velvets or in guardsmen's scarlet and blue.
They did keep up their reputation of being among the
smartest in Europe, however, and gave a confused impression of diamonds and other jewels, and of clothes no
less lovely because they were less vivid than the men's.
Some raised seats arranged about the walls on one side
were for the archduchesses and the older ladies of the
court; and for the wives of foreign representatives there
were seats on the other side. I had heard there was to

be a seated supper for all these, while the gentlemen and we, the dancers, were to sup at a buffet. Also, I was told that at court, because the Emperor never sat down, but moved continuously among his guests, we would stand for the cotillion and between dances.

Another curious detail was connected with the presence of several ministers of the government, who were self-made men and had been named to their high rank because of their talents. These kept apart, knowing none save one another or a few foreigners. The Emperor spoke to each member of his cabinet, and then they stood about rather helplessly, but apparently contented with a lot which aroused my curiosity by its lonesomeness. I found on inquiry, that all the cabinet came by right to a court ball; but only for the time he was in office was the self-made man asked, and he, as did all others who had not sixteen quarterings—or four generations of noble birth in every direction—knew he had no right to a court presentation. Therefore no such man ever asked to meet the proud aristocracy who formed the élite. It seemed quaint to accept such a situation in such a submissive spirit, when their brains were admittedly necessary to carry on the administration of government, and I was surprised to think these men the moment they left office went quietly back into their earlier spheres.

I heard further that a woman who married one of the nobility, but did not possess the requisite sixteen quarterings, not only could not go to court herself but destroyed the chances of her children and grandchildren. Four generations must pass, even if the Emperor ennobled her in her own right, before the stain of her plebeian blood could be eradicated from the family! This seemed strange to our American ideas, and not without

a note of the grotesque in its excess—but Austria claimed
to be the most exclusive court in Europe, and I suppose
one must sacrifice something to such a reputation ! Anyhow, it suited the Austrians.

In a few moments our procession had moved slowly
down into the centre of the splendid company assembled, and as the Emperor turned and bowed to the
Duchess of Cumberland the dance music struck up—
such music as ears rarely hear—a Strauss waltz by an
orchestra unrivalled in all Europe, for by imperial command Strauss himself held the conductor's baton, and
none but his own music was played for the dancing.
Ears of sixteen and feet as young were keen to follow the
call of such rhythmic strains, and I was delighted when a
young secretary from Italy's Embassy asked me to dance.

When we ended our turn, up came another and another,
and a great number of the Austrians also were introduced, and soon I had forgotten the treasures of the palace and the formalities of court, and was waltzing with
the intense enjoyment I had always felt at dancing-
school.   One officer or civilian dancer looked like another
to me, and their names were a jumble in my mind that
night.   Leaving this question to straighten out at leisure,
I gave myself up wholly to the joy of the exciting music,
the perfect floor, and the admirable partners, who probably represented the best dancers in Europe.   Once I
encountered the Emperor passing in the throng and he
smiled amiably and said, "I see the ball goes well"; but I
do not recall any other incident of mark.   The younger
archdukes were introduced and we danced, but they
were not so good at waltzing as most of the other men,
and my interest in them was lessened at once.

Finally came supper, and my Hollander appeared with
an amused look, to ask if I recognized him and remem-

bered our engagement. Then he dragged me off for some sort of light food. We were joined by a number of other men, and I had a pleasant time of it; and as soon as the music played we rushed back to waltz again and again, until at some signal the party was over, the royalty bowed and retired, and every one began to push forward toward the various doors, each group in a hurry to reach the exit nearest his or her carriage.

I had suddenly realized I was in a great crowd alone, when my father touched me on the shoulder and said: "Suppose you come home, little girl. Was it nice?"

He and my mother looked no more tired than I felt, and she had had a gay time also. In the carriage, which Franz had managed to produce at the desired moment, my father said, laughing, "I don't know what I shall do, chaperoning two such belles here in a strange country"; and he added: "I was very proud of my little girl to-night and had a great many compliments for her." And my mother said, rather elated, that the Emperor and the Duchess of Cumberland and various archduchesses had all noticed me and spoken of the way I danced and held myself. And then by way of training she added: "I hope you won't lose your head and hold yourself less straight; you will lose all you gained to-night if you grow careless."

I had not spoiled my pretty gown, either, and that pleased my mother, as she had seen several others torn by the smart officers' spurs. When we got back home I was quickly sent to bed, so I should not be "green," for next day there was to be another party, and a long season of them to follow. So I quickly laid aside my finery and tumbled into bed, not feeling in the least weary, but only with a blissful jumble of memories as an end to the great day of my first ball.

After that there were a lot of splendid fêtes, in which I had rather more than my share of pleasure, it was said. The young men's faces became less confused in my mind, and several were so kind that I rather felt they belonged to my own special little circle. A few I met later in America or in Russia, where our old warm relations were renewed with pleasure. Two more court balls occurred, as brilliant and official as the first; also a third gathering, called technically a "Ball at Court," which was a fête more intimate and gayer, about half the size of the court balls, and where every one sat down to supper in one banqueting-hall. Diplomats and officials of the government were usually omitted from this party. We were asked, and felt much honored, and the Emperor said by way of explanation, "Your little girl likes dancing so much, I thought it would amuse her to come"; and it seemed various colleagues were quite frankly envious and surprised over our good luck.

There were balls at several embassies, the French ball being perhaps the most attractive, because of the ancient frame the Lobkowitz palace offered and because also of the becoming candle-light. There were several private balls in the huge palaces of some of the great aristocrats, one at Count and Countess Harrach's, where one almost got lost in the many salons, filled with all the imperial family and the court, as well as society. It was here I saw for the first time the pretty custom of a host accompanying each married archduchess to her carriage, preceded down the stairway by two lackeys carrying flambeaux—in this case represented by candelabra of many branches trimmed with lighted candles. The Harrach palace was one of the oldest in the city, and was filled with beautiful things dating back through centuries of family history. One felt transported to the days of

Maria Theresa as one looked on at the perfect fête given by candle-light. It was a picture with a perfume of ancient times.

The ball at the Marquis Palavicini's was more gorgeous as to its flowers and the proportions of the vast rooms, where the same number of people did not seem a crowd, and where the light was brighter and the jewels and gowns showed more individuality; but it was less quaint than the first or than were the fêtes given in several of the older palaces—such as the soirées of the old but still beautiful Countess Clam-Gallas, a ball at the Larish palace and one at Prince Hohenlohe's, as well as two balls at the Duke of Cumberland's. These last deserve a word of special mention.

The Duke and Duchess of Cumberland possessed great wealth, and he was the eldest son of the blind old King of Hanover, whom Bismarck had dethroned. Various countries had refused this king a hospitality which promised to be indefinite; but the court of Austria, true to its traditions of birth, accepted the exiles and made them welcome. The old blind refugee had lingered for a time, and then died, mourning his lost throne. His son had never used the title of king, but had taken his father's second title, which was English. He styled himself Duke of Cumberland, was phenomenally ugly, and about fifty, cultivated and amiable, though far from a brilliant man. The duchess was fifteen or more years younger in looks, with a very pretty figure, complexion, and eyes, and by her charming manner won many friends. In society she was received with sympathy, and went without her husband frequently to the balls, even very informal ones, where she danced with an enthusiasm equal to my own. It was an unusual thing to do in Vienna, as none of the archduchesses, once married, seemed to dance much, but in the Duchess of Cumberland such action was never criticised, since in spite of it her dignity was maintained. Her clothes and jewels were perfect and her manner was always gracious and gay. She was surrounded invariably by a group of friends, her corner in a salon being one where conversation and laughter never lagged. She was the youngest daughter of old King Christian of Denmark, and her two sisters were the then Princess of Wales—now the Dowager Queen of England—and the Dowager Empress of Russia.

The Cumberland palace was out of town, at Penzing, and stood in a great park, where the duke and duchess lived in royal state and entertained constantly. Large Sunday luncheons regularly took place there, and musicales. Two balls, besides rather informal small and very agreeable parties, occurred during the short season I was out, and we were fortunately of those invited, for my father had met the hostess, when the latter was a young girl, at the Danish court, and she had at once declared they were old friends, when they met again in Vienna. She had charming children, two boys and several little girls. The eldest boy came often to play with my small brother, or the latter went to Penzing. My father and the Duke of Cumberland found much in history and politics to talk of, while the duchess and my mother were most congenial, too.

When I was taken to their first party my father pointed out some of the interesting collections of which the palace boasted, and chief among these the Hanover silver. There was one room, a large one, with silver furniture— not just painted, but of metal, modelled and chased most beautifully, while their table silver was famous both for its taste and vast quantity. When the Cumberlands gave a ball the entire company sat down at tables where the centrepieces were subjects of conversation, and one gasped to think that the whole supper was served on silver plate, change after change occurring for the various courses, the supply apparently inexhaustible.

The duchess to me was the attraction of her own fêtes, as of any others where she chanced to be, and I always felt her sympathy with my own craze for dancing. Once I found her in a side-room having her tulle draperies mended, and she looked up and laughed to see I had turned in to help my own rags, of the same material, with pins.

"These spurs are dreadful," she said gaily. "One feels quite ashamed to be in such a condition, but it is great fun to dance, and I enjoy it, even if it is silly and I'm too old. Your dress is all right now. Run back and dance some more."

The Hohenlohes had a palace out on the edge of the city, surrounded with something of a garden. It was one of those imperial palaces built in late eighteenth-century style, and the effect was of an American colonial country house—no very high ceilings except in the ballroom, which, as I remember, was square, with columns and a round dome. This room was lighted by many windows on three sides. Prince Hohenlohe lived here, and filled one of the great posts at court; I think he was the Grand Master of Ceremonies. He was short, rather red-faced, and had grown a bit heavy with years, but he had charming manners, and seemed to enjoy his own party and to wish others to do likewise.

All the appointments were well carried out, especially the flowers for the cotillion. As it was spring, these were largely lilacs, and the big bouquets made a charming effect in the dancers' arms. They had been brought in clothes-baskets and the latter were standing about on the

outskirts of the circling pairs. My partner seized one
to lay my flowers in, and having piled that full, a second
one was brought and also filled, thus leaving my arms
and chair free. As we drove away in the early dawn my
father was delighted with his little girl's success, and
said, pinching my cheek, he would soon have to hire a
truck for my bouquets. Even Franz was rather excited
to be hoisting two clothes-baskets and tying them on the
top of the legation landau, overflowing with flowers, but
it was my last ball in Vienna, and all my partners of the
winter were trying to show their regret at my departure.

One funny and very attractive custom in Vienna was
that of the picnic balls. Either a group of young men or
a group of young couples, anxious to repay kindness or
merely to do their share of entertaining, clubbed together, planned and carried out a ball in some one of the
restaurants or hotels rented for the occasion. Such
fêtes were always well arranged in every detail, with excellent supper, floor, and Hungarian gypsy band. Those
giving it considered their guests paid them a compliment
by staying later than was done at private balls, and to
make such parties a real success one had to take one's
morning coffee before going home to bed. About the
only one of the royalties who went was the Duchess of
Cumberland, and save the girls' chaperons no non-
dancers were asked. A few mothers were invited to
play hostess, and there were card-tables to amuse such
of the elders as cared for gaming.

The prettiest feature, and one I have seen nowhere
else, was that each young man at those balls supplied his
own cotillion flowers. Naturally each tried to outdo his
rivals, and it made for very fine and ingenious bouquets.
The men displayed their taste, and we counted, among
the girls, who should get most. I remember O'Neill,

who, in spite of an Irish name, was the Chargé from Portugal, had his bouquets all of violets, and to my joy a large one always came my way; while young Count Larish had always roses; and there were those who had roses of one color only. Others used nothing but white or purple lilacs, or all daffodils, narcissus, or valley lilies; and some stupid or unfortunate ones who did not know of this detail's importance left their flowers to the vendor's taste; we girls rather disdained their lack of care. The smart Austrian men's club, the young diplomats, and various other groups each gave functions that season which were among the gayest. Altogether I had twenty-three balls in a few short weeks, besides many agreeable soirées.

One of the Emperor's little granddaughters—the daughter of Princess Gisela, of Bavaria—became engaged to the young Archduke Joseph. He was wealthy and belonged to that branch of the imperial family living in Hungary. They seemed vastly in love with one another, though not at all a good-looking pair of fiancés. We little realized that this boy was to be commander-in-chief of the Austrian armies in the great World War twenty-one years later!

At the end of the season there was also a wedding at court, which was the occasion of much pomp. The Archduchess Margaret, a most charming girl, was married to the heir to the Württemberg throne. It was a pretty ceremony, with a few of the diplomats invited into a loge of the imperial chapel to see the pageant. The bride was well worth looking at, for in her long white robes her tall slenderness seemed particularly fine, and her delicate face was quite lovely. Her beautiful stepmother, Maria Theresa, looked as young and radiant as usual. We heard the imperial family thought the match appropriate and satisfactory, and I wondered as I watched the contracting parties, who knew nothing of one another, if they would find even a moderate share of happiness in such a union. She would be a queen in time, it was thought. Poor Margaret's fate was different, for within a few short years she died, a victim to the lung weakness which even before her marriage had marked her with a fragile look. Of course the Emperor, archdukes, the court, and the guardsmen assisted at these ceremonies, but they were no longer new to me, so, though I liked the color and the light, I was not quite so thrilled as I had been at first.

I fancy a good deal of gossip about Vienna's ways was handed about in the diplomatic corps. Its members never got the true versions of personal stories, but only the somewhat twisted accounts given them by outside hangers-on—German teachers and such, who went from house to house circulating a good deal of nonsense, with some truth, alas! Various tales were told of the Archduke Otto's dissipations and his disrespect for all things serious in life—how he abandoned his wife, whom my mother liked extremely and found always very sad; how he had one morning, after a drinking bout, taken a ride on horseback through the city, and seeing a funeral had stopped it, while, on a bet, he made a hurdle of the hearse; how even the tolerant Emperor had talked to him, trying to quell this unruly nephew. We heard it whispered also that Francis Ferdinand, the heir apparent, was much disliked; that the Emperor despaired of teaching him the way to win his subjects. Then we were told the empress was given to fits of depression, which made her quite abnormal and difficult to deal with. There was endless gossip, also, as to the vices in the circles of high finance.

After whispering over all this the talkers would straighten up and some one would say with great decision, "I don't believe a word of it! That person doesn't look as if he did such things; and people exaggerate so. Still, they do say"—and the whispering would begin anew.

Later as we came home my mother would ask father if he thought the story they had been told was true, and he tolerantly would say: "Well, I don't know; but if it is, there isn't anything we can do about it." And so the question would drop for a time.

One family whose members kept tongues wagging was that of Prince Philip of Coburg, who took high place at court when he chose to appear there as visiting royalty. He was an exceedingly important-looking man, about forty-five, handsome still, though somewhat heavy. He wore his uniform with great elegance and received with amiability at the splendid parties which he gave. He was rather above medium height, with thin, close-cropped hair, a clipped beard, an aquiline nose, and very keen, clever, amused eyes. He was very intelligent and cultivated, an admirable talker, well up on all questions of the day. I do not remember why he chose Vienna to live in, but I fancy there must have been some excellent reason. He was connected with both England and Germany through the Coburg family, and he had French royal blood through his mother, who was a daughter of King Louis Philippe. He was connected with Belgium and Austria, too, by his wife, who was the pretty sister of the widowed Austrian Crown Princess Stéphanie. He seemed to know all sorts of interesting secrets, diplomatic as well as personal, and he had great capacities, yet apparently he did nothing much but shoot, collect books, and talk. He had the reputation of intriguing overmuch, and he was not popular, but apparently did not care. He had been an intimate friend of the dead crown prince, and was with him at the party where Rudolf and the Vetěsra had died. Perhaps for this reason one saw little of him at court. My father and he had many a long talk, however, and the former maintained that Prince Philip was, in spite of his defects, one of the most interesting personalities he had met abroad. For some time, even after we returned to America, letters were exchanged between them.

Now and again an official function was given at the Coburg palace. It was a huge, dark, forbidding pile—rich but ugly in effect, and of a bad period. As one entered one was surprised by the height of the impressive stairs, and on every step stood two retainers, one at each side, in the family hussar uniform, we were told. It was of Empire style, and these two long lines of men were most effective. At the top of the staircase Prince Philip received alone, and made us feel most welcome. He told us if we would turn to the right we might find the princess. We did so, and found Princess Louise sitting in one end of the great salon with her sister, while various vague guests, who had said good evening, were looking uncomfortable and edging toward the doors.

The two sisters looked much alike. Both had hair overfrizzed, the color of spun gold. Both had beautiful skin, were fair, with rosy cheeks, and both had very handsome figures dressed in the height of the fashion. Stéphanie was known to have had a miserable existence until her widowhood, and—rather unjustly, because of Rudolf's popularity—she was made to bear some blame for his end. One felt she suffered from this, while, perhaps from a fear of criticism, she was timid to excess. It made her always try to get into a corner, away from every one. I felt a keen sympathy for her, her smile was so strained; yet really she was glad to talk a little, and always said something gentle and amiable. I was told the Emperor was very friendly to his poor daughter-in-law and tried to help her in various ways; but, on the whole, her life was sad and extremely dull and empty—until later she made it over by marrying again. Her sister was said to be content with finery and the gay life she led. Prince Philip of Coburg did not seem either for or against her, but quite indifferent; and when he spoke of her it was with perfect amiability. I fancy he had once looked her over, perhaps, and decided that though they had no single subject of interest in common she was entirely presentable and undisturbing as an element in his life.

When the rooms filled at their party, the prince left his place at the stairhead and moved among his guests, stopping to speak with a group here and there—a charming host, smiling and gracious. The main part of the gathering listened to a fine programme of music in the big ballroom. I sat in another room at the rear and he asked me in passing where were my parents, and said he was looking for them to take them—and me, if I would like to go—to see his mother. I showed him where my parents stood, and joined them with him after a word of excuse to my companions. He took us all through a suite of rooms to where, at the end, in a smaller and more intimate apartment, sat his mother.

She was a most picturesque figure. A lace cap much beruffled covered her head of white hair, elaborately and most carefully dressed; her strong face had massive features and sharp, quick eyes, still very piercing and intelligent. Her figure standing must have been majestic, for even sitting she was straight and strong-looking. She wore a gown of dark, rich silk or brocade, with some beautiful lace about the neck and wrists, and a few jewels in old mountings. Near her, against her little sofa, leaned a thick cane with a crook handle meant really to lean on; I believe she was a victim of gout. Evidently her son bowed down to this old lady's will, and her face and manner well became her reputation as one of the most capable managers in Europe. She was just saying she was too old to see many people or to appear at a party, and so she sat back comfortably in her quiet salon with such people as her son cared to present being brought in to her. Her talk was to the point, and her questions were sudden and concise.

Some two or three people who had been with her took their leave when we came in. Then she turned to us, and spoke to my parents of how she had heard so much of America from her father, King Louis Philippe, who had found a welcome in the United States while he was a wandering exile. She made one or two inquiries as to how this or that place had developed, and if we had ever been here or there. She spoke of my grandfather and asked some questions about him.

Finally she turned to me and said: "You have brought your little girl out to Vienna, Mrs. Grant. Do you like it here? Do you have a pleasant time?" I made some banal, acquiescent answer, and she continued: "Well, you would; you look made to enjoy life." Some other people appeared in the doorway, and the old lady, turning back to my parents, ended our visit to her with a few pleasant words, short and energetic, like her gestures, and always to the point.

As we wandered off, leaving our places to the newcomers, my mother told me I must remember this presentation to the daughter of the last French king, and my father added: "You won't see many old ladies like that, pet. Even now she keeps all Europe busy watching her, and she had a great brain and wields real power."

On the way home in the carriage my parents spoke of her again, and of her second son, Ferdinand, who was at this time, or shortly afterward, placed in Bulgaria by his mother's will and influence. Many people criticised Ferdinand more than they did his elder brother, telling of his faults, but he won his way and played a great rôle in European politics until the World War. If Princess Clementine had lived long enough she would have enjoyed thoroughly watching his star rise, finally seeing him the Bulgarian Czar and a great factor in Europe's history.

There was another character in Vienna whom I saw and to whose house I often went—Princess Pauline Metternich, unique in her generation. She was at that time about fifty years old, and still possessed a very fine figure. Otherwise her appearance was more remarkable than beautiful, and she did her best to live up to her reputation for intelligence and eccentricity. Her evening dresses were always of bright hues, preferably green or yellow; she wore large aigrettes, at different angles from any one else, and had splendid jewels, which she wore in quantities. Her face was worth studying—large, restless eyes which saw everything, and could be very sympathetic or humorous, reflecting her passing impulse; a short nose with an amusing tilt, and a very large, thick-lipped mouth, with sudden, generous laugh always ready, as well as a funny story or quick repartee. The mouth was exaggerated by brilliant red paint, not only on the lips but all around them, augmenting the size of this feature beyond all bounds; otherwise one had no impression of artificial make-up. Tremendously smart in her clothes, houses, and turnouts, this queer princess was a figure as well known to the Vienna populace as was the Emperor himself. She organized and planned all their public charities, and whether it was Old Vienna of the Middle Ages reconstructed and set up in the Prater for strangers from all four corners of the globe to come and see, or whether it was merely a great public ball for a minor charity, Princess Pauline Metternich's genius carried through the enterprise to a successful termination, with all the world of her city ready to work and play under her leadership.

She had her relations, as her rank and blood indicated, at court and among the aristocrats; and, besides, the high finance, the Jewish circles, the bourgeois, and the small shopkeepers knew her well. She helped each in turn, spoke the patois in its broadest form, and had a cheery word for every one. On the Ring or in the Prater, where she drove out in an extra large and high victoria swung on big springs, with magnificent horses, and lackeys in knee-breeches, the crowds stopped to see her pass, and doffed their hats. All the interesting foreigners who came to town found their way to her with letters of recommendation, and they, as well as every kind of person in Vienna's varied strata, were seen at her agreeable parties. She knew how to entertain one evening the Emperor, the court, and all society, and keep the function from stiffness, and another evening six or eight would gather about her tea-table informally, sure of a brilliant conversational treat.

The princess was admittedly a genius, and her light shone very brightly on the background of Vienna's rather narrow-minded society. In her work she was ably seconded by her quiet, well-bred, and charming daughter, Princess Clementine Metternich, who apparently was in no way like her mother, and shunned a prominent rôle, though she had many friends and much intelligence. The old prince depended a good deal on his daughter, was most amiable in showing interest in his wife, but one fancied he was rather fatigued by her ways at times, and a little uncertain as to what she might do next. He was her own uncle. He had therefore seen Princess Pauline grow up, and I heard had no cause to regret his match. She had been a great success wherever he had placed her, especially in Paris, where the Austrian Emperor had sent Prince Metternich as ambassador to the court of Napoleon III. At that post he had done good work, it was said, and the princess had taken a unique position, had become the intimate friend of Eugénie, and had driven boredom once and for all from the life of the French court.

I never heard of but a single failure on the part of Princess Metternich, and the tale of this was repeated about Vienna as typical not only of her daring, but of the Austrian aristocrats' unbending attitude about certain things. Baron Rothschild and his very pretty wife wished to make their way in the society of the gay capital, and Princess Metternich, whom they knew, took upon herself to try the ground before they made a venture. She went to Prince Schwarzenberg, who was to give a large soirée.

"Will you let me bring my friends Baron and Baroness Rothschild?" she asked. "But I don't know them; and, besides, if I asked them, they would invite me in return; and I do not want to go to their house or meet their friends," answered the old prince.

"I will see that you meet them beforehand. They are Jews, but if you ever went to their house you would meet no Jews there." "Then, my dear Pauline, if I could go to the Rothschilds' house and meet no Jews, tell me . why people should come to my house and meet Jews," was the final and decisive reply.

The story was much repeated. In the end, though, the Rothschilds, I believe, went to court, and though they made many friends and were received by a number of the broader-minded Austrians and most of the diplomats, they were blockaded by the leaders: Liechtensteins, Schwarzenbergs, and so on, who formed the ultrapowerful group at the top of society. The little baroness, who was both pretty and charming, seemed rather crushed; and before we left Vienna she died, after a long and distressing illness. We had seen a good deal of the Rothschilds, and liked her as much as she and her sister, the lovely Madame Ephrussi, had both been liked in Paris society.

I had enjoyed my Vienna season thoroughly, and had danced to my heart's content. Aside from this, I had seen much that was interesting, and had made a number of warm friends. At sixteen one becomes easily attached, and I felt I belonged to these Viennese whose language I spoke and among whom I had grown up. It caused me sincere and deep distress when we began to pack and when we moved to the hotel. The household furniture was returned to cases from which four years before it had been taken. At the ancient Hotel Munsch daily there were numbers of kindly people who came to say good-by, and then came again, seeing we were to remain still for a week or so. I was very tearful over abandoning my share of these nice friends and I had quite made up my mind that never again should I feel at home anywhere or establish relations such as these had been.

At last the day of departure came, and we went to the station in the old carriage, accompanied by the same

Franz who had met us early one morning more than four years ago. Franz was in tears, and I was nearly so. My parents also were sad, to leave what had been to them a very pleasant post. Flowers and sweets were brought to us in quantities; many Austrian friends were there to see us off, and nearly all the colleagues came in a large crowd. There was great excitement, and as we pulled out of the station waving hats and sounds of good wishes followed us.

CHAPTER VI

GOING HOME

WE travelled slowly to Southampton and from there embarked for home. The sea was gentler with us in July than it had been in early March, 1889, and the fine weather gave us pleasure for once, in our nautical experience. We were carrying back to America many agreeable memories. Besides Austria, my parents had been to Hungary on a short stay for the twenty-fifth anniversary celebrations of the King's coronation. They had seemed to think those fêtes more splendid than anything Vienna produced. They had also been to Rome, received there by both the Pope and the King of Italy; and, finally, they had spent a few days in Paris with Mr. and Mrs. Reid, who had given them an opportunity of meeting numbers of interesting French people, among whom the Reids had taken a fine position.

Besides these social trips made together they had taken us children over much of western Europe. My father personally planned every journey so we should get all that was educational from our wanderings. His own earlier travels, his knowledge of history, architecture, and art, with his intensely alive mind, made everything vivid and interesting to us. He drew our attention to all that was worth while, whether in light vein or of serious nature. My mother was generally anxious to rest during our trips as much as possible, and my brother was still very young to go sightseeing continuously, so I found myself often my father's only companion on the expeditions we undertook. I was as strong as he, and my absorption in his favorite interests pleased him extremely. I was just of an age to understand and follow him blissfully. Once we went to Naples, where, as my brother had been ill, we spent a month sunning ourselves, though the wind even there seemed cold that winter. We visited all the delightful points about the city, and I had a horrid fright in climbing Vesuvius, at that time in eruption. Our little invalid soon regained his strength, and we returned slowly to Vienna by way of Rome and Florence, making a lovely tour.

Still another time we journeyed through Styria and Bohemia, stopping off at Ischl and at Prague, and from there going into Bavaria. As we wandered on toward the north we visited a number of the picturesque small German cities so rich in old buildings, history, and museums. Augsburg, with its streets of the Middle Ages; Nüremberg, a still more perfect example of that same period; the small German rococo courts; Weimar, with its Goethe traditions; the Wartburg, with memories of Saint Elizabeth and the famous singing contest; Coburg and Hanover, with English and German influences noticeable; Potsdam, with its stories of Frederick and Voltaire, and its later evidences of imperial residence; Berlin, Kiel, and Hamburg; Lübeck and Bremen, the free cities—all these we saw. Then on by boat we went to Copenhagen, looked on scenes where Hamlet had lived, and from there into Holland and Belgium, with their spic-and-span little cities, their quaint beauty of architecture, and their art treasures. Finally we travelled up the Rhine, stopping off at numerous cities, visiting castles, museums, churches, palaces, and battle-fields with enthusiasm, which never knew fatigue.

I loved it, and the stories my father had to tell were thrilling. He knew all the primitive legends, as well as statistics he absorbed from guide-books, and he passed on his lore to us children: tales of Hans Sachs and of Lorelei, equally those of battle-grounds near Metz. He was indifferent to what small discomforts we faced when off the beaten track and taught us to be so. We found we liked the varied hotels and fare as much as he, and we occupied some amusing quarters in vague German towns, where people were unused to foreigners. Even if sometimes our food seemed very queer, the beds were of fine old mahogany and the rooms were scrupulously clean, with gay cretonnes and neat pillow-cases, trimmed with typical crocheted or bobbin lace. It was hard to say just what we most enjoyed: the beautiful Schwarzwald and the Thüringerwald, the fine Gothic cathedrals' architecture, the treasures in the Green Rooms of Dresden's huge museum, the primitive paintings of Memling, Dürer, Holbein, or Ten Eyck, the later glories of Rubens, Rembrandt, and Vandyke, or the market-places, with their small carts and gay colors. Old Dutch and German façades made one fancy that among the picturesquely dressed good-natured people Faust and Marguerite or Hans Sachs and his guild's members might step out. It seemed as if it would be easy to meet Lohengrin and Elsa, or Tannhäuser, or Elizabeth on any of those green hills with castles, as my father brought them to life in his tales.

It was before the day of motors, before the time when ancient walls and fortifications had been thrown down to make room for modern boulevards. Tourists went on foot then or in whatever was the national horse conveyance, and were easily content with the meals and comforts of each country, even when one candle lighted them to bed. So we learned to drink beer and eat Schinkenbrod with perfect satisfaction; and even to take "com-

pote" with our meat. I never learned, though, to like
the Germans' table-manners. It sounded, at some of
the long "tables d'hôte," as if a lot of animals were feeding from a trough, and where there was the possibility of
doing it, we tried to eat before or after the natives did.

On one of our trips we stopped over at Ostend for a
few hours between trains, and went strolling along the
broad beach walk among the gay throng there. Coming
from the opposite direction toward us we saw the tall
figure of King Leopold, surrounded by several gentlemen. He advanced with long, slow strides, towering
above other people, and these all turned and stood making way and bowing as he passed. His roving eye stopped
on our small group of four, to which his attention was
probably attracted by the fact that while every one else
was in light summer clothes, we were just off the train
and wore dark costumes. He glanced keenly at my
father, stopped instantly, holding out his hand, and then
said, calling him by name, "What a pleasant meeting!"—
with a very amiable smile. "How long are you to be
here? Will you introduce me to Mrs. Grant? And are
these your children?" He spoke with each of us a little; said his daughter had written him of my parents,
and how much they were liked in Vienna, and he asked
a few questions about our trip. He was so extremely
tall that he leaned a little over us as he talked. His
manner was very democratic. He had magnetism and
was very clever-looking and thoroughbred, but not handsome as to face. His size made him majestic, however,
and he was not ungraceful or clumsy. After a few minutes of conversation His Majesty straightened up.

"Well, I am very sorry you do not think our Ostend
attractive enough to linger here for a little longer. I
should have enjoyed seeing more of you, but this meet-

ing has been a pleasure to me, Mrs. Grant, and I trust
you will come again. Good-by and bon voyage!"

He raised his hat and passed on up the street in his
casual, easy way, while we turned, to find ourselves the
centre of a large number of idlers, gathered to hear the
King and see the odd-looking foreigners who knew His
Majesty. We were soon lost in the moving ranks of
people again and went on to find our train and continue
our journey.

I think, perhaps, though four years in Europe broke
up the regular schooling which composed an American
education, it gave me other things quite as well worth
while, and to my brother it gave these without spoiling
his home studies, for at the time of our return to America
he was still under twelve years old, and able to take up
his work in the proper atmosphere at the right moment.

When we landed in New York we went at once to old
Cranston's Hotel on the Hudson, where my grandmother
was stopping. She was well, seemed delighted to see us
and to have our long sojourn abroad ended. My parents
had made a delightful plan, which we were to carry out
immediately. We were to go to Chicago and pay a
lengthy visit to my mother's family. The World's Fair
was in full swing, and my beautiful aunt, Mrs. Palmer,
was president of the woman's division. At a time when
American women were new to the game of civic work
they had obtained recognition in connection with the
World's Fair, and were on their mettle to do their best.
My aunt had accepted the presidency after some hesi-
tation. It meant heavy physical labor in the organization and carrying out of the great movement, much entertaining, long office hours, crowds, meetings, possible
strained relations, and many other things uncongenial to
her; but, on the other hand, to carry the effort through

to a successful finish meant real glory to the women of the country, and no one had more qualifications, mental, physical, or material, to offer. So Mrs. Palmer was elected, and the Woman's Building was made one of the most artistic in the White City on the Lake, while the celebrations held there and at the lady president's splendid home were things the board was proud of.

When we reached Chicago, in late July, the exposition was already in full swing, and my aunt, though tremendously occupied, was accustomed to her rôle, and played it easily, gracefully, and without for an instant being flurried or ever showing fatigue. She was forty-two then, and radiant, with fresh skin and brilliant eyes, in the prime of her great beauty. Calm, amiable, quick, and capable, she managed her heavy duties with a gentle manner and sweet smile which bewitched her aids and made them doubly willing and enthusiastic. She was seconded by a number of distinguished women, too numerous to name, but who ably represented Chicago and many other cities in America. There were women who had come from abroad as well, bringing exhibitions from their far-away countries. It was a totally new departure, this woman's movement, and every one was watching it with deep interest.

That summer left none but pleasant memories, both of the affections of the family circle, still complete, and of the excitement and interest of the World's Fair. When it was over we left Chicago with regret, and I had discovered somehow that life at home was much better even than it had been in Vienna!

Early in October we went to New York. We were very poor, my mother told me, and it would be a painful experience, after all the comforts of our Vienna life, to settle down as modestly as we now must. Grandmama had sold her New York home and moved to Washington, established for her old age, so we were to live alone, and my parents chose the big metropolis because of a business opportunity my father hoped for, and because my mother liked that city. She decided it was where she wanted me to make my début, and my brother to get his schooling.

We found a tiny three-story house in West 73d Street, and my parents took it for the winter. It was new and, though so small, somehow our furniture, which had come from Vienna, was crowded into it. We spent a pleasant season there. My brother was settled at school, and though I was to have neither a coming-out tea nor a ball, I was to be allowed to accept parties to which I was invited. I greatly looked forward to an experience so different from what I had seen of the official world in Europe during the previous winter.

Our life was not anything like what I had known of New York before. In the old times my interests had been confined to the two rooms we occupied, where we slept, studied, and played the days away, our only change being meal hours with the family or a walk in Central Park, with a dancing-class once or twice each week, and an excursion to the shopping district of the city two or three times a year. Now, with slow horse-cars changed to cable on the main lines, 73d Street did not seem nearly so far from the centre of movement as had my grandparents' home in earlier days. Then instead of the quiet I had known before, we now led an agitated life, more so even than had been those last gay months in Vienna.

I found it did not much matter our being poor, except that one could not give big parties or have many fine clothes, and that street-cars replaced the legation carriage. But others gave so many entertainments it would have been difficult to fit any more into the season, anyhow, and my lovely aunt sent me two pretty gowns. When one is seventeen and overflowing with the joy of life, money is of no special importance! College friends took me with parties to football games and college proms or to cadet hops, and by the time our tiny house was settled, there were callers enough to make the rooms seem even smaller than they were. These Americans were my own people, and in spite of the four years and more spent abroad, I found they felt the same way I did about everything. I had no cause to regret or miss Vienna.

My parents, too, had many friends who were glad of their return to New York. They were much invited, while I got more than a pleasant share of invitations through the same kind sources. I had imagined, and so had my mother, that having been away so long would make coming out in New York extremely difficult, but if anything it was just the opposite. We found American society rather liked European traditions. It was still in the phase where people composing it were limited in number and where leaders were acknowledged who bore names distinguished in colonial or revolutionary history.

Ward McAllister, an important figure locally, was not yet too old in years to lead at dances or to decide arbitrarily upon the invitations to the Patriarchs' Ball at old Delmonico's. Every one knew every one else. The same orchestra had been playing for a generation, and its programme was fixed, while the entry of guests and the opening of the Patriarchs' Ball was a very stately affair. Middle-aged women wore stiff silks, fine jewels, and old laces, and younger guests felt anxious for invitations, grateful when they came, and worried over the fit of their gowns. There were certain reigning belles or beauties of New York whose reputations were established, while the ambitious from other cities came to be presented at "a Patriarchs'" much as abroad they went to court. The Carnival's queen from New Orleans, or a new beauty from Richmond or Baltimore, was always received and examined by the dowagers and critics quite seriously, was passed upon as having good manners and bearing—or not—as well as fine feathers and complexion! When approved she was invited to further assemblies and private balls, and she often returned and stayed permanently in New York. But the Patriarchs' was the crisis in her career.

A group of men—not boys, but club-men of age and standing—had much to do with placing a girl. If they approved her looks, were introduced promptly, called on her and danced with her, the youngsters followed suit; and provided she could hold her beaux she found herself an established success, with every cotillion and supper engaged months beforehand, with bouquets galore, which she carried to dinners, operas, or balls—daily boxes of violets and avalanches of flowers when the holidays came round. Every girl on Sunday afternoons, throughout the season, if things were going well, considered twenty to thirty young men callers but a proper number.

Besides these acquaintances, there formed a group of more intimate friends, who, however poor one was and however little one entertained, dropped in to lunch or dinner, took one walking on Fifth Avenue, made long evening visits in the off-season, and seemed to enjoy a cup of tea late of an afternoon, even when the carnival was at its height.

To me, after Europe, there seemed a delightful informality about all this, and I fitted into customs which —compared with those of present New York—seem of

another age. I had a kind protectress in Mrs. Rhine-
lander, who was a great power in the city. Hers were
the quaint looks and attitude of an earlier generation,
and she could boast the blood of ancient colonists, of
course. It was she who saw to it that I was invited to
my first Patriarchs' and to two or three other of the
ultra-smart functions in the early season. At her high
tea on Sunday evenings I met and made my first intimate friends. Her sons and their comrades were of the
all-powerful club set, while the younger women of their
group were distinguished both for looks and for fine
breeding. A background of ancient family portraits and
old silver brought from Dutch or English homes by
ancestors added their charm to these gatherings, where
conversation never flagged. The company bore names
of generals who fought for liberty, of signers of the Declaration of Independence, or of those who had shown
themselves statesmen or administrators of mark through
history. Because "noblesse oblige," these guests had
both manners and culture, and with tolerance toward
others they combined some severity toward themselves.

There were many people even then in New York who
had great fortunes—as money counted in those days—
and these lived in large houses within easy reach of one
another, many of them about Washington Square.
Younger couples were moving up-town, and it caused
almost distress and much criticism to see them branch-
ing out, doing new things. Various old ladies threw up
their hands, shaking their bangles and wondering what
society was coming to, with scandal being talked, and
the drinking of cocktails at the clubs, and so much
flirting!

Yet New York was extremely attractive. On Sunday
mornings, especially on Easter Sunday, every young and

pretty girl or woman walked a few blocks on the Avenue in her best bonnet, violets or roses pinned to her gown and a prayer-book in her hands. She was invariably accompanied by one or more admirers, making conversation.

High place in society was duly given the general in command at Governor's Island and the admiral who commanded at the Brooklyn Navy Yard, and they, with their staffs, were the central figures of official entertainments. Mrs. Vanderbilt, senior, a widow, living in retirement, left her sons and daughters, each with a fine house, the duty of entertaining. Old Mrs. Astor received much and with great dignity and splendor. There were a number of others, also, to hold tradition's fort, making any newly rich strangers, who were candidates for recognition in New York, feel they had a thorny path to tread before they reached the pinnacle of their ambition and became members of the Four Hundred.

It was just the end of the era of ancient ways, and I saw the beginnings of the new invasion, both as to ideas and people. Fine old ladies with smooth bandeaux, or hair scalloped on their foreheads still wore loose gowns of taffeta, satin, or velvet and old lace, because their age permitted nothing more frivolous. White stockings, with black, flat-heeled, and silver-buckled slippers, clad their comfortable feet, and they were served by retainers who knew the foibles of the household, in which each servant took a personal pride, since usually they had been in their places many years.

New York in the early nineties was really a very quaint place, where one had time of an afternoon to talk and visit for pleasure! In early spring, after business hours, many a young man could be seen driving good horses in Central Park, with one of the season's belles seated beside him, in a smartly turned-out runabout, while dowagers in handsome victorias would nod amiably in passing, and then turn to look again and gossip, all from sheer interest as to whether an engagement would be announced soon or not.

Our home life was quiet and modest to a degree, but full of contentment. My father was busy with some writing, preparing a new popular edition of my grandfather's book, with annotations of his own, also with more maps and pictures than the original volumes had held. This soon had a large sale, and the work was of a kind my father most enjoyed. My brother loved the American ways, and had plunged with zest into his school life at Cutler's. He was doing well in his studies and was becoming a great, tall fellow. His health gave my mother some anxiety, as she felt he was perhaps outgrowing his strength, and she spent much time devising new means of building him up, and did so with marked success. She rather dreaded the strain of West Point for him, and said all she could to persuade him to take a classical course in college and then go into law. But the boy himself wanted to be a soldier, and stuck to his ideal, while my father, I think, was content to have the third generation follow in his own and my grandfather's footsteps, choosing a career for which by nature my brother seemed well qualified. Finally, having finished at Cutler's at sixteen, the boy took one year at Columbia College, and then entered West Point. His appointment was given him in rather an interesting manner.

Once during that last winter of my grandfather's life, when we lived with him in New York, my father, to distract the invalid from his terrible suffering, had talked of his boy's future, saying he hoped the youngster would go through the Military Academy and then into the army, as they both—the elders—had done. With a sudden inspiration he added he would like the boy to go, not from any single district of the United States to West Point, since they of the army belonged to all the country, but that he wanted very much the boy's appointment to come to him from the President, as a matter of sentiment. He continued: "Father, I've never asked you to do me a favor, but I think if you will write it, I would like a letter from you to the then President of the United States, asking him to appoint my boy a cadet." I heard my grandfather was greatly pleased, and the following day he prepared a letter and gave it to his son for use when the sturdy four-year-old toddler should need it. It was short and simple and contained this request:

"May I ask you to favor the appointment of Ulysses S. Grant—the son of my son, Frederick Grant—as a cadet at West Point, upon his application? In doing so you will gratify the wishes of   U. S. Grant."

By chance General Sherman was present when the note was finished, and my father read it to him. General Sherman exclaimed over it, and my father said: "Why don't you sit down, general, and indorse this? My youngster will be very proud of such a paper some day." Sherman was pleased to do so, as follows:

"It seems superfluous that any addition should be necessary to the above, but I cheerfully add my name in the full belief that the child of such parents will be most worthy the appointment solicited.

W. T. Sherman."

When my brother was ready for West Point, this double petition went to President McKinley, and the latter not only complied with the request it conveyed, but, adding a little note, he returned the precious letter to my brother, who treasures it to this day.

The boy, with his strong character and fine brain, developed well and did credit, both at West Point and afterward, to his name and bringing up. Graduating among the first of his class, popular with his comrades and those under his orders as well as with his commanders, he has always filled difficult posts and filled them well. My father was vastly proud of him, and took immense comfort in the very words "my son"; and though the active work of each in their common profession kept them far apart, my brother repaid his parents for the care and devotion the latter had offered him in their time. Especially gratifying to my father and my mother was my brother's marriage with Miss Edith Root, the only daughter of an old friend admired and loved by our elders.

We were all much together during my girlhood, and our home circle had a warmth which drew relatives and friends into its sunny atmosphere. I danced and dined, and was taken to opera or play, or to drive, with kindly people, and I enjoyed myself more and more as months and years flew by. I grew in experience, and in spite of the lack of money, I had as many worth-while things as those girls of means among whom I went, for I enjoyed all their pleasures and carried no responsibility.

I went to Washington and made my début there, too, at a ball given for me by Mrs. John McLean, a chum of my mother's. After her, others of my mother's friends followed suit in entertaining me, and at the capital, as in New York, I was much spoiled. Before the first of these big functions I had gone to show myself in my best evening dress to grandmama, who said she wanted to see me. She received me in her parlor, where she was sitting after her dinner, and on a little table by her lay a box.

"Well, dear, you look very nice," she said. "I'm glad to have my pretty granddaughter going out. It makes me feel young again myself. Now I want you to wear your pearls with that white gown, so they will bring you luck as they did me. Grandpapa always said they were yours—my namesake's—after me, and I am too old and wear mourning too deep to use them ever again. If I kept them they would be just in the bank, and I would rather have you enjoy them and wear them on your young neck while I can see them there, than to have them lie all closed up where no one gets any pleasure from them, and with you waiting for me to die."

So she opened the box and took out the string of beautiful pearls I had so often handled in my childhood, and which I remembered putting on her neck.

"They are Julia Grant's pearls and will bring you luck, and they look very pretty. Do they feel nice?" she asked with a smile as the clasp snapped.

I loved them, and I was vastly proud of their size and sheen and of the fact that they were mine. I had never owned anything so grand, and I naturally prized them doubly for the memories connected with them and for the fact that grandmama had given them to me herself for my first big American ball.

Washington, though the capital, had little in common with Vienna, but I liked society there just as much or even more than abroad. I visited the White House several times, and was impressed with its dignified style and sober beauty. It was a building to me typical of our American ideals, exactly the place where our first magistrate should be housed. It had such a simple, homelike atmosphere, with enough of space and grandeur in the proportions of rooms and porticoes to make one feel the good quality of the people who had built it. The gardens were enchanting, and suggested a repose no other city palace I had seen possessed. I was glad to have come into the world in such a nice place, and I thought the whole city of Washington exceptionally attractive.

My grandmother lived there in an agreeable, sunny home—comfortable and content through her last years, surrounded by friends of other times, visited frequently by her sons and keeping her daughter with her always, for Aunt Nelly was a widow and had returned from England with her children to live again in her native land. Something of an invalid she was, yet able to move about and enjoy the Indian summer of what had been a difficult existence bravely faced. It made grandmama very happy to have her. She seemed glad, also, that we were in the United States again.

Each spring and fall she stayed with us in our little New York home, going and coming from her cottage at Coburg, for which Elberon and its damp climate had been exchanged. We always loved grandmama's visits, for she was a cheery person, keenly interested in everything, childishly intense, and, though her eyes were failing, she still had many resources. She lived much in the past, and the family persuaded her to dictate her memoirs. She began with enthusiasm, putting intense frankness into them. She would say to my father: "Now, Fred, I'm doing this, and I'm enjoying saying just what I think about every one since 'way back. Later it will be interesting, because it will show what people were, but I don't want all this published for several generations. Some one might get mad, because I'm telling how they really felt and acted."

Grandmama was visited by large numbers of persons

in her last years, and she kept her charm of conversation. No occasion was more worth witnessing than when one day Li Hung Chang, the viceroy, passing through New York, expressed a desire to see her. She was with us at the time in our house in East 62d Street, where we had moved during my second season. Everything was arranged for the great man to come with his numerous suite and pay his respects. The Chinese Bismarck was tall and gorgeous to behold, surrounded with secretaries and interpreters. He and they were all dressed in the most vivid silks. He had been to my grandfather's tomb to plant in tribute two trees from his native land, for my grandfather had met him in China several times. They had had long conferences, and the old gentleman had then said with simplicity to his visitor: "You and I, General Grant, are the greatest men in the world!" Now his tribute to my grandfather's memory and his call of respect to the latter's widow seemed very touching.

In spite of his eighty years or so, and his fragile health, the statesman was still of fine presence. He came into our parlor and sat with Oriental calm as his attendants brought in bales and packages: the gifts he offered. Some wonderful ancient statuettes in ivory and wood, some cups of rare old porcelain, and some jades were for my mother and father; several rolls of beautiful rich silks, appropriate both for dress and furniture, splendid brocades, and several admirable embroideries were for us—things not to be found in modern shops.

These were distributed about, with a flowery word of compliment from the donor, carefully translated by the interpreter to each recipient in turn.

Then with equal care a large covered piece of furniture was brought into the room and unpacked. It turned out to be a wheeled chair with every mechanical device for

putting an invalid at ease, and arranged so the occupant
could run the chair herself. Our visitor was obviously
delighted with the hideous ultramodern capacities of
these appliances, and had them all exhibited. He turned
to grandmama with all solemnity at last and had the interpreter explain he had seen this marvellous machine,
thought of the poor widow of his friend, and had immediately purchased it to offer it to her in her old age; he
hoped she would enjoy and use it! Grandmama, who
in spite of her seventy odd years and heavy weight was
very spry and never thought of infirmities, was surprised
and even indignant at being called old or thought of as
decrepit. Yet she was much touched by Li Hung
Chang's attention. Between gratitude, amusement, and
annoyance, her face made a queer study, but she rose
to the occasion and thanked him charmingly. They
talked lengthily of their mutual memories, of China, of
my grandfather's illness, of actual politics. Several
times Li Hung Chang brought up the subject of age, and
would say, "You and I are very old"; and afterward
grandmama spoke of it with mixed heat and fun. "He
is at least ten years older than I am," she would repeat.

He spent the whole afternoon with us, and the visit
was most enjoyable. The polite Chinese—both he and
his suite—drank tea they probably thought horrid compared with the amber brew they knew, and ate light
refreshments they also probably hated. But their faces
and manners never betrayed anything but the suave
politeness of the Far East, and long after their departure
that highly colored group was pleasantly referred to in
our talk, while their beautiful gifts were much enjoyed.
I received as my share of them a box of perfumed flower
tea and a roll of silk the color of spring green, possessing
a sheen of moonlight. No Western hands could produce

such quality and dye. In my Russian home, where I used the material, it was much admired, and was only rivalled by another material I had also from the Far East. This other was of wonderful Japanese weave— coral red, deep violet, and white flowers on a ground of dull gold. It had been a present from the Mikado to the White House baby at her birth, and was sent to make me a court robe! I could not cut up or wear such splendor, but had had a frame constructed, and I used it as a screen in my salon, where it glittered and glimmered softly in the midst of treasures of old Europe. The work of deft Oriental fingers and looms more than held its own in such company, and won the praise of connoisseurs. One hates to think such beauty has been wantonly ruined by the hands of Bolshevik destroyers!

As the months flew by, my father's time was more and more crowded with useful work. The new edition of my grandfather's book finished, he did some writing on his own account—war articles for various magazines. Then he found himself becoming intensely absorbed by the local political situation, both in New York and nationally. He was associated with many of the eminent men of the day, renewed old or made new friendships which were both interesting and useful. Among these the veteran Roscoe Conkling, who died soon after; Senator Root, whose talents and character already placed him in the forefront of the great; Joseph Choate, Senator William Evarts, General Sherman, and General Porter, ex-President Harrison, President McKinley, and the political bosses Senator Platt and Mark Hanna, passed through our parlor, dined at our table informally, or came to talk with my father about the interests of the country, state, or city, and the aims and work of the Republican party.

The effervescent Roosevelt was daily gaining more prominence in the midst of many other men of mark, and one felt his remarkable talents and magnetism. Amusing, interesting, with a quick, warm sympathy and a charm innate, Roosevelt was the keenest, the most intense and urgent personality imaginable. He and my father were quite intimately thrown together, for they were made co-workers in the Police Department when a reform wave swept New York. They often disagreed as they discussed the reorganization of the police force and the cleaning up of New York's tragic and criminal districts. Roosevelt talked a great deal, always rapidly and persuasively. He was much more of a politician than my father. The latter would listen with sincere enjoyment to his brilliant partner. Then after some time he would say in a very quiet voice: "Well, that is one way of putting it, but did you notice this? Or suppose we just think of this other side a minute"—and in a few concise phrases my father would lay out his own views. Frequently Roosevelt would say cordially: "Now, that's true! I think that, too! You go ahead and do that just as you say, and I agree!"

He had unlimited enthusiasm and energy, and my father, less loudly expressive, had the latter quality, combined with patience his colleague was glad to depend on for carrying out their plans.

My father was fond of the men under him—was sympathetic to the dangers incurred in their work and to their needs, and he won great affection from them in return. He eliminated pitilessly elements which were bad. Both graft and lack of courage were largely suppressed, and for some time after his term of office New York's police system was a model. The men's standards were raised to a point that made the force a credit and drew into the service a type of American who was an honor to the city.

Years later I remember a conversation between Roosevelt and my father which typified the former's best qualities as I recall them. He had become President, and Mr. Elihu Root was Secretary of War, while my father had an important army command. When in New York the President stopped across the street from us, and he occasionally dropped in to see us with the informality of earlier years. We were at dinner when the door-bell rang and he joined us. As of old, he was soon arguing with my father, this time about some military measure. His animated phrases rapidly followed one another, yet my father differed.

Finally the latter said: "Well, Mr. President, why don't you consult your Secretary of War? Perhaps I am prejudiced, but I really don't agree with your point."

"I have," said Roosevelt with impatience, "and he thinks just as you do; that is why I came to you."

"I'm poor comfort, then, for I don't see my way to changing my view either." "Well, I'm sorry," said the President. Then he added with a mixture of admiration and discouragement all his own: "The trouble is that Elihu Root is always disagreeing with me, and he is always right! I suppose now I will have to go and do this as you and he wish."

Roosevelt had great enough talents to be honest in admitting those of others, and he seemed always ready to act on information from people who were expert advisers. It was one of his biggest traits, and did much, I think, to add to his reputation. Also, he was never sulky or obstinate if contradicted, and he was quick to praise others. He won friendship and co-operation by this attitude. Altogether, he was a most interesting personality.

My father's work became more and more serious, and he was obliged to stay in the city even through the summer months. My mother remained with him, keeping our house open and fairly comfortable even in hot weather. I went visiting friends in the environs, where there were many pleasant house-parties. Also I went much to West Point. There my father loved, with my mother, to join his old comrades as often as he could. My Aunt and Uncle Palmer had a cottage for two summers at Bar Harbor, and they took me there. I thought I had never seen any scenery more lovely than Mount Desert in its setting of blue sea and sky, and I loved the life. After these seasons the same kind relations invited me to join them at Newport, and I made my début in that gay, smart resort, where I had a lot of friends already among the New York group of merrymakers. Habits then were simpler than they became later at Newport, and we were a crowd of carefree youths, who rode and picnicked, or went out crabbing and catboating, who danced and dined, played golf or tennis, as the spirit moved us. We prided ourselves on being the jolliest group Newport had ever seen, and we loved the place and our healthful life.

I remember only one year with a shadow—cast on our spirits by the Spanish-American War. Already in the spring, with the promise of war, my father had volunteered his services. He was in doubt as to how he would be used, for a few weeks while he waited—meantime he prepared his uniform and kit. Our house was full of paraphernalia—saddle and harness, uniforms, arms, and such—and constantly men came and went who wanted my father to join one or another of the volunteer groups

going to the front.   He refused all these positions, though
he helped several to organize, putting his old army experience and wisdom at their service.

Then came a call which appealed to him.   A hard-
working infantry regiment of the National Guard, modest of pretension and comparatively poor of pocket, sent
him a delegation.   The members were offering themselves in a unit to our government, for service under fire.
They decided they must have a commander who was of
Regular Army training, and they knew my father's life.
At a meeting, the day before, they had chosen him—
would he accept?   He did at once, and for a few days
we lived in a turmoil of excitement, for no sooner had
they volunteered than the government ordered them out
to camp on Long Island, saying that after two weeks
they would go to the front.

My father had everything he needed for this sudden
departure except his horse.   But he was so impatient to
start and to be with his regiment from the first moment,
that he would not think of waiting for a mount.

"If the men can walk, I can," he said, "and these
early days are the time for us to learn to know one another and work together.   They aren't experienced yet,
and would not have asked me to command them if they
didn't want me now."

So early one morning, only three days after his acceptance of this call, we found ourselves in Brooklyn at the
armory where the 14th Regiment was assembled, ready
to march forth.

I had heard much of war and fighting.   In our family circle the subject was among those most frequently
discussed, but this was my first experience of the bustle
of departure, of running messengers and quick orders
silently obeyed.   It was also the first I had seen of weep-

ing women and girls, of children held close for consolation after a last good-by kiss. Though that day's trip was to be but a few miles long, and we had hopes of meeting again before the troops sailed for serious work, hearts were heavy in the crowd of little family groups. The men were stepping out into the street putting their feet on a road of which the end was invisible.

A command or two rang out. I did not recognize my father's voice. I had never heard him use those clear, ringing tones before; and then he walked slowly up and down the lines, glancing over the rows of clean-looking young chaps, who hardly looked like amateur soldiers. It was a fine regiment of men, many of Scandinavian blood, and I could tell from my father's pleased expression how much he liked them. He, himself, had not been in uniform for about fifteen years. I was surprised it became him so well, and how he seemed to throw off the weight of time. He stood trim and straight, looking his best, alert and keen, not at all showing his forty-eight years. It was the beginning of a new career—not at all, as he thought, a military incident—this answering to the call of patriotism.

Two weeks my father spent with these men. It was hard work for them and their commander, who became very proud of their rapid progress. Then he was ordered off by the War Department to a training-camp in the South, where through sizzling summer weather, he fought malaria and dysentery and trained raw young recruits. They moved on rapidly to the front, where he, the camp's commander, longed to go. He suffered a short, sharp attack of the prevailing malady, but, refusing to give up his work for a trifle like ill health, he continued his duties till he could hardly stand and the doctors said he was all but dying. My mother was wired for. Then, after a week of nursing, my father's magnificent physique answered to her care, and he was back in camp again. At last, late in the summer, came the much-desired orders sending him to the front. He was promoted to the rank of brigadier-general, transferred with the same rank to the regular army, and named military commander on the island of Porto Rico.

There, interesting occupations and many curious experiences were my father's lot. Propaganda had been made against Americans by the Spanish, and he had some difficulty in persuading the natives they would not be punished or ill treated by him. When good feeling was established after the fighting, many natives of all classes came to see the commander, and in good faith offered him bribes for this or that advantage over a neighbor, or to effect the loosening of various rules which he had made. They were amazed at his invariable refusal either to meddle in their relations among themselves or to change any of the new regulations, so one man should be more favored than another.

When his peculiarities as compared with the former administrators on the island were finally understood, my father suddenly found himself very much appreciated for his honesty and loyal ways, and was frankly complimented on them. He brought my mother down to the Porto Rican capital, when things became settled, and her talents for entertaining completely won the natives' hearts. Both my parents always spoke of their stay on the island as one of great pleasure, where their interests were manifold and their efforts well worth while. In spite of the dreadfully hot climate and the insect life and snakes which had to be fought as daily enemies, they loved their home there, it seemed.

At Newport through that summer I think we scarcely

felt the war, though sometimes a weary man would come up from Washington with a face strained by sleeplessness and fatigue. He generally could only stay twenty-four hours to rest and breathe the fine air. Certain of our ballroom partners were missing, we noticed—gone with the Rough Riders generally.

The time between July, 1893, and September, 1898, had passed very quickly, and my girlhood had been gay with the sunshine, which health and youth and a family circle without serious troubles made. Except the cloud of the short war, none rose on my horizon, and there were only problems such as any girl must face who is comparatively poor in a circle very rich. My clothes were simpler than those round me, and fewer in variety, but they were pretty, and the necessary economy about them and in my habits made me perhaps enjoy my pleasures more. I was greatly spoiled, and had many warm friends among my contemporaries of both sexes. I had rather a broader life than most of these young people, for while they were kept in one small circle, I had acquaintances of a wider range both of age and fame. I knew and met my father's friends quite often in our own home and outside, and these men were of intense interest to me, as was the work they were doing in civic and political spheres.

My father held that in a government of the people, such as ours was, all must take a share of responsibility and effort. He set an example in this matter. He was greatly distressed at the way the strong, fine elements of the country, and especially those of Anglo-Saxon blood who had originated its ideals, were standing back, letting less worthy men hold power. He thought those who had come recently to our shores, though ill prepared and needing education, were unduly allowed to influence our laws.

He hated the vice and sluggishness which had crept into public life, poisoning the nation, and he had a deep contempt for those who—thinking only of material gain—left all national affairs to men lacking in patriotism. Never did he lose faith or patience, and, all devotion to his country, he never felt able to go into anything merely for his own advantage. A fortune decidedly modest satisfied my father, but though he preached economy and industry to his children, he was always glad to give us any simple healthful pleasure, and was our best educator and adviser.

We lived much for one another. My mother was greatly pleased that I had a good time in society, where the first year she took me about herself, and watched my every act with greatest care. Keeping me to European ways by her constant criticism and advice, she prevented my being too much spoiled by American freedom. Afterward, as I became more used to local customs, she allowed me to attend various parties where only young people were invited. I even paid some visits quite alone. I think I never abused my liberty, and it was far from that of other American girls anyhow, for until I was engaged I never received a note or letter or wrote one which my mother did not read. She and my father never allowed me to go swimming with the gay free groups of boys and girls I knew, or to ride a bicycle. Even in those days this was considered exceptionally severe, and in modern times it sounds impossible. But I was so used to giving my parents absolute obedience that it never occurred to me to question their wishes in such matters.

I was allowed occasionally to drive or walk with certain men by special permission, and to ride horseback with some young cavalier when a horse was available, but I was never permitted to invite a man to be my companion at any sport or even to call, as mama thought that pushing, and I never sat out a dance. All this seemed not to matter, though, and I had a beautiful time in New York, Washington, and Chicago. I renewed my visits to my aunt in the latter place frequently and with great happiness.

Being the only girl of my generation in our family, I was greatly petted. My two favorite cousins were like dear brothers, my four bachelor uncles, all young, gay, handsome, and fond of society, made a delightful group —half beaux, half chaperons, ready always to bring their friends or to enjoy anything with me. My uncle and lovely aunt put all possible pleasure into my girlhood, too, and gave me much, which otherwise our own limited means would not have offered. It was they who gave me, as one man said, all the advantages and fun of riches without the disadvantages, and took me to Newport or Bar Harbor each summer. My uncle, grown delicate with advancing years, in spite of many aches and ailments, was most patient with my frivolities, and even pretended to get fun from them. Often he teased me over my beaux. He called them by amusing names which he invented to suit the peculiarity of each, and he constantly made fun of me and my never-ceasing enjoyment. But he was all kindness and generosity, and he liked, apparently, to see us youngsters have a good time. I loved to talk to him and get his keen-witted opinions. He had a terse intelligence and a warm appreciation of all that was strong and fine, honest or beautiful under the foam and froth of the summer colony's occupations, and his judgment of men was admirable and always thoroughly to be trusted.

My aunt, slim and graceful, with hair grown silvery

white, had kept her freshness and seemed more beautiful than ever. She went about a great deal, and was the acknowledged centre of any gathering where she appeared, while her wonderful brain and gentle nature won her exceptional admiration. Her expression was always so serene and gay, that I instinctively felt the quality of her nobility of soul and character. To be with her was a joy and a great privilege to me, and I was always happy in a companionship which began then in earnest and stretched on through my life. She had no daughter, and gave me something of the affection she could have lavished on one. Besides, she had a talent of comradeship both in silence and in talk, which made her presence an ideal one. I never saw her cross, selfish, or hard, yet she inspired one to do right, through suggestion more felt than heard, and her own mind was so quick, brilliant, and unpretentious with it all, that unconsciously one flashed the light back and was at one's best. A rare woman, whose influence carried with such as met and knew her, even long after she died. I felt a deep devotion for her, and always found her ready sympathy and understanding a great comfort.

Whenever the question of my marrying came up, I found in her a true friend whose advice was easy to follow, as it coincided with my own ideas of what was right. I was grateful that in spite of our small means I was not pushed into a "brilliant match," so called.

My father said to me on one occasion: "Little sweetheart, I don't want you to get married at all. If some day there is a really fine man, and you feel you can't do without him, then I'll be resigned to lose my little girl and let him take care of her; but remember, life is a complicated problem at best, and often a constant struggle. So one ought at least to be armed for it, and to feel that whatever comes, even if health and wealth should blow away, one is tied to a man whose personality is enough to fill one's horizon with real values which are worth while. If you don't find a man like that, keep your liberty, and stay with your old father, who loves you, too, and will take care of you always."

So I had no weight on my mind, and only felt joy in going about in society. I felt no interest in my men friends other than their intrinsic value drew. There was an advantage in keeping a worth-while lot of hard-working young fellows and older men about me who were not shy about joining a circle where their feelings were never otherwise interpreted than as they were meant. Poor men were received at our house with the same enthusiasm as were richer ones, and brought their gifts of conversation or their modest prides and ambitions, always sure of a cordial understanding and of an atmosphere of recognition for their quality.

My mother and father generally liked my friends, and cultivated them with pleasure, and father enjoyed immensely talking with what he called nice youngsters, who always wanted to spread their plans out and ask his advice, whether they were in the army or in business. They were all fond of my parents, and often in the years which followed, whenever I returned to America, I found many agreeable faces of men I had known in youth still gathered about my old home.

CHAPTER VII

MONTHS OF TRAVEL

IN the early autumn of 1898 my mother was to join
my father in Porto Rico, where he was military commander. She did not want to take me with her for
fear of the climate and the roughness of a newly conquered
country. Uncle Palmer had passed a bad summer at
Newport, and was being sent abroad by his doctors to
spend the time of cold weather on the Nile. My aunt
was taking her two boys along for a year's travel before they settled down to business. They had just graduated from college. The Palmer family proposed to take
me abroad with them, and I was perfectly enchanted
when my mother accepted for me. There was a great
scrambling to prepare, for this decision was reached suddenly. It seemed an ideal arrangement to me, and a
unique opportunity of seeing places and things as yet unknown.

London we were only to pass through; in Paris we
were to stop for some time, and I had heard much of
that gay capital, but had never been there. Then we
were to go through Italy, land in Egypt, and after our
Nile trip we expected to return slowly through the Holy
Land to Constantinople, and from there through Greece.
I had not dreamed of going to any of these places, and
such an opportunity coming after four years of very gay
society life satisfied a desire for something more serious.
It was a party, too, after my own heart, because, except
for my uncle's fragile condition, there was no probability
of sadness. We were five congenial souls starting out
on what seemed the perfection of a holiday.

And, indeed, through the early part of our travels all went well. Though the voyage across the ocean was stormy, London seemed comfortable and agreeable, to me; much more so viewed from the ancient, smart, small hotel we stayed in, than it had seemed ten years previously from the big caravansary we then inhabited. We did a little shopping, mostly for the men, and moved on to Paris, where we scarcely stopped, so anxious were we to reach the southern sunlight, which was to help my uncle. In Rome we lingered longer, and already felt the warmth and light were helping him. Roses were tumbling over the walls of palaces and ruins. Our invalid liked Rome so much that my aunt and I stayed there with him, till the day before our steamer sailed from Naples, while my two cousins went on ahead to see the latter city and make some excursions.

During the two weeks in the Italian capital we were very quiet, driving about the environs, resting, or reading books we felt would prepare our minds for the great deserts and the Nile's strange beauty. We saw no one save two old friends—Doctor Nevin, pastor of the American Church, and Father Farelly, of the American Catholic College. Both were men my parents knew, and most interesting individuals. Both had known me since my childhood. They came, and came again, to sit with my uncle, my aunt, and me, and the invalid greatly enjoyed these broad-minded, unprejudiced men who were of the world as well as of religion, with brain, soul, and body well balanced. They were playing fine rôles and working hard among their flocks.

Nevin had been a young soldier under my grandfather in the Civil War, and had later joined the church, because, he said, if he had not done so he might have gone to the dogs, he had so many faults. He was a militant churchman, and had much good in deed and word to his credit. His cultivation and fine nature made him friends and admirers among the rich and powerful, whom he exploited without scruple for those humbler and poorer. To these he gave also most of his own salary. He made his church and its services beautiful, and his own home, in a modest but quaint old house near by, was as attractive as was the man himself.

Scrupulously clean, with whitewashed walls and rough stone stairs, the entrance-hall of the simple rectory was quite empty. One climbed to rooms unlike any others I have ever seen, for there was no single note of decoration in them; high, bare, whitewashed walls, a big fireplace, where burned a log; a huge desk in a sunny corner; two or three tables of old Italian workmanship of good period, and several stiff wooden chairs. On the tables lay bits of Renaissance brocade, adding dull notes of color; and a few books, some old, some modern, were scattered about. The rooms were lighted deliciously, with ancient Roman lamps burning oil, and the whole atmosphere seemed classic and austere. There was one note of comfort only—on each side of the fire was a leather chair, low, deep, and inviting, with between them the splendid fur of some forest king which Nevin's gun had killed. Many a multimillionaire spent an hour in one of those armchairs, talking of what good he might do to his fellows, guided by his host's wise advice, and many a sad man or woman unburdened there a weighted soul or conscience, and went away comforted.

Doctor Nevin was wise in his generation. He knew well when to aid or support, and when to reproach his visitors. He was also a delightful friend with whom to tarry an hour in the restful surroundings created out of so little. Beyond, there was a dining-room where six

could eat and where the meal prepared and served by his
single old servant was as short, simple, and excellent as
all the rest. Another and larger room of the rectory he
called his museum. It was full of a wonderful collection
of heads and skins, for Nevin was one of the five or six
best shots in the world, and had explored the Americas,
Asia, Africa, and Europe in his occasional vacations,
bringing back trophies which thrilled the huntsmen of
his acquaintance, and even many who were unknown to
him. He was an admirable horseman, too, and knew
his Rome better than did most, having lived there thirty
years. Nevin loved both its art and history, as well as
its humanity, with all his heart.

Monseigneur Farelly had the charm and brilliancy of
Celtic blood, plus American training and long discipline
controlling it. He was tall, strong, very handsome, with
distinction both of manner and expression, and he also
loved Rome, where he had been many years. When I
went there a child with my parents he had escorted us
through the Vatican museum, and his enthusiastic words
had made us forget time and space. With age he had
but mellowed, and his sunny Christianity, sense of
humor, and kindly understanding won all who met him.
He went little into society, as he was a hard worker and
a specialist at education, but his influence at the Vatican
was great, his judgment very sure, and the friends he
cultivated in relaxation appreciated his presence among
them as an honor. His rapid career was no surprise to
us. Once or twice he or Nevin dined with us in the restaurant of the Grand Hotel.

Nearly all Rome's smart people frequented this place,
among the earliest of its kind to open in Europe. There
were many beautiful women and famous men sitting
about on one occasion I remember, and the soft lights

and pretty music added their attractions to the scene. Nevin knew every one worth knowing, and as he bowed he would tell me who they were.

The Duchess Graziolli, famous for her successes and elegance, who was in her prime, was the star of a party; Lady Randolph Churchill, still lovely in spite of her fifty or more years, with a long career yet to run, was the centre of another group, and there were many others famous for their looks. In one corner a large table was surrounded by young men, the jeunesse dorée of the diplomatic corps, said my guide. It seems they "messed" here, and regularly had the same table, where they came to look over those present. They appeared a well-groomed set of men, seemed to talk gaily, and they came and went informally, laughing, jesting, nodding, known at many a table, where pretty faces lighted as salutations were exchanged. It was an agreeable impression of modern Rome we gazed at, grafted on the wonders of its ruins and history, which for the moment pink silk curtains shut out into a December night. I was very much pleased when my aunt said: "Mr. Palmer and I like Rome so much and he is feeling so much better, that we are almost sorry to be leaving. Perhaps when the trip is over, on our way northward, we may stop here again."

"Do that, and I will show you all the sights and be your cicerone. As for you, young lady, I'm your father's —even your grandfather's—old friend; so I'm going to claim the privilege of my gray hair and take you riding with me all over the Campagna. Who doesn't know it from a horse's back, at the hours of slanting shadows and purple skies, hasn't at all been initiated here."

This from Nevin, and I was glad to think of the pleasures in store in such delightful company. The old

PRINCESS CANTACUZÈNE, 1907.

sportsman was an escort worth having and something of
an autocrat whom women usually tried to please.

"If you think me too old a beau, you may invite any
one over at that table of smart youngsters to go, too.
I'm as good a chaperon as I am a guide; you'll see."

We went away a few days later, and in the back of
my head was a vague question, whether Rome was not
too agreeable and beautiful to be leaving for still more
ancient places.

The Mediterranean was blue but rough, and we were
glad to wake one morning to the clamor of an unknown
tongue, the splashing of oars, and the bumping of small
boats. Our cabins were steady again. We dressed and
packed in haste and were soon ready to land. It is quite
useless to describe Oriental light and atmosphere to those
who have not seen it, while such as have, know without
description its intense, luminous qualities. I loved it
from the moment I emerged on the deck of our small ship,
and my enthusiasm grew steadily through days of turquoise skies and tawny deserts. Aside from the scenery,
with the strange, mysterious figures moving on its background, carrying a weight of traditions thousands of
years old—aside from our delicious, lazy luxury of life, I
loved the East, as I saw it there in Egypt, just for the
splendor of its opalescent sunset each day, and the mar-
vels of its sapphire nights. One waited with impatience
for the renewal of the pageant of light and color, and
each time one's powers of enjoyment were greatly taxed.
One felt strained with sensations. No wonder people
born in such surroundings worshipped the sun-god and
the Nile!

In Cairo we did much that was amusing. The restaurant and terrace at Shepherd's were as picturesque as
any "revue's" stage, with their mass of inharmonious hu-

manity running over the latter's edge into the streets.
There were smart women come to winter there, painted
and bedecked with jewels and fine clothes, in latest Paris
style; smart English officers in every sort of uniform,
from those returning worn and shabby from the Upper
Nile, bound on a short vacation, to those just come from
London ready for their work; Turkish officials, and Egyptians in uniform or in frock coats with turban or red fez;
natives in national silks; Bedouins, camels, peasants,
donkeys, French nurses, babies, negroes; veiled women,
dignified and silent, with lovely eyes; push-carts and
European shops; blue beads and false antiques; old rugs,
fine arms, and poor imitations; cool drinks, warm tea;
Vienna waltzes, Sousa two-steps, both played by orches-
tras of crashing military brass; shrill voices squabbling;
small gray animals of burden braying; finally, now and
then, if an interval occurred in the din, one heard the
soft chant of a muezzin from some towering minaret,
calling to prayer the prophet's faithful people. All these
impressions, crowded on one's senses, made one dizzy.

Sometimes we had a clear view of a group or a single
figure. Thrice we had rather rare experiences. I went
one day by chance into a mosque, where the proportions
were superb and the soft gray of carved and perforated
stone stood cool against the burning noonday sky. Here
and there, at some point of vantage architecturally, a
mosaic in gilt or in bright color reflected the soft light
which penetrated there. Standing about were a number of noble figures, tall and solemn, in long, straight
draperies or smoothly moving in genuflections; then with
their foreheads on the floor they were prostrate in prayer
or deep in meditation.

My cousin had two letters of introduction, one to a
native newspaper man, the other to an Egyptian sheik,

and both these men were very kind to us. After calls had been exchanged, they invited us, the one to dinner and the other to his daughter's wedding reception. Both these feasts were exceedingly interesting, and to our European eyes had their amusing side. The dinner was the most difficult social experience I ever had, for my aunt and I were included in the invitation, and accepted, though we were told, of course, the ladies of the host's harem could not appear, since gentlemen would be present. When we arrived at the party we were first ushered into a room indescribably hideous. Harsh blue damask was stretched on the walls, and two long mirrors framed in rich, shiny, ugly gold frames hung opposite each other. Coarse, stiff lace with damask curtains over it hung straight down at the windows, and a heavy French clock, of the worst workmanship and period, stood beneath a glass globe cover, before one of the mirrors on an otherwise empty shelf. Round the room was a row of bent Vienna wood, cane-seated chairs, and at one end stood a table of the same workmanship, with a thin white marble top; such a table as one sees on the sidewalk in front of a café. It was about three-quarters of a yard in diameter and was uncovered. It seemed an accident among the other furnishings. We had been there a few moments, and had thrown off our wraps, when my cousins came in from the outside hallway, and with them our host and several other men—seven or eight in all. We women had worn high gowns, as we did not want to offend Oriental ideals and habits more than we could help. For a few minutes we conversed through an interpreter with the master of the house, and discovered that the other guests were his brother, his son, his secretary, his son-in-law, and so on. It seemed a clannish party. We spoke of Egypt's beauty, of the building up

of the country, and, except that they all flashed a little
when the Turkish officials and English administration
were mentioned, the whole conversation seemed dull and
rather flat; but they were pleased with our enthusiasm
over the beauty and picturesque qualities of Cairo.

Soon servants brought in trays of things. The little
table had a circle of chairs put round it, enough for nine
or ten of us, and we sat down elbow to elbow, about a
yard off from the table, which became an island in our
midst. My aunt and I were placed side by side. The interpreter sat next her, and then the host, and on my left
was one of the relations, who spoke a little feeble French.
Soup came in cups, and though to us it had no taste, we
drank it; then there was a dish of something like fish
which—put on the table, where a pile of plates and a
handful of forks were laid as well—had to be eaten. I
think I remember some potatoes in another dish, also a
quantity of bread—a mountain of slices. My aunt was
invited to help herself, then I, and we did, with a fork
and plate of our own choosing. We took the plates on
our laps and ate. There were no napkins, so we used
our handkerchiefs. I remember cool water was brought
in thick, cloudy goblets, which stood in a row on the
table's edge.

We had soon finished, and so had the Egyptians.
They ate in silence, with evident fear of the forks and
great expenditure of effort. They watched us, and I
decided it was the first time they had tried such instru-
ments, which, with the table and chairs, must have been
introduced for our special benefit. When a lamb, almost
whole, boiled with rice and covered with watery sauce,
was brought in on a great platter, they gave up and
frankly used their fingers, helped by bread. This dish
had a sweetish, sickening flavor, and seemed loathsome

to my Western palate, but to the Egyptians it was obviously excellent, and we pretended to enthusiasm and ate
a little just to seem reasonably polite. A sweet dish
followed. I had a fleeting idea that it must have been
prepared in the same pan as had been the meat, but a
little of this also had to be forced down our throats—and
then came on fragrant Turkish coffee, served in little
cups. That, at least, was perfect. Conversation lan-
guished. The natives probably suffered as we did in
attempting foreign fashions they disliked. We were all
glad the feast was ended, and after a number of compliments had been exchanged we took our departure.
For twenty-four hours we felt quite miserable, and even
now a certain sickly smell of cooked lamb and sometimes
the taste of it turns me pale, while I fancy those natives
swore never to touch forks nor perch on chairs again.

The other entertainment I saw was much more picturesque and interesting. My aunt and I, with the two
cousins, drove through narrow streets in the old part of
the city one evening, and stopped our landau at the entrance of a large, important-looking building. There we
descended, and on foot went into a courtyard, where every sign of a great function was visible. There were rugs
and silks spread on the walls and ground or making cano-
pies, stretched on poles and columns. There were cushions and small, low tables; some higher tables, too, with
Western chairs. There were men in Oriental uniforms
and flowing robes, others in the official frock coat with
red fez. Native musicians were playing vague, wailing
music. Attendants moved about, serving food. The
scene was rich and beautiful, a nice background for some
of the handsome, swarthy faces. The weird lighting of
lanterns and torches heightened all effects as they flared
or lowered again. It looked to me as if confusion reigned,

probably only because my Western eyes were used to a different style of entertainment.

Some one who seemed to be a master of ceremonies greeted us, and then, turning our escorts over to his aids, he showed my aunt and me to a staircase, where he mounted a short flight. We followed. A door opened ahead, and we saw we were in the harem of the sheik. We were at once introduced to his oldest and first wife. She was an old wife of the Khedive's brother, we afterward heard, whom the latter had passed on to his friend as a special mark of favor! A small white-haired woman with gray eyes and a face still young, good features and a clever expression, she evidently held all present in respect, as she bustled about giving orders which were promptly obeyed. Through an interpreter she told us the marriage ceremony was over, and now was the entertainment, but soon the bridegroom would come and fetch his bride, to take her home. He had never seen his wife yet. Refreshments were given us and the old lady asked us to be seated.

The room was large and as garish as possible. It was in blue, of French taste, in a bad epoch, overcrowded with miscellaneous furniture, ornaments, and junk. Such rooms seemed the height of fashion in Cairo. Cushions were strewn all over the floor, hundreds of them, and on these lounged a lot of women, old or young, but all heavy and dark. Most of them had big brown eyes and pretty hands; otherwise they were ugly, and their looks were not improved by their wearing Paris-fashioned frocks without stays. It made them seem bunchy and ungraceful. They talked among themselves, smoked cigarettes, ate sweets, and they looked at the bride and evidently chattered about her. The latter sat apart, a gentle-faced young creature, as lumpy as the others.

Some finely mounted old jewels sparkled on her fancy, absurd frock.

The room seemed in great disorder, and the things standing about included a sewing-machine, a music-box, a piano, gilt clocks and candelabra, boxes of candy, dishes, and so on. There were some soft, comfortable chairs and sofas, covered with damask. The curtains were drawn and the atmosphere was stuffy.

We divided general attention with the bride. For a time especially our clothes were of interest, but the old lady was the only one who talked to us. She was frequently interrupted. It was not very satisfactory conversation, and we never got beyond the first polite nothings.

Soon there was a stir. A great noise on the staircase announced the groom. He was ushered in by eunuchs, and came forward, led by our hostess toward the young bride. All the other women jumped up and surrounded them. It was impossible to follow further movements amid their din of laughing, crying, talking, and excitement. My aunt whispered to me she thought we ought to leave them to their family party, so we worked our way to the door, and found our own companions below, wondering how they could signal us and quite ready to return to the hotel. I got a curious feeling as to the dull sloth and emptiness of these Orientals' lives, and I was glad when we left the hectic capital and started up the Nile on our pretty steam yacht *Nitocris*.

We had visited the pyramids by moonlight and made various other charming excursions, but Cairo and Alexandria did not hold my enthusiasm after the first days. The rest of the trip was a wonderful experience, of pretty villages and bazaars, of imposing ruins, and especially of the dignified, graceful natives, walking with swinging, heavy draperies, carrying jars or baskets on their heads. Donkeys and donkey-boys, who were like imps of bronze, accompanied us. Their tales were always false but most amusing, and we loved the excursions we made each second day. On the day between we moved up the broad river, with its long-drawn-out panorama of beautiful shapes and colors either side of us. The land's picturesque value and the lovely lines of sails about us were a real joy. Our crew was enough to inspire an artist, and there was material for many a picture in their poses as they ate their food, or bent and rose to say their prayers out on the decks. We were a congenial party, all of us delighted by our trip save my poor uncle, who was growing steadily worse instead of better, and whose condition gave us much anxiety.

Finally, on our return to Cairo, after the classic tour to the First Cataract and back, we sadly gave up the rest of our contemplated journey, and took the first steamer for Brindisi. We hurried to Rome, where my uncle remembered being comfortable, and where he liked the doctors. We reached there just in time, for on our arrival the invalid took to his bed, and various medical lights were called in to his aid. They said there was no danger, that he would be better soon, but he was too fragile to go farther north for some little time, and he must be kept quiet. My aunt devoted nearly all her time to him, only occasionally making herself free to go out with us of an evening. In Rome I could not run about only with my cousins, as at home. I was left, however, with much time on my hands during the day, and as I had been too young to remember much of my sightseeing with my parents, I decided to take this up quite seriously again. We would have a month in the Eternal City, at least, and I meant to enjoy it.

CHAPTER VIII

ROMAN GAIETIES

ROME'S gay carnival season was at its height and we had not been there many days when old friends of my parents and aunt found us out. Soon our evenings were filled with charming parties.

I made friends with some young people, among whom were nearly all those gilded youths whom I had seen dining at the Grand Hotel in December, and of whom Doctor Nevin had told me. Lunches, dinners, soirées, and balls followed each other. We were even asked to a small afternoon reception and tea by the Queen-Mother, a beautiful, graceful woman with delightful manners, who already knew my aunt and my parents. We also went to a court ball, which was well done in every way and very pleasant, though not possessing the quaint historic and picturesque qualities of the Hapsburg court functions. In general one gathered that Roman society was new and cosmopolitan, having nothing much in common with its ancient background's rare beauty. Americans, English, and Russians camped out in magnificent palaces and gave rich fêtes in them, but they did not fit into their surroundings. Even at court, the halls were comparatively modern, and the mixed crowds lacked something of Vienna's old-time dignity. Yet the King and Queen were popular and very agreeable. People wore fine clothes and jewels, and to us the good music and floor appealed strongly.

It seemed complicated to keep track of the families who belonged to the White, or royal, party, and those who had remained faithful to the Black traditions of the

193

Vatican, though I noticed feeling still ran high, and of the older generations, members of the two groups scarcely ever met or mixed.

The most interesting experience we had was to assist at a high mass celebrated in gala robes by the Pope in person. Léo XIII was then very old, and had not for some time appeared at any function, but we were given tickets for a mass in the Sistine Chapel, and accepted. I was anxious to see the church in all its splendor, and to hear the famous choir. Besides, it was rumored that if he was well enough His Holiness was to appear, though no one counted on this. In black, with lace mantillas on our heads according to etiquette, we went early. On the threshold of the papal palace I was seized by the feeling of a fairy-tale being acted for my benefit. The staircase, always magnificent, was lined with Swiss guardsmen dressed in costumes designed by Michael Angelo. On the streets one would have taken them for crazy masqueraders, but on this background, for which it was designed, the dress of the Renaissance was quite appropriate in its gorgeousness. The chamberlains and gentlemen in waiting, the *monsignori* in purple, and the cardinals in crimson, the priests and officers of the papal household in their uniforms, were all so much necessary color against the finely proportioned gray stone walls. In the chapel the light was dim and beautiful, and the frescoes rich and dignified. We took our places, and after a short wait the rumor circulated and was soon confirmed that His Holiness would himself celebrate mass.

Soon after this we heard a distant chanting, which announced the coming of the procession. Prelates of rank, brains, and distinction made up the larger part of it. Chief among them the thin, sharp features and the keen, shining eyes of Monsignor Merry del Val stood out, dark and powerful. Great things were predicted of the young Spaniard, and I was interested to see how he had developed. I had known him in Vienna, where as a young student preparing to take orders he came sometimes to visit his father, then Spanish Ambassador to the Hapsburg court. Now his father was transferred to the Vatican, and many were the tales circulating of the Pope's reliance on this son.

As the chanting and music reached their zenith, came the Pope, surrounded by his intimate court. Seated on a throne, which I am sure he owed to Michael Angelo's genius or to Cellini's, His Holiness was borne high above the congregation's heads, and about him were carried various emblems and banners. Six or eight huge fans of splendid white ostrich plumes were also held on each side of his throne, waving gently and catching the light of hundreds of tapers. The shrivelled figure and face of His Holiness, moving along high up in the uncertain light, looked pure almost to transparency. High-bred, intellectual, worn with fasting and with age, the face was one of great nobility in repose. He turned slowly from side to side to bless the crowd of his children, who looked toward him with reverence. All in white, he caught the light and seemed surrounded by a halo.

Both then and afterward, as he drew himself to his full height at some point in the service, hand and arm raised in benediction, one was struck with the sublimity of his ethereal presence. It was the very spirit of religion come to life, and not for long, for the old man looked very frail. I believe this was his last public appearance. It was a very grand one, for the music and surroundings, as well as that picked crowd of devotees, seemed all worthy of the central figure. Somehow I felt the Church

of Rome, in this Pope's person, gained in spiritual beauty
what it had lost in luxury and power since earlier days.

Doctor Nevin had been as good as his word, and had
arranged a fine mount for me to wander over the Campagna in his pleasant company. He was as perfect a
guide as elsewhere my father had been, and he knew his
subject and loved it so well, that I was never weary of
his talk of the ruins we saw, or the villages and villas we
visited. Often we went together in the delightful tête-à-
tête of old and sympathetic comradeship, and though we
were many years apart in age, we grew to be warm
friends. Sometimes my cousins came on these excursions,
and little by little various others were asked to join our
party, till it grew into a large one, keen for the pleasures
Nevin arranged so well.

There were three or four young men among the diplomats I had met who were especially polite about accompanying us on these picnics, and who, besides, felt it their
duty to invent other sightseeing expeditions in and about
the city, visiting with us palaces or museums. One of
these, a Russian, was only temporarily attached to his
embassy, to ease somewhat a tedious stay he was obliged
to make in Rome, because of his bad health. A soldier
by profession, also a sportsman who made his mark
among the élite of the Italians, both at riding and in
handling the ribbons over a smart team of four horses,
Prince Michael Cantacuzène was in the south recuperat-
ing from a horse-show accident. He had little if any
duty on the embassy staff, and seemed glad—in spite of
his reputation of hating society—to run about with us,
whether to balls or in more sporty occupations.

My uncle grew better and we were soon to push on to
Cannes, where with early spring the doctors said he
would find the change of climate and the sea air bene-

PRINCE CANTACUZÈNE.

ficial. Somehow our departure was rather saddening. We had all enjoyed the season of gaiety, and felt we were leaving pleasant friends who would be missed. At the last our rooms were continuously crowded with people and I had no quiet talk with any one individual.

I discovered a variety of rumors had floated round us, and that I was supposed to have refused every man in our sympathetic little circle, from old Doctor Nevin down. It seemed just as well to be leaving while this glory lasted. Several of our group spoke of coming to join us in Cannes for a vacation, and each one was to write me more of his plans. They all kept their kindly promise as to this, giving me the opportunity of straightening things out so there might be no misunderstandings. All save one did this, for I had not been on the Riviera a week when, on walking into the hall of our hotel with an armful of bundles and an open box of candy, I found Cantacuzène seated in a deep chair reading. He dropped his book and came toward me. I had only just had a letter from him saying he was leaving Rome, going direct to Paris, having given up his proposed stop on the Riviera, and his sudden apparition surprised me so much that my arms fell and the sweets and bundles scattered over the floor. When my aunt and cousins joined us Cantacuzène was still gathering up the horrid things. The family were all very glad to see him, for he was an agreeable fellow. He explained with energy that he had been on the verge of starting for Paris when a telegram from the Grand Duke Kyril had brought him to Cannes for a few days' visit, and that he was spending the evening with this old comrade. We were also dining out, so we all parted, making an engagement for the next day some time.

At dinner I chanced to sit next to the grand duke

himself, and by way of conversation I said to him how nice it was that he had brought Cantacuzène to the Riviera.

"I did not," said Kyril. "I was glad to see him when he appeared in my rooms this evening, but it filled me with amazement. All winter he has stuck in Rome—I don't know why—and now, when I gave him up, he came. I had to turn him out, since I was already engaged for to-night, but to-morrow I will know why he has suddenly elected to arrive. He seems unusually capricious!"

It was evident Kyril's story and Cantacuzène's had not been compared before the telling, and that some mystery surrounded the latter's actions. I was given further food for thought when a day or two later an old college friend of my cousin announced to me that I would be making a great mistake to tie up to any foreigner, no matter how nice he was. "Grants belong in America, and I want to argue the point seriously with you."

As he spoke he looked across the table to where the Russian sat, making himself agreeable to Princess Clementine of Belgium. She was a delightful person with whom we had made friends, and whom I had visited at San Rafael. Mr. G—— scowled and I laughed.

"I assure you that no foreigner wants me. You see all the girls who marry English, French, and Italians have fortunes. I'm too poor to be in danger. Besides, I don't think I should care for foreign life save as an incident such as this trip has been. Don't let my peril weigh on you now, therefore, and if it will allay your anxiety for the future, I can safely promise you to keep myself free for any American who may appeal to me in time."

"I suppose I must be content with this solemn promise," said Mr. G——, and we passed on to other subjects.

Whether it was the fine weather and the beauty of
Cannes, or the powers of eloquence which he displayed
and his disregard for the European necessity of a dower,
within two days from that of the luncheon I found myself, in spite of my intentions, engaged to Prince Cantacuzène. Ours was a somewhat complicated position,
for we were far away from both our immediate families,
and for many days we kept the telegraph-wires hot.
Finally we had official consent from all our parents, and
were able, with my aunt's help, to make some plans. April
was still to be spent in the south on my uncle's account,
then we were to go to Paris, our party augmented by
my fiancé. There the official announcement would be
made, and I was to order my trousseau. On the 1st of
June we were to sail for the United States, while Cantacuzène returned to his country, to take up regimental
service during the summer manœuvres. He was to join
us in the autumn again for the wedding. We had known
each other but two or three weeks before becoming engaged, and had been a month together since then. Now
the summer was to mean a long separation, and we were
to see one another only shortly before our marriage day.

I was called a gambler by some of my friends at this
time, but though generally a slow, careful person, on this
occasion I was not at all hesitating or agitated over what
seemed a risky business, perhaps, to others.

I knew nothing of Russia—even its geography and history were hazy in my mind—nothing of the society or
family in which I was to take a place. Such Russians
as I had met I liked, and I had found their point of view
similar to my own. My fiancé knew beforehand I was
quite poor, yet he had not hesitated over this fact. He
was a liberal-minded, hard-working individual, and seemed
popular and well liked. His name carried me back to

those Vienna friends, of whom I had been fond. Without any doubts on the score of what my future background would be, I had accepted his proposal to go and live with him in his far-away home. It sounded attractive.

That summer in America was spent visiting various members of my own family in my mother's company, and then with her I went to Newport to await my fiancé's arrival. I seemed to have a series of new and strange impressions of my home and its inhabitants. People's amazing capacity to absorb queer stories about totally unimportant details dazed me, as well as the manner in which this taste was catered to. All my family was entirely satisfied with my marrying some one I liked and felt to be attractive; yet the papers came out with lurid accounts of my Grandmother Grant's despair over the match, giving dramatic tales of interviews with her and with me. My trousseau, which had remained in Paris till I could pick it up in the autumn on the way to our new home, was said by the papers to be lost, then to have arrived; gowns which did not exist were minutely described, especially one with "real gold coins sewed all over it," and one covered with "real fish-scales"! These were as completely non-existent as were the fairy palaces and various extraordinary family traditions with which Cantacuzène was supposedly endowing me. The long descriptions of family jewels were equally foolish. Such jewels, gowns, and background as there really were, were neither spoken of nor photographed at all.

Another quite amusing phase was that of the anonymous letters I received, full of violent praise or blame, sometimes calling me names for abandoning my country, disgracing my Americanism and my family by marrying a title, or else showing deep sympathy toward me for all I must go through in darkest Russia, living under a

European ruler, giving myself and my fortune to an adventurer who sought nothing but the latter—as if I had any money! One of my correspondents even went so far as to offer to marry me himself if I would break off with this foreigner!

The summer passed, as Newport summers do, though I went to no balls and naturally saw less of my men friends than in other years. My chief occupation was the writing of many notes necessary to thank people who sent me wedding-gifts. The latter came in by every mail, and the express companies were working overtime. Some of the things were lovely, and a special room in my aunt's house was given over to them, that they might remain spread out to be admired, examined, and packed at leisure.

The first days of September brought my fiancé, and after that a round of dinners began, given in our honor by kind friends. Our time was much of it spent in the open air, riding, driving, or yachting. A few last details were discussed and settled connected with the wedding ceremonies. There were to be two of these—the Russian Orthodox, and one in the tiny Episcopal chapel at Newport.

The Russian ceremony was to be performed first, and (by special dispensation) at home, the priests coming from New York and bringing all the necessary paraphernalia with them. It was a most beautiful service. The icons and the tapers, the incense and the chanting made a charming effect in the quiet room. No one was invited save our ushers and our family party, with Bishop Potter and Doctor Nevin, who had come all the way from Rome for the occasion.

It was the first Russian church service at which I had ever assisted, and though I was one of the chief actors in the scene and necessarily anxious not to do anything wrong through inattention, I managed to enjoy the pageantry, and I found in it an admirable dignity of ancient traditions, beautiful and rare with us.

The chanted music, without any instrumental accompaniment, was especially admirable and the kindly face of the old priest inspired respect; his deep intoning was rich with harmony and I loved it, though I had no notion of the words he used, which were in Slavonic. He and the bridegroom engineered us all through our parts, and every one present was greatly delighted to have witnessed the service.

At the American chapel, also, the wedding was a very pretty one; as simply carried out as possible, according to our wish, for both Cantacuzène and I disliked extremely the idea of exaggeration or show. There were a few autumn flowers and leaves on the pews and a screen of feathery green about the altar. Bishop Potter, my parents' old friend, and Doctor Nevin, who had seen the birth and growth of our romance, divided the service between them. My cousins and uncles and a few of my best men friends were ushers.

My gown was the simplest possible. The veil of tulle had no flower or jewel to attach it to my hair. The one note of magnificence in the whole proceedings was my husband's uniform. He wore his regimental white cloth with red-and-silver trimmings, high black boots, and golden metal helmet, with the imperial eagle of Russia on its top in silver, which caught the light and added its glistening note. Every one was very much excited about the groom's fine clothes, and his thoroughbred type, face, figure, and manner came in for favorable comment from all who met him for the first time that day.

The little chapel was filled with friends from the vicin-

PART OF THE CANTACUZÈNE WEDDING PARTY AT NEWPORT.

ity of Newport, and others who were interested enough
to come from Washington, Chicago, New York, and elsewhere. No one came to see a show. They knew there
would be none. Some army officers, comrades of my
father, were in full-dress uniform out of compliment to
my husband, who was an army man. I was given away
by my handsome cadet brother in his West Point uniform.

My father having been sent out to the Philippines in
the early spring, I had not found him when I returned
from abroad, and he had written us he expected to come
back before our wedding. As the summer passed his
work in Luzon and Samoa had become more arduous,
and constant trouble with native chiefs made him feel
that his duty was to stay there, not asking for the leave
he had meant to take. Consequently he wrote and wired
he did not want the marriage to be deferred, but wished
us to ask the President, if under these circumstances the
latter would not give my brother permission to leave
West Point and to replace him for the occasion. Mr.
McKinley kindly granted this request.

During the week of my wedding my father was in four
battles, but from the firing-line out in the wilds a runner
carried back a telegram and sent it from headquarters,
so it was put into my hands as we returned from church,
and my father's message of love, blessings, and congratu-
lations was the first to reach me.

A most amusing incident occurred as we left the
chapel. Nearly all of Newport's village people had
assembled in the street about the brougham which was
waiting for us, and Cantacuzène, with me on his arm,
was greatly and audibly approved, when we appeared at
the church door. Feeling we were rather conspicuous,
and disliking that above everything else, he hurried a
little and we climbed into our coupé. When the door

closed and while the footman was going round to his place on the box the crowd's curiosity got the better of their discretion and they pressed against the little carriage, looking in at the windows. In an instant my husband was dragging down the shades, indignant at this invasion of privacy, but the good-natured, interested crowd put their own construction on Cantacuzène's actions, and a voice shouted: "Sure, he's kissing the bride; three cheers for the prince." Up went the curtains again, but this did not spoil the pleasure of the multitude, convinced of its own divining powers, and we finally got under way, a hearty ovation ringing in our ears. I do not think the American public ever gave a foreign bridegroom such a warm reception.

Afterward, at the house, where my aunt had a delightful breakfast prepared for the wedding-party, the same informality reigned and every one seemed to have a lovely time. There was no crowding—in salons, on balconies, and lawns were scattered cosey parties, family, and friends comfortably seated gossiping, when they had eaten luncheon under a great marquee tent. The weather was warm and soft, and every one congratulated me on the pleasant omen and on my luck that the equinoctial storms had held off so late, for it was September 25.

There were a great many interesting people at the wedding who had gathered for love of my parents and interest in their child, but I have little memory of any individual faces. My grandfather had come from Chicago with his four sons, and he was, at eighty, still well and strong, though cataracts were developing on both his eyes and he used a cane to prevent false steps. He and my Grandmother Grant found each other in the company, and taking each other's arms they were wandering about talking, in the gayest spirits. They travelled back in their memory twenty-five years to the time of my parents' wedding, and all the company enjoyed their pleasures and their reminiscences. We had some anxiety for their safety, for grandmama, too, was grown old and very heavy, and her eyesight was extremely bad. Our fears were misplaced, however, and they survived the heavy lunch and other pleasures of the day, and were photographed with our wedding-party, standing together.

We left Newport that afternoon, on a yacht loaned us by Mr. Walters, the kindest of friends, and we sailed the next morning for France. A few days in Paris to gather up our various trousseau trunks, and then we took the north express bound for Russia.

CHAPTER IX

THE RUSSIAN HOME

ON the frontier of my new home country I was keyed to the highest pitch of interest and curiosity. What was it which made every one say I would find both the land and life so different from the same things in the West, and why should I feel so far away, as I was told I would?

At once, of course, I heard the unknown tongue, in which long sentences seemed to be spoken as if they were each one a single word. I saw strange square-built figures with broad, stolid faces, standing about. They said almost nothing, made no gestures, and answered agitated questions with patient, quiet voices. They were *mujiki*, wearing to me very odd costumes and white aprons, also caps of a queer shape. They carried our baggage adroitly and seemed very strong. Officials in various uniforms, fine-looking, heavy-built men, who wore their clothes smartly, were most busy examining passports and baggage. The travellers who were Russians had a lot to say, and seemed excited over their explanations. Those who were foreigners stood petrified by the difficulty of the language, but were perfectly cared for by the railroad people.

On the outskirts of this and every other station were little groups of people standing, sitting, or stretched out asleep, eternally waiting among their bundles. These were the peasants and the Jews, each in the dress of his caste. The first were generally silent, the last were almost always talking, and their sharp, roving eyes spoke of discontent.

We were met at the frontier by a clever-looking old

man who had been with my husband's grandfather, then with Cantacuzène's father, for years, and had become the majordomo, or house steward, since the death of my father-in-law. He took our tickets, baggage receipts, and passports, also all responsibility, and telling us to go and eat the dinner he had ordered for us in the restaurant, he marched off to care for everything.

After our meal we walked about among the picturesque groups, before old Auguste came to tell us our special car had been hooked to the train going south, and we must get into it. After twenty-four hours' more travelling we arrived at a tiny station which was then the nearest to the old château of Bouromka, and there, when we alighted, my husband's brother met us. He was a fourteen-year-old, charming, round-faced boy, with a cheerful smile, and with a keen sense of humor lurking in his handsome eyes. He had brought me a large bunch of violets, and while we chatted with him the contents of a big lunch-basket had been unpacked by the servants and laid out for our benefit. We ate with hearty appetites, for since the frontier had been crossed we had had only such food as old Auguste could prepare in our car. The home-made food seemed delicious, though some of the dishes, unknown to my Western palate, I thought I should like better with time. It seemed a funny way to travel, to have to take so many things and people along to be comfortable. Auguste had brought bed-linen and everything needed with him, and I learned this was really necessary, as soon as one left the main lines and the express-trains.

My brother-in-law had arranged to perfection our drive to Bouromka. Over the undulating steppes three relays of dapple-gray trotters, each set harnessed four abreast, dragged us in a huge, luxurious landau. Another carriage followed with Auguste and the bags, and a third vehicle carried our trunks. At the frontier of the Bouromka estate a gala equipage, called traditionally the "golden carriage," which was used for all ceremonious family occasions, awaited us. Hung so high from the ground that a ladder of four steps was used to climb into it, this carriage had a platform out behind, where between the springs two footmen in Cossack dress stood holding to straps and looking very handsome in their blue, scarlet, and fur, with the family eagles fastened on their breasts. Cantacuzène and I sat on the main seat, and my brother-in-law on a small one at our feet, with his back to the high box which the coachman occupied.

All the men wished us health, happiness, and welcome to Bouromka. The superintendents of the estate met us with the traditional bread and salt on silver dishes, covered with towels which were embroidered by the women of the estate. They kissed my hands, while my husband embraced each of the old servitors heartily. They had seen him grow up and were his devoted friends, it seemed.

We were established in our lofty turnout. Its six horses were launched full tilt. Harnessed four in a row with another pair ahead, this relay, even with that heavy equipage, made excellent time. The horses were all white and were decorated with gay ribbons, as were the men and the carriage itself. I felt myself unworthy of all this grandeur; I ought to have had on something much fancier than a dark-blue tailored suit, for as we passed through each village the peasants looked at me with curiosity in their smiling faces. We pulled up in the midst of a crowd on each public square who offered us always the traditional bread and salt, and whose health Cantacuzène drank as he thanked that particular village for its welcome.

Some had made arches of straw and flowers, tied with bunting, for us to pass under. All the people seemed to me most sympathetic. The villages were as picturesque as were the costumes, and I felt I was going to like Russian life and all it seemed to mean of tradition, good feeling, and interesting duties.

The loaves of bread, the lumps of salt, with the platters and towels, were piling up under my brother-in-law's care in the bottom of the carriage. It grew dark and we were met by two more men in Cossack dress, who were on horseback and carried flaming torches to light us on our way. Soon after this we swung into the park, and, taking the main avenue at a gallop, we reached the house entrance through a mass of brilliant figures in peasant national dress. As we pulled up, a brass band began to play on the lawn, the front doors were both thrown open, and ever so many people met my eyes— all apparently retainers of one kind or another—with Cantacuzène's mother, in a light gown, and the village priest, standing together as central figures.

We were fairly carried out of the carriage, and our outer coats were removed, I scarcely know how. Then we found ourselves pulled or shoved toward the princess. When our greetings were over we moved into the ballroom, which looked enormous. It ran two stories high and there was room in it for all the people. Here a welcoming thanksgiving service was celebrated by the village priest, or "pope," and during that, I had time to get my breath and look around. The service in Slavonic I could not understand at all, of course, but I knew it was in the nature of a Te Deum in honor of my husband's return to the old home with his bride, and I was aware that while they listened, as respectful devotees, to the words of the priest, most of the retainers kept their eyes fixed on me—from curiosity, doubtless, as to what the new member of the château family would represent in their lives. I was, on my side, deeply interested in their kindly faces, many of which had intelligent expressions. Their background also attracted me extremely.

The room's proportions were really imposing, and seemed the vaster because of the softly shaded lamplight and the rather scattered furniture. It had been a ballroom, but was now used as a general living-room, evidently, with big, soft chairs stretching out their arms invitingly, and many books, periodicals, and games scattered about. A billiard-table, a grand piano, a phonograph—all offered themselves in different corners, while screens of plants shut off spots where one might sit for cosey conversation or a card game. There were large glass cases with family souvenirs and relics, marble statues, attractive-looking paintings, and a great chimneypiece of carved wood.

Most of all, I was struck by the floor, in the great open space between us and the priest. It was inlaid in the most complicated designs; of oak foundation with white maple, red mahogany, and bits of mother-of-pearl, its surface brilliant with polish, rich with many coatings of pure beeswax—a work of art such as I had never seen in any other country. Afterward I learned this floor was hand-made, hand-laid, and hand-polished for generations by patient people, who showed by their care of detail a true love of beauty and their instinct for good taste. In its way it was as splendid as the high-panelled ceiling or the chanting of the choir, which carried out perfectly their share of our thanksgiving service.

On a table stood a collection of icons which were to be ours, and with which we were to be blessed. Some of these were ancient and rare, offered by the family or by

friends; others in modern enamel or beaten bronze were
donated by the house servants and the superintendents
of the estates. Incense burned, voices rose in beautiful
strains, and the whole scene was most touching, with a
charm different from any I had ever experienced. It was
a far cry from Newport, New York, and Paris to this new
life just opening, and somehow, in spite of its strange-
ness, it attracted me more than I could express. I began
at that first moment to feel a deep sympathy with the
nation which created such a frame and lived in it, filling
it so well.

The princess, my mother-in-law, was a Frenchwoman,
and her looks, gestures, attitudes, and ways were different from those of the others present. She was very
handsome, and was dressed in the latest fashion of Paris.
She moved more quickly than did the Russians, and she
wept from excitement. Her eyes roved about, alert to
catch and correct any imperfection. She made an excellent effect and stood out in sharp contrast to the background of Bouromka life, which she greatly appreciated.

The service over, we remained where we were, I standing between my mother-in-law and my husband, and
from the old priest down to the youngest servant-maid,
every one passed by us to be presented to me and to kiss
my hand. Many of these faithful people were very old
in the family's service. Two tottering old chaps had
known Spéransky, who died in 1829! Many dated back
to serfdom times, and practically all were born and
brought up on the estate. My husband's old nurse wad-
dled by, rolling in fat, with a new gold brooch on her
ample breast, and when she kissed my hand, after hug-
ging and kissing Cantacuzène, I thought her so motherly-
looking I kissed her with enthusiasm on both her ruddy
cheeks. She gave me a comfortable hug and a smile in

return, and from then on I had in "Grandmother Ann-Wladimir," as she was called, a stanch ally.

Soon all the servants and I were extremely friendly, and, through almost twenty years, I always saw only signs of their good-will and understanding devotion. It was the qualities of these simple, lowly country folk which first made me fond of my new home. Afterward, as I grew to know them and their compatriots better, the same traits made me admire all classes of Russians for their utterly simple dignity, their patience, and their courage, with so many other traits as rare and fine as these.

After our reception, followed a long dinner with all the bigwigs of the place at table. It seemed a dull ceremony, since I could not communicate with my neighbors, though I was fairly simmering inside with questions. I was very much pleased with all my new friends, but I was glad, nevertheless, when bedtime came, and the guests withdrew, leaving me to rest and to make the acquaintance of my new maid.

It took a little while to get used to the size of the old house and its complicated plan, and I was always getting lost and asking my way about. There was much I liked and much that was amusing at Bouromka. The average American housekeeper would have gone quite mad from the inconvenient arrangements. The pumping by hand of all water for that enormous establishment; the fetching and carrying necessary; the mere fact that two men spent their entire days cleaning, filling, and lighting kerosene lamps; that we all lived with doors and windows unbolted, even open—French windows standing wide on the terraces through summer nights; that all one's treasures lay about in complete safety for years, generations even; all this seemed amazing! Yet it was true that we, with our possessions about us, lived thus always in old days in Russia. Confidence begat honesty and loyalty apparently, and the atmosphere was such as made one feel the world worth while.

Outside, the country was very beautiful, and I never could decide whether I loved the flat steppe-land best, with its splendor of harvests waving and its chocolate-colored furrowed fields so full of promise, or whether the woods and meadow stretches were more admirable in their green peacefulness, with cattle feeding and streams flowing gently by. The number of our animals and the variety of work on the estate were as absorbing as the witchery of scene, and it seemed to my American mind interesting and amusing to think how self-sufficient we were, seventy versts away—about forty-six miles—from post, telegraph, railroad, and electricity. Yet life was entirely civilized and comfortable, and everything moved as if by well-oiled machinery.

After two or three days the princess departed for St. Petersburg to conduct my young brother-in-law to school, and we remained on for two weeks or so through the golden magnificence of the early autumn. My husband took me over the whole of the estate, and during that first stay in the Russian country place I grew to know much about the way of running it with its wheels within wheels. Originally it had consisted of thirty thousand déssiatines (of about two and two-thirds acres to a déssiatine). With the abolition of serfdom half of this had been given to the liberated peasants by the Emperor, and the government had paid a nominal sum to the landowner for the confiscation. Later, through three generations, various reasons led to further sacrifices of a small part of Bouromka's land, but thirteen or fourteen thousand déssiatines were still ours. Interweaving its borders with the peasant-commune lands it made a fair sight, and gave one the feeling that one was lord of a small kingdom, with all rights and responsibilities belonging to it.

The village outside our gates was very picturesque, but it gave me a heartache to see the wretchedness which reigned there, and the unhealthy looks of many of the people. Situated on the green, sloping banks of a tiny lake, it was ideally pretty and showed the Russian deep-rooted instinct both for the practical and the beautiful. Cattle and people both drank and bathed in the crystal water. Their homes, smothered in trees and gay flowers, were of a charming general effect from a distance. Close by it was different, for the thatched roofs all needed mending, were blown about terribly, and let in rain and snow. The houses themselves had usually crooked walls with tiny windows fixed in the plaster. One saw evidences of poverty, misery, filth, shiftlessness, overcrowding, and discomfort. To me it was deeply distressing to think the people who, when serving in our house or on the estate where conditions were better, showed us sunny faces and sang gaily over work, which they carried out with quick intelligence, in their natural state and their own village homes lived in such a sad, unhealthy way.

Alcoholism and the village usurer undermined our peasantry physically and morally, and they seemed too dulled to realize the situation or to help themselves.

My husband's father had been dead a long time; my mother-in-law, in the hands of her superintendents, during her children's minority, was exploited by these men almost as much as were the peasants, and, besides, she had been away from the country place a great deal. She had done much to better the château and other buildings on the estate, but she was facing large annual deficits caused by overexpenditure and underproduction. The people were not considered part of her responsibility. I do not know if this situation was the same all over Russia, but I was told Bouromka was a model of prosperity and the Little Russian peasants were happier and cleverer than those of the north.

For a long time it seemed difficult to understand why our people should suffer so much more than the inhabitants of other lands. By degrees I learned the influences which had been at work for centuries, and these Russians then made an even greater appeal, especially as through the years between 1900 and 1914 I was carefully watching their development.

I dug down into their history, which seemed to give the explanation of many traits I found in them. They had originally, in prehistoric days, drifted backward and forward over the great steppe-lands—essentially nomads, tending their flocks, living in tribes. Strains of Oriental blood influenced these early Slavs' habits and minds. Then civilization in two forms reached them. A militant Viking group had come in from Scandinavia, while from the south merchants and travellers brought Byzantium's influence to bear. The nomads grouped themselves, settled down, founded towns, and learned what government was. A period of civilization extending over several centuries followed for these various principalities—Kieff especially taking its place among the brilliant courts of the times—and Russians fought against Bulgarians, Hungarians, and Poles, making a reputation and carrying their conquests almost to Byzantium itself.

From out of the east then appeared the hordes of Genghis Khan, and, passing over the steppes, swept all opposing armies before them, capturing cities, sacking, burning, stealing Russia's rich possessions. The domination of the Tartars was long and cruel, since they exacted tribute so difficult to produce, it meant almost slavery to our people. During the conquerors' stay the peasants learned to toil as never before, and this developed the silent patience, which is still so marked a national trait.

Some of the nobility lingered about the Khan's court; the rest, on the contrary, stood off and plotted against their foreign tyrants.

Thus a warlike spirit came to be born, and little by little the nobles gathered round the strongest of their number. Several efforts were ineffective, but finally Russia won, and emerged from her domination by the Tartars the stronger and the wiser for the yoke carried so long.

Several things had Russians learned—first, above all, the strength there was in fighting together as an organized whole; second, the advantage of centralization for constructive work.

After the enemy without was disposed of, the grand dukes of Moscow seized the reins of government, keeping the centralized power to themselves. In the midst of this autocracy there were, however, quaint paradoxes which made for more democracy than anything western Europe knew at that same epoch, and which neutralized much that was severe in the new régime.

The ruler chose his wife from among his subjects, for her beauty, virtue, and intelligence, and he called on his nobles for advice. So Moscow's court was nationalistic and patriotic, and the council of "boyars," or nobles, divided responsibility in a way with their ruler. Furthermore, at various times, when the succession gave rise to discussion, an open election was held on the palace place, where a new and generally a popular man was chosen to reign. The nobles had much influence and intrigued among themselves for more, as was the habit of that day at every court in Europe or in Asia, but they also did most of the fighting and all that was done to civilize the provinces.

Our peasants had been forgotten through centuries of history. Since they had first attached themselves to the land, they had remained on it, ploughing or harvesting, turn and turn about. Outside of this they prayed according to ancient ritual, while their only culture was in the music and poetry of their own souls. It broke out into legends, tales, and songs never written down by them, but religiously passed on by word of mouth from generation to generation. Now and again some genius emerged from their midst and made good in art or science, religion or statesmanship, and the high-born aristocrats readily gave way for an humbly born man, who, through his self-made success, took his place in their midst. Strange these contrasts, symbolic of all that is Russian!

With Peter the Great the period of Muscovite Czarism, national reserve, and Oriental coloring ended, and a new era was inaugurated. Conscious that his people were a century or two behind Western monarchies in their development, he decided to push them forward by his sheer strength and force them into position among the nations. Every one knows the history of his colossal effort—how with infinite imagination, talent, and enthusiasm he created a new Russia. His capital was moved to a fresh site and built with magnificent conception on European lines. His courtiers were taken from their gorgeous costumes of the Middle Ages and made to wear Versailles' styles. Education and art, a fleet and an army, industry and commerce, were all built up in one man's reign on plans brought from abroad; and a new machine for gov-

ernment—the bureaucracy, as it was afterward called—
was created, to avoid the powers of the aristocrat and to
get men better trained.

It was the middle of November when we went up to
the capital from Bouromka. One felt a great change in
the climate going north. In the government of Poltava
the autumn was only fairly advanced. Heavy rains had
set in which made our ploughed fields fertile but turned
our roads to quagmires. Six horses harnessed to a great
"berline" like a landau could scarcely drag it through
the heavy mud which oozed over our hubs, and our
spending the winter in that special spot on the road was
apparently among the possibilities.

The long trip in old-fashioned trains with no conve-
niences, to me was an amusing adventure, for we had
space and provisions and plenty of servants along. All
this changed after some years, but I remember with interest those funny arrangements, the piles of hand baggage and the ready, helpful people, who through atavis-
tic traits of a desire to please, doubtless, knew how to
make us travel easily. I am sure our party resembled a
modernized edition of the nomad prehistoric Russians I
liked to read about.

It was easy to get used to the methods of my new life,
since there was room and time for everything. As always
in old Russia every one kept in excellent humor, so I
remember the two-day trips as one would a novel kind
of picnic, to me full of the unexpected.

We were to go to the home of my mother-in-law on
arriving in the capital, and she had offered us a part of
her large apartment for all winter, or till such time as
we found one in which to settle ourselves. She was to
send her carriage to meet us at the station, and we were

to have the feeling of a home-coming, she had said with much enthusiasm.

It was a drizzling morning with dirty snow covering the streets thinly. Scarcely light as yet, the place looked dull, and a very raw, icy wind swept across one's face. The carriage, through mistake or neglect, was not there, so perforce we drove across the city in a queer vehicle called a "droshky," with a driver as odd as his turnout, conducting a horse which had a night's work already in his weary legs, I'm sure, from the slow way he moved.

That drive was my only bad experience in the magnificent city which I was to love so dearly as my home through many years, but it was horrid, and it seemed miles from the Warsaw station to the Fontanka, where the Princess lived.

When at last we were safely landed at her front door and made our way up the great staircase into her well-heated rooms, our spirits rose. The Princess received us with as much excitement as in Bouromka, but with less ceremony, and I was at once introduced to my husband's sister and her husband. The former had extraordinary distinction; small and fragile, she was the quintessence of fine breeding, with gentle hands, and eyes of great beauty. Her rare intelligence, wit, and sweetness were all her own. Shy as a rule and not demonstrative, she was of those of whom the French genius spoke when he said: "The most attractive women never draw attention, but always hold it."

I found her very simple and winning, and we at once adopted each other as sisters. During twenty long years we have been that, and faithful friends besides.

Her husband, big, warm-hearted, charming, made himself my kindly comrade immediately, and I found him also most sympathetic through a long relationship.

We liked our rooms, which the Princess had had arranged with some furniture my husband had sent from his bachelor quarters in Rome. Our American wedding-gifts soon arrived, also, and with a little living in them our quarters became cosey, in spite of cathedral-like proportions.

By degrees I realized the city's splendor, which thrilled me, and I even had a taste of its gay society life almost at once.

Taken all in all, though, I had a bad time at first, for, arriving in November, by Christmas I had already spent three weeks ill in bed, while at the end of January I went to bed again, to remain till Easter, with a grave case of typhoid. Then a slight relapse kept me ill or convalescent until the end of May.

When my brain was not more or less clouded, I felt · deeply depressed by so much illness, but my young husband was a most excellent nurse, and he and his brother and sister were amiably ready to amuse me and cheer me through the slow hours of recovery.

In June we moved into our own new apartment on the banks of the Neva, and though it was much smaller than the Princess's home, we were enchanted to establish ourselves. We both loved the great river, which was a constantly changing picture.

My mother had come to me during my illness in the winter, and in the summer she returned for six weeks, taking the long, fatiguing trip with much patience.

In July our first child was born, a splendid fat boy with Cantacuzène eyes of deep brown. He was lusty and healthy, and I was immensely proud of this new member of the family. As soon as he was old enough to travel, we took our son and heir to old Bouromka, so that he should meet the members of his family, from his grand-

Lake in the park.

A wing in the château.

BOUROMKA 1899.

mother to his young cousin, who had preceded him into the world by a very few months.

Again we spent a long southern autumn at the family country place. This time, returning to our establishment for the winter, I felt myself an old married woman, for whom St. Petersburg was really home. Great interest and happiness lay before me in the following years, where there was so much to tempt my enthusiasm and curiosity.

My husband had a sailor brother but fifteen months his junior, and the latter returned from the Orient about the time young Mike was born. Boris at once adopted me and the baby, of whom he greatly approved, and after meeting this member of my family-in-law, I felt I truly had every reason to congratulate myself on the lovable circle my husband had given me through our marriage.

With a pretty home to look after, full of things which we liked, with a fine son and an agreeable husband, I was taking a new start in Russian life. I felt well and strong after all the care connected with my various illnesses, and looked forward to seeing something of St. Petersburg's court society, and to meeting the various people of world renown whom I knew largely composed it. It would be nice, I thought, to take part in court functions, for the Russian Emperor was considered at that time to be the most brilliantly surrounded sovereign in all Europe, and these fêtes were famous for their splendor. I had grown to love the magnificent buildings and broad streets, whose proportions seemed finer to me than in any other capital in Europe I had seen, where the rows of palaces, the great cathedrals, and the old fortress on the banks of the Neva made architecturally a sight at which all foreigners marvelled. Especially was it beautiful under the heavy snow of mid-winter, with the dull red northern sun, or during the white nights of mid-summer, when our capital clothed itself in mother-of-pearl tints. At such times, with sunlight or moonlight on the river, the buildings, silhouetted dark against the sky, gave one a picture never to be effaced from memory.

I listened to the many church-bells, and at Easter, especially, I loved to see the crowds of humble citizens moving toward their shrines in reverent groups. Russia at prayer was deeply sincere and appealing!

CHAPTER X

FIRST SOCIAL IMPRESSIONS

GETTING to know people in St. Petersburg was an interesting experience. It was not like meeting a society when passing through some foreign city, with the idea that one would be moving on soon and that mutual impressions made were only of casual importance. Some of these Russians were now my relatives; all of them potentially were my friends, and I knew I must live among them through the remainder of my days. They were different from any companions of my past. I had the feeling they were much simpler and more natural. Etiquette existed, a good deal of it, but its hand was less heavy in St. Petersburg than in Vienna. More of my actions seemed left to chance and my own choice than had been the case in Austria.

Peter the Great had established a grading of rank, and the rule was that no army officer below the rank of colonel could go to court and take his wife to palace entertainments, unless she or he were attached to the person of some member of the imperial family. In the latter case they went officially as part of their service. An inherited title did not change this court position at all. One could be head of a princely family, yet have no court rank, though every colonel, even of humble origin, all over the empire had a right to go to the big court ball and take his wife. Birth counted historically and socially, but not officially, while official bureaucratic rank, military and civil, gave one certain court rights. This was impressed on me at once by my mother-in-law, and as my husband at twenty-four was a lieutenant only,

even with the prestige of his being in the Empress Dowager's own Chevaliers-gardes, and with all the pleasant
relatives and our social position, he could not take me
to court nor go himself, unless he should be ordered there
on duty. He did not want to leave his regimental service, so it looked as though we would be obliged to wait
for years before I should have the official right of being
presented to the two Empresses, which was, of course,
the first step to court recognition.

In the lives of several women this had been a handicap during all their youth, I heard; but I was more fortunate, and almost at once the difficulty was cleared
away from my path.   First, at a small ball at the palace
of the Grand Duke Vladimir, the Grand Duchess Marie,
our hostess, came and took me by the hand, saying:
"Come, Joy, I have been talking to the Empress of you,
and she says I may personally present you to her"; so I
was taken up to where the young Empress stood, and
the Grand Duchess said a few kindly words, and pushed
me forward into the little empty space kept clear about
the sovereign.   The latter was exceedingly quiet and
timid.   After two or three perfunctory questions, which
I answered, she fell into her usual attitude of silent distraction, so I curtseyed and wandered off.   However, I
had actually talked with Her Majesty, which made every
one say that I must ask a formal audience at once, not
only of the Empresses but of all the Grand Duchesses
as well.   Once one had bowed before Her Majesty, to
neglect these latter would be wrong, apparently.

Shortly after this came another pleasant surprise.
Quite from a blue sky I received a letter from the senior
lady in waiting of the Dowager Empress, who said the
Duchess of Cumberland had written asking Her Majesty
to receive me kindly, as my parents had been the latter's

friends in Vienna. Consequently I found myself one morning called to an audience at the Anitchkoff palace, the residence of the Empress-Mother. The latter showed herself as gracious as she always was.

The news of all this irregularity soon spread about. As the presentations had then been accomplished, however, I received invitations to a number of court functions, and forever after had a perfectly ideal time. Of course my special honors raised a clamor, since a number of women similarly situated were waiting about, on the side-lines, for fate and years to bring them recognition, while I was invited everywhere and enjoying myself extremely.

I was fortunate in several other ways. Firstly, my husband had grown up on terms of constant companionship with several of the younger Grand Dukes. The Grand Duchess Marie had given us a little dinner so I should know all these. That evening the Duke of Edinburgh, brother of King Edward VII, had dropped in to the party, met me, and told every one present my family history, and how he had met my grandfather long ago. When he had finished I was firmly fixed, with all my background in the minds of those present, and my road became socially easy.

Sponsored thus, and being young, full of energy, and with a great desire to please my new compatriots, I was able to take my place immediately among the gay young matrons of the imperial capital.

It seems, however, that the younger Empress, after seeing me, had said to some one that my ball-gown was cut in a deep square instead of the classic court décolleté, which was straight across and off the shoulders. This little sentence was repeated and magnified till it was made into a severe criticism of me and of American manners in general. It amounted to nothing after a week, but at the time it made me more prominent, and won sympathy for me. I forbore from complaining, naturally; but the fact that there were many women present with gowns as square as mine, since a grand-ducal entertainment was counted a private ball, made the blow at a well-meaning, helpless stranger work all in my favor.

Afterward I discovered that a strained feeling existed between the women of St. Petersburg's aristocratic group and the young Empress. It had developed soon after Her Majesty's arrival, and grew rapidly, encouraged by the wretched plotters, whose game it was to control their Empress for their own ends. Following the incident of my gown, four or five young women deliberately wore square-cut gowns to the next court ball, and when the Empress's severe remarks were repeated to the town the culprits defended themselves with some energy. Gossip and bitterness followed, all of which seemed both amazing and unnecessary, but showed how the wind blew already in 1901.

My husband's regimental comrades and their wives were, many of them, about our age, and they made room for me in their midst with a hospitable enthusiasm which went straight to my heart. As the first regiment of the empire the Chevaliers-gardes represented the pick of Russia's young sportsmen, and the *jeunesse dorée* of St. Petersburg's social life all followed the lead of these officers. The Dowager Empress was our honorary commander, and came to the regiment fêtes in a pretty uniform, consisting of a dark-blue cloth skirt like the material of our officers' trousers, with a white silver-braided uniform coat (fitting her still ideal figure to perfection). She wore on her head, instead of the officers' metal helmet, a little close white cap with a small tuft of pure white ostrich feathers. Her proud carriage made all this very becoming, and her manner with the officers and us women was perfection. She was always popular everywhere, it seemed, but in the regiment she was especially admired. It was whispered about, on the other hand, that the young Empress disliked the Chevaliers-gardes, because they belonged to her mother-in-law; also that she was jealous since her mother-in-law had the command of the first of Russia's regiments, and that she was always ill disposed toward members of our group. It sounded as if relations were a good deal strained between the Emperor's mother and his wife; but though this may have been the case, I never saw any indication of it, and I put these rumors down to gossip.

My first years in St. Petersburg, till the outbreak of the Japanese War, were the most brilliant socially I saw there. The Empress-Mother did not appear often, but when she did so, she took first place at court. She wore black gowns always to mark her widowhood, but she usually had them covered with jet which scintillated; and decorated as was the upper part of her dress with "orders" and splendid jewels, she did not suggest anything sombre. Her conversation was as gay and agreeable as she herself was. Putting each one at his ease, she seemed most human and womanly, an inspiration to do one's best, whether in the performance of serious duty or merely in the telling of some nonsensical tale which would make her and others laugh. She had kept about her a lot of quite intimate friends who felt and showed for her sincere affection, and this she repaid in kind. Her manner was exactly that of her sister, the Duchess of Cumberland, and I felt somehow I had always known her. She received in a large red damask-hung and damask-furnished salon, with quantities of flowers about her.

It had a double-sized bay window; so as much light as a winter day in St. Petersburg offered could be enjoyed. Pretty ornaments covered scattered tables, and most of these things looked like souvenirs, the kind a woman gathers through life. Though nearly all the trifles were luxurious, they suggested intimacy and sentiment rather than money. The atmosphere of cosiness and warmth was underscored by Her Majesty's cordial reception.

The Anitchkoff is a large palace of a bad period— 1860 or thereabouts, I think. Its entrance-hall was vastly high, overheavy in its decoration, the staircase long and wearisome to mount, but made attractive by a wonderful series of Hubert Robert's panels, the best I have ever seen. I traversed a number of severe, classic reception-rooms, fitted with paintings, mirrors, bronzes, and statues, where a little furniture was stiffly arranged. I was told this palace was last done over for the wedding of the present Empress-Mother to the then heir to the throne, some fifty odd years back. The couple had still lived at home there, even when Alexander III inherited his crown, and they went over to the Winter Palace only for functions, continuing to entertain their friends and bring up their children in this frame, which was their personal creation. Souvenirs of their travels and of the small events of their unofficial life filled it.

In the largest reception-room I found the grand mistress and grand master of the Empress-Mother's court and two ladies in waiting, with a master of ceremonies. Two or three other women who had had, or were to have, audiences were also there, and our small talk was conventional. I was the newest interest to their circle, it appeared, and evidently its members were very curious as to the reasons for my being presented to our Empresses when I had no "official rights." They had heard from Her Majesty of the letter from Vienna, and all that, but were glad to have a few moments in which to put a certain number of discreet questions. I had not quite finished answering all these when a huge negro, dressed in a multicolored Venetian costume of the sixteenth or seventeenth century, opened the door to an inner room, and ushered out a lady who had finished her audience.

The master of ceremonies next escorted me to the door and the black, decorative, smiling doorkeeper threw it open again in silence. When I had made a curtsey on the threshold and another as I kissed the Empress's small hand, all ceremony seemed at an end. The Empress wore but two rings, I noticed—a great, beautiful, polished ruby and her wedding-ring. Over her simple black gown she wore two fine long strings of pearls. Afterward I was told these were some Alexander III had personally given his wife, which she used constantly, in preference to the many strings of larger pearls she owned.

Her Majesty asked me to sit down. There were several comfortable chairs, with little tables by them. The latter seemed covered with bits of old silver, tiny animals carved in precious stones by Fabergé, or various enamels of his making, a small clock among others—things such as any one might have in a sitting-room; and the Empress herself looked at home here. She took a chair and pointed me to one just beyond. Then she asked me a lot of questions about my parents, home country, and our Vienna life. Incidentally, I was able to tell her a little of her sister. It was to me a pleasant half-hour, one I always remembered. I was extremely touched by the simple kindness this greatest lady in Russia took pains to show a young stranger, who still had her way to make in a new country. When the time came for me to go, the Empress-Mother rose, and I again kissed her hand and made my curtsey. She said good-by, and that she felt sure I would like Russia; also that she would see me often probably; all this with a gentle, low voice and pretty smile. It was easy to realize why people were devoted to this womanly sovereign. Afterward I saw Her Majesty frequently—sometimes at a parade, or carrousel in the regimental group, or at a court ball, sometimes at a dinner-party, at the Grand Duchess Marie's, or at the Grand Duchess Xénia's. Always at least a pleasant word and a sweet smile were my share of her attention, and always it was a happiness to be near her person.

Once her kindly attitude and tact saved me in a very painful and false situation, which I owed to the German Crown Prince. The latter—I think in the season of 1902—came to St. Petersburg for a week's visit. It was at a time when the German Emperor was trying to win ours over, and when he was harping on the fact of his first-cousinship with our young Empress—the Kaiser's mother and the mother of our Empress were both daughters of Queen Victoria: the Princess Royal and Princess Alice of England.

The German Kaiser hit on the plan of sending his eldest son, then still unmarried, out to Russia to visit the regiment of which Wilhelm II was honorary commander, and to spend a week at our court. Our Emperor attached to the Crown Prince three officers with a number of minor secretaries, as the visit was official. At the head of this group was old Prince Dolgorouky, one of our Emperor's "adjutant-generals," then a "general of the imperial suite." Further because the visitor was young and a sportsman, and because he spoke no Russian and hated to use French, my husband was chosen, together with an A. D. C. of His Majesty, as attendants.

Cantacuzène, one of the best horsemen in Russia and a keen polo-player, attracted young Wilhelm. Their conversation was always in English, which Wilhelm liked, and used with great facility. He and my husband got on excellently.

The delegation went to the frontier in the imperial special train, to meet the distinguished visitor and bring him to St. Petersburg. Our Russians were greatly impressed with the discipline and training the Crown Prince had been given. On no occasion did he show signs of boredom, and when he held official receptions he found themes for discussion as well as amiable compliments for the least interesting of those people who were presented to him. The young boy patiently made the trip into the provinces, to the garrison where the Kaiser's regiment was quartered, and made his proper speeches to its officers. He also patiently talked or listened to the two elderly generals attached to him, taking great pains to please them, and succeeding perfectly, for I heard each one of them comment on the admirable education the Kaiser gave his sons. Cantacuzène thought the Crown Prince had a disagreeable face but a good manner, and in all branches of sports they really found a lot in common. The Crown Prince clung to Cantacuzène, who was the only young member of the group of Russians attached to him.

Among the Germans in attendance on the Crown Prince was General von Moltke, afterward Wilhelm's chief of staff in the World War. There were a lot of highly titled officers who wore very tightly fitted uniforms. All of them were big, red-faced men, and none of them were much liked by our Russians because of their stiffness and artificial politeness. I do not think any woman among us looked at them twice; certainly no

one wasted time discussing them.   They were completely
heavy and dull.

When the Crown Prince reached St. Petersburg he was
established at the Winter Palace with his German and
his Russian suites in attendance.   There was to be a ball
given for him at the German Embassy, and one at the
Winter Palace, while a third and smaller dance was
arranged by the old Grand Duke Michael, the last of
Alexander II's brothers still alive.   The Grand Duke
was a magnificent personage, well over seventy, who for
some reason of relationship—perhaps because he already
knew his granddaughter Cecilie was to become the Crown
Prince's bride—felt he should throw open his palace in
honor of the young visitor.

After his first court dinner and an afternoon official
call at the German Embassy, the Crown Prince unfortunately had fallen ill with a sharp case of influenza.   It
kept him in bed nearly a week, and this broke up the
court ball, which was countermanded.   The German
Embassy ball came off without him.   The old Grand
Duke Michael did not recall his invitations, either, and
happily for himself the Crown Prince was able to attend.
The palace of old Michael-Nicolaïovitch on the river-
bank was one of the most spacious and finest in St.
Petersburg.   Courtly and handsome, with his tall, well-
proportioned figure, the host stood at the head of his
staircase alone to receive his guests, of whom just enough
to fill his rooms without crowding were invited.   As each
one of us came up and curtseyed, his air and words as well
as his graceful bow and cordial hand-shake gave a sensation of sincere welcome.   For some of us the Grand
Duke even found pretty compliments to pay on our
gowns.   Every woman was glad to have worn her best
for such a smart little function.

The Empress-Mother came to her uncle's party, the Emperor and his wife also—a rare honor, for during the fourteen years between my marriage and the Great War I do not think they graced parties given in the capital more than five or six times. All the Grand Dukes and Grand Duchesses came, of course. Beyond the members of the imperial family and their courts in attendance, there was no guest who was not of the gay, ultra-smart set of young, married dancers, with the best of the crack guard regiment's bachelor officers added for extra partners. The floor was perfection, the gypsy orchestra the best in the capital. My husband, being attached to the Crown Prince, was living at the Winter Palace and was to arrive with the latter's suite. So I went alone, and found a number of guests already assembled. Every one had to be there before our imperial family or the Crown Prince made their appearance. The German Embassy members all came, the only diplomats invited. Only the Ambassador and Count Lüttwitz, the military attaché, were married men. Countess Alvensleben was said to be an intimate friend of the German Kaiser. She was quite old and plain, dressed atrociously, was very dry in her manner, and did everything by rule. She even arranged her hair stiffly with a green erection on top which we disrespectful youngsters called a tennis-net, and she had a way of saying "Nun, also!" before beginning a sentence, even in English or French, which caused us all great joy. She was rather easily annoyed and tried to dictate to us. The little Lüttwitz woman was American born, but had become so German that she spoke her mother tongue with German construction of phrase, and called her husband "my man" in English! Lüttwitz was most unpopular and we always felt sorry for his wife; but her German affectations got on the nerves of a good many who, like myself, tried to be nice to her at first.

As I came into the great ballroom there was loud talk in a group at one side of the door, and I turned toward the commotion with curiosity, leaving Prince Obolensky, who had just been reminding me of our engagement to dance the mazurka and be partners for supper. Countess Alvensleben was holding forth, and on the outside edge of the shifting women Countess Lüttwitz turned around and said to me in English: "We are just arranging the women, so we can take them up and present them to our Crown Prince when he arrives with Their Majesties. Won't you come too? You are one of the best dancers, and I am sure.would like to be presented to His Imperial Highness."

I promptly replied that if he danced well, I should like very much to have the Crown Prince presented to me, but I did not expect to be presented to him. "I've never been presented to any man. Our Czarévitch is always introduced to ladies like any other gentleman."

"But it is not the German court etiquette; and the Crown Prince would be surprised to have things otherwise. He will not dance with you if you are not properly presented to him by Countess Alvensleben," insisted the little Countess, beginning to look hot.

It struck me as supremely funny that this American woman should have reached such a mental attitude, and with a laugh I replied: "My dear Countess, this isn't Berlin, this is St. Petersburg, and *our* etiquette says the gentlemen of Russia ask to be presented to us. I am told by my husband that your Crown Prince is most polite; I fancy, therefore, he will follow our customs during his visit. If not, and if in order to dance with him I have to wait in a line and be presented to him, I am quite sure I shall be content to enjoy this ball with my Russian partners. So please don't have me on your mind at all." And I moved over to the far side of the ballroom without waiting for her answer. Afterward I was told that the Countess Lüttwitz said she did not think me rude, but she and others thought me indifferent! I felt like inquiring did she mean about her Crown Prince? But I refrained.

A number of other women joined me and we stood as far from the entrance-door as possible. We still were there, when the music struck up, and in the doorway appeared all the royalties; among them the Emperor's brother Michael, who was one of my favorite partners always, and a perfect dancer. He came across the room, and took me out for the opening waltz. When we finished it he invited me to be his partner for the mazurka; then he said: "I'm going to bring our cousin and introduce him to you. You will like him, and he dances awfully well."

He went and fetched Wilhelm from the crowd at the door and brought him straight to our side of the ballroom, introduced him quite informally to me and then to all the other women who had followed me over there. The Crown Prince showed no sign of shock at this breach of etiquette, and being, for the first time since his arrival, in young, gay company, he proved his enthusiasm and his admirable qualities as a dancer at once. He asked me to waltz and I accepted, feeling a wicked joy as we passed the corner where the ladies from Germany stood looking with stony expressions at my excellent partner and me. We circled several times in their neighborhood. Naturally they were cross, especially as Wilhelm, having also asked me to be his partner for the mazurka, and hearing I was already engaged to the Grand Duke

Michael, went off and arranged for the latter to waive his rights in the guest's favor, since this was to be the Crown Prince's single ball in Russia.

Everything went swimmingly; I danced every moment till supper-time, which I was to take at a gay little table, arranged by Prince Obolensky, my partner. The Crown Prince was designated to sit on the right of the Empress-Mother at her table, since he was the guest of honor. Some important old lady was to be on his other hand. Prince Dolgorouky came up to us, explained the plan, and said as the Empress-Mother would be placed next our host, Wilhelm must join the other lady and escort her to supper. The arrogant petulance of the young German showed for the first time. "I won't; I have already asked a partner, the Princess here, and she must come with me to Her Majesty's table!" he exclaimed.

I then ventured to take part in the conversation. "Really, Sir, I couldn't sup with you; firstly, because I wouldn't for the world intrude at the table of the Empress-Mother; secondly, because I mustn't drop out of my own party, and here is Prince Obolensky come for me. So thank you and au revoir"; and I moved my hand from within his arm and turned toward my waiting supper partner.

The Crown Prince seized my hand, so I could not withdraw it, and turning to the old Prince Dolgorouky, said quite rudely: "I told you, I won't; either the Princess comes to this table where I sit, or I won't go. Arrange it as you can."

I protested with some energy: "Really, Sir, it is impossible to change the plans of our host. You are leaving and will not feel the consequences, whereas I, who belong here, will be accused of having attempted to push myself forward, and I cannot consent to that. You must excuse me."

The Crown Prince looked furious, and protested again
so crossly that old Prince Dolgorouky, who was an accomplished courtier, turned to me, saying: "Will you
remain with His Imperial Highness while I see what can
be done?"

People were going to the dining-hall, and, of course,
save this headstrong guest, the royalties must have been
all seated by that time; but I knew I could count on
Prince Dolgorouky's tact and kindness, and my original
partner had assisted at the little scene and understood.

He smilingly said to me: "I will stay with you till the
question is well settled."

Wilhelm at once replied: "It *is* settled; take my arm,
Princess, and come with me to supper."

As Prince Dolgorouky had disappeared in that direction, it seemed to promise a rapid solution to go to meet
him; so I again took the Crown Prince's arm. He was
too ruffled to talk, and I was seriously annoyed by my
situation. I desired nothing more than to escape with
Obolensky, who remained quite near, where I could
transfer to him at a moment's notice.

We reached the door, and I really felt I should like to
cry. I seemed helpless to handle my arrogant companion. But we met Prince Dolgorouky returning toward
us, and he said: "Will you come to this table where Her
Majesty is? One of the Grand Duchesses has ceded
you her seat," he added, turning toward me.

The Crown Prince at last let my arm loose, and, as we
approached, the Empress-Mother looked up and smiled;
Wilhelm bowed low over her hand and I curtseyed. She
stretched me her hand, and I kissed it. Looking amused,
she said to him, "Will you sit here?" and to me, "Sit
just beyond."

I moved away from her chair and around the Crown

Prince's, reaching the rear of the one which the Empress had pointed to, when to my own and every one's amazement old Countess Alvensleben, appearing out of space, stepped between the table and my chair, and plumped herself down into it, saying: "Nun, also! Dass ist jetzt mein Platz!" (Well, now, this is my place.)

The Empress-Mother looked as if her merriment would get beyond control, and the Crown Prince looked as if an explosion of violent temper was to occur. I felt I should certainly cry in another moment. One of the gentlemen who was two seats from the German Ambassadress rose.

"Princess, sit here," he said. "With Her Majesty's permission I can easily move to another table and you must take my place."

"Yes, sit there," the Empress said, and gave the charming Russian courtier and me a radiant smile.

The supper was sadder than would have been the one I had planned with Obolensky, but I talked with Prince Dolgorouky, who was between me and Countess Alvensleben, and who was looking greatly entertained.

Forever after Prince Dolgorouky had a lovely time attacking me about the way I put people's supper arrangements out of commission. He did not have much to say to the German Ambassadress that night, and the Crown Prince never once spoke to her either. I did not look at the latter, nor did I recover my spirits till toward the end of the meal.

At dessert I heard the Crown Prince say: "Princess Cantacuzène, Princess Cantacuzène!"

Prince Dolgorouky suavely remarked, "I believe His Imperial Highness is speaking to you, dear Princess," and as I turned that way: "I have been trying to attract your attention for a long time to drink your health,

Princess," said the Crown Prince, and he added some conventional compliment.

I wondered if Countess Alvensleben was enjoying herself less than I was? She looked deadly, and I expected gossip to follow my trail. Of course there was some talk, but it soon died out, for Her Majesty was afterward as lovely as she had been in the sudden emergency, while Prince Dolgorouky told the story truthfully and amusingly, advantageously to me, bringing out the arrogance of our young visitor. I had already a host of friends in St. Petersburg by that time, and they would not have believed me apt to put myself forward, or inclined to shove myself into a party at the Empress-Mother's table, even had they heard I tried to do so.

For years, though, whenever I saw Her Majesty, the latter would ask me if I had news of the Crown Prince, and once she said, "I never will forget his face and manner that evening, when Countess Alvensleben suddenly took your chair!" and she laughed. I was always grateful the Empress was so gracious and had such a sense of humor.

Through years following this, each 1st of January brought us a telegram of greeting, or some souvenir, from the Crown Prince: a small painting of himself on horseback, a photograph of him with his fiancée, three or four water-colors showing the ancient uniforms his regiments had worn, a picture of his eldest son. Once when I went through Berlin, His Imperial Highness, learning I was there, called me on the telephone and invited me to "go with my wife and me to the play and to supper." I accepted, and they came to fetch me with the utmost informality, the Crown Prince descending and coming into the hotel after me and returning me later to my door. That was a quiet, pleasant little party. I felt surprised at the simplicity of their life, and at the apparently agreeable relations between the pair. They, his brother Auguste Wilhelm and the latter's wife (both fat and deadly dull), with an aide-de-camp and myself, composed the party of six. We sat in upholstered armchairs, placed in that space where ordinarily in our theatres the first row of the orchestra would be. They had chosen *Samurun*, a pantomime, so I would not have to be bored listening to German talk, which they thought I did not understand. Supper was served between the acts in an attractive little dining-room in the theatre building. The Crown Prince was amiable with his wife that night and they seemed a congenial couple. A year or so later, when they visited Russia, I had the same impression again. I heard much gossip, however, tending to contradict this, and I could not forget the pettishness he had shown at that ball long before. I could more readily believe in his defects than his virtues, so when the war came I had no scruple in throwing away or turning to the wall the various souvenirs he had sent us during ten or twelve years.

The Crown Prince was to do me one more ill turn, however, which might have ended badly had it not been for Russian chivalry and intelligence. It was in the early part of February, 1915, that one day I was asked for on the telephone by General Rauch, an old and prized friend of ours, and at that time one of the important men in the departmental command of the capital. He begged me to receive him at once and alone. I acquiesced, of course, wondering at his strange request; and when within a few minutes he appeared he looked more anxious and solemn than I had ever seen him before. Often it happened that people we knew came to me, asking to have some message passed on to the Grand Duke Nicolas

by my husband, who was temporarily his aide-de-camp,
and who held a rather filial position with his chief. Cantacuzène had stayed at headquarters during his conva-
lescence from his wound, and as he and I were both
known to be discreet, and our letters went back and
forth by the grand duke's private courier (not subject
to the censorship), we were used this way frequently. I
fancied General Rauch, knowing us well and being a
faithful friend of the grand duke, might wish to make
some communication, so I said: "What is the secret,
dear general? Can I do you any service?"

"No," he answered, "except by replying to a few questions. Were you expecting any mail from any one
abroad?"

I began to enumerate the various members of my
family who regularly wrote to me, but Rauch interrupted: "You have no correspondent in Germany?"
"No," I said.

"Can you tell me then what this is?" he asked, and
he drew a large envelope from his despatch-case. "Perhaps it is addressed to some one else?"

I took the big envelope and read the address. "I am
the only Princess Cantacuzène, née Grant. It is for me
and is peculiarly addressed; it says only 'St. Petersburg,
via Rumania.' I didn't know mail still came through.
It has a large red seal with 'W' and the German imperial
crown. Yes, I can tell you without looking further what
you will find in this, general, if you open it; it will be a
portrait of the Crown Prince of Germany, or a picture
of something which concerns him. He sends me some
such souvenir each year, for the 1st of January. I had
not had one this year, but I confess I thought it was
because His Imperial Highness had intelligence and chivalry sufficient to realize that in war-time his remem-

brance would be obnoxious and, possibly, compromising.
Perhaps this was sent me through the stupidity of some
secretary left in charge in Berlin, who forwards these
things for the Crown Prince each year, and has this season used his habitual list without corrections."

Rauch examined the envelope with care. "No, this
bears the stamp of the 'Fifth Army,' which is the one
young Wilhelm now commands on the western front.
Also, it bears the signature of his Hofmarschall—marshal
of his court. I'm afraid it is sent by the Crown Prince
himself. What do you think you better do about it?
The big envelope arrived this morning at the censor's
and made a sensation. The matter was brought to the
chief there, who rang up our department, as he knew
enough to realize he mustn't accuse you lightly. I asked
to handle the matter—said I would take it off his hands.
I am satisfied (if you tell me you have not received or
written a letter) that you are telling the truth, and I will
satisfy the chief at the censor bureau. This is my end
of the business, but I should like to know what you are
going to do yourself about it?"

I said, firstly, I would make him a present of the picture, which he promptly declined; secondly, I would at
once write the whole history to my husband, asking him
to inform the commander-in-chief, so that if the latter
ever heard the story from another source, he would not
think I had tried to hide it; thirdly, I would tell Prince
Orloff, also, so he would be in possession of the facts, in
case Madame Wiroboff had the story from her spies and
tried to use it to my detriment. It would be so easy for
her to say: "People are telling of Soukhomlinoff's treach-
ery—here is the wife of an aide-de-camp to the ultra-
Russian grand duke who corresponds with Germans;
and so on!" And I would need a strong defender, in-

deed, at court to stand up for my loyalty. None could be better than Orloff, though, whom the Emperor knew to be absolutely truthful.

Finally I said: "Dear general, if you won't accept this as a gift, to whom shall I offer it? I don't want it in the house."

And Rauch replied: "I think all your measures are wise. Suppose you ask your husband or Wlady Orloff what to do with the thing."

I asked if I could not send it back. I thought that the best way to revenge myself for the nasty trick of the arrogant Crown Prince. I felt sure he had wished to prove that, no matter what he and his armies might do to our Allied forces, his prestige in the eyes of those who had known him remained unimpaired. Or else he had done this thing to compromise my husband and myself and make trouble, simply. Either way it seemed horrid and I was keen for paying him back.

I wrote my husband, who told the story to his chief. The latter laughed, said I had acted right, and to think no more of it. Then I told Orloff. He felt as I did—it would be fun to return the picture, and we tried to do so through one of several channels. The German censor would have prevented its reaching its destination by ordinary mail; of course none of the neutral embassies would let their couriers handle it. We learned this by consulting the American chargé d'affaires; neither could any member of the Red Cross undertake the carrying of so undesirable a packet. Evidently this picture was to be a white elephant on my hands.

My mother-in-law, who became greatly excited when she heard the tale, said I ought to tear and disfigure the portrait, and then return it, writing an insulting letter, too, but my anger was rather cold than hot, and I did

not feel such action would express my sentiments. Orloff said, laughing, he thought I ought to show it in a
large frame to the public as the latest manifestation of
German ill-breeding and arrogance. One must be indeed both ill-bred and arrogant to send a woman with
whom one had had only two or three meetings at parties, one's portrait done in war paraphernalia, with
trenches in the background, when the war was against
her people, and when such a gift might throw suspicion
on her, besides!

I persuaded Orloff to put the ugly thing in his safe and
keep it, which he did, till the moment when I was leaving Russia.   Then he returned it to me as a souvenir of
one of my friends, he said, and to recommend me to
Trotzky-Brönstein in case we were captured by the Bol-
sheviki on the frontier!   This did not happen, luckily,
and I believe Wilhelm has sent me no more pictures of
himself.

CHAPTER XI

THE COURT AND SOCIETY

IN Russia the diplomatic corps was very large, and most countries sent us their best representatives. The American Ambassador, Mr. Tower, who was there when I married, lived in a palace on the Neva's bank, where he entertained with a series of quiet dinners the élite of the capital's intellectuals, as well as the court group. The other embassies were then all rather quiet, save for an occasional dinner or soirée. One shone above all others during the period between my arrival and the Japanese War. It was the French, which in riches surpassed all its colleagues, and held a place second to none in St. Petersburg as Russia's friend and ally. The French Ambassador had quarters which occupied a large space on the French quay, and commanded a fine view of the Neva. He used lovely furniture, tapestry, silver, and works of art from the royal collections of France. As a peevish rival of the Marquis de Montebello said to me once at a banquet given by the latter: "We have kept our King, so our ambassadors can't be using royal property!"

The inspiration of the feasts, receptions, and balls which succeeded one another at this embassy was the Marquise de Montebello, a woman of exceptional beauty and wit, with a large personal fortune which she spent lavishly; a brilliant talker and very "enfant terrible," she amused even the most blasé. She had a gift of arranging successful parties, and putting the right people together. She grew to be the intimate friend of various

245

prominent or smart Russians, especially various members
of the imperial family. She gave a large formal party
for the sovereigns, small suppers with the older grand
dukes, pretty cotillions with but thirty or forty couples,
well chosen, for the younger royalties, especially for the
Emperor's brother Michael, who was very fond of dancing. An extremely unpretentious youth he was at that
time, admirable at all kinds of sport, and always ready
to enjoy an informal gathering. His riding was exceptional, both in races and in the horse-show ring, and he
saw quite a lot of my husband, who was then one of the
best horsemen in Russia. I had met Michael Alexan-
drovitch at a dinner the Grand Duke Wladimir gave,
very soon after I made my début in Russian society.
Andrew-Wladimorovitch, a son of the house, brought up
the stranger and said something which sounded vaguely
like an introduction. I was talking in another direction
and stretched out my hand, which the stranger took and
bowed over; then as I turned again to my conversation
the smart-looking young officer withdrew. I noticed he
had a well-set-up look, and wore the aiguilettes of an
aide-de-camp to the Emperor.

After I finished talking with the man near me, I turned
to a woman at my side, saying, in all innocence: "Who
was that trim aide-de-camp the Grand Duke Andrew just
introduced to me?"

She looked astounded. "You don't mean to say,
Julia, you really don't know? It is no less a person
than the Czarévitch, heir apparent to the throne of all
the Russias, and you treated him in such a casual manner; I wondered what on earth was the matter!"

"There wasn't anything the matter. He looked exceptionally nice, and I couldn't possibly tell his name by
looking at him. I hope he won't mind my liking his

modest way of going about, getting introduced to strangers properly, instead of exacting official curtseys due his position."

Michael asked me for the mazurka and supper when dancing began that evening. He liked my treating him simply, it turned out, and always after we were frequent partners—in fact, at the court balls I was invariably his partner, either for the mazurka or for supper, or both. My husband and I were generally invited to his table, and were also included in any little fête given for him.

St. Petersburg was probably, during those years, the most brilliant capital in Europe. Besides the embassies, there were a lot of aristocrats, rich, lavish, highly cultured, who were fond of entertaining. Good taste and money had created ideal frames for dinners, theatricals, dances, suppers, and music. Our women were handsome and well gowned, and both men and women were most unpretentious, cultivated, and clever. I liked them thoroughly, and I felt immensely at home among them; also, I liked their occupations and amusements. Every one had serious duties, fulfilled with great success, but they also possessed a rare faculty of putting aside their work and plunging into any pleasure with a zest no other race can boast, I think. It is a rare quality, especially as their unfeigned enthusiasm led to no excess. In all the years I was in Russia I never met in society any man who had had more to drink than was good for him, nor did any act or word ever go beyond good form and good taste. It was all instinctive breeding, as was the invariable kindness shown a young stranger who had dropped into their midst. They helped me in every way to make good, in spite of my ignorance of their customs and their etiquette.

Aside from the ordinary run of parties, there were

often rather unusual and unexpected picnics—when at a dinner or after the play some one would say: "Let us go troika-driving to the gypsies to-night." Then the men would begin to plan and telephone. Troika sleighs would arrive, we would all bundle up warmly and sit in these gay, carpet-covered, bell-bedecked vehicles with their prancing horses three abreast. We would skim over the river's ice and the hard, smooth snow on the islands, go far out of town, with the moon creating a deep-blue fairy-land about us, and the air nipping any part of one's face left exposed. Ten miles or more we drove out, one horse trotting at such a rate that the others on either flank must gallop to keep up. We felt dizzy with intense cold, rapid motion, mounting excitement, and the winter's beauty.

Suddenly we pulled up. It was the gypsies' settlement we had reached, and there, though all looked so quiet in the low-ceilinged, dull, badly lighted house, we found an excellent supper, as if by enchantment, waiting for us. Smoking dishes—Russian; fruits from far away, champagne and tea. It seemed delicious, for our appetites were sharpened by the air. Soon we passed from the supper-table to long benches ranged about the walls of another room, equally low, dingy, and ill lighted. In trooped the gypsy singers, two-thirds of them women, dressed in crude colors which seemed violent contrasts even in the semigloom. As they settled themselves, every one lighted cigarettes and our glasses were filled. The health of each guest in turn was drunk, with a little verse sung to her or him by the gypsies—a pretty initiation. These strange people, who came from no one knew where originally, whose voices had a wail of the Orient which deeply stirred one's heart with things left unsaid, had wonderful répertoires of weird songs. Most foreigners were bored after a time, but I always loved expeditions to these gypsies, who were so different from their race in other countries. About five in the morning we drove home again through the early, freezing air.

Besides gypsy parties, there were many other original, gay, curious affairs. Supper at some palace, where, asked at half after midnight, we sat at table till five or six o'clock in the morning, listening to a fine Russian singer. She was installed generally at the table with us, her accompanist, a man with a guitar, standing behind her chair. Between courses and when the meal was ended, she would sing old Russian legends, popular folk-songs, anything any guest asked for. The singer had no caprices, and the guests were all sympathetically vibrating and would join in the different refrains. Strangely enough, most of the music was sad; at least I felt as if a scintillating pattern of golden sound was woven into a background of sombre gray, with just a recurrent note which aroused one's wildest energies before it died away. The Russians seemed to bare their national soul in their peculiar, lovely music.

We danced the whole night through, if we danced at all, and balls had a vim I never saw elsewhere. Beautiful flowers, perfect floors, rarely too crowded for comfort, stunning jewels, brilliant uniforms—every one certain enough of his position to be quite natural. Night after night one danced, till hot coffee was served—the Russians' usual morning meal—and many an officer went straight to early drill with his regiment without going home to sleep at all.

Irregular sleep apparently did no one any harm in Russia. I found it did not at all disagree with me to come home with my arms full of flowers and my dress ragged at the lower edge from spurs, about the time our children were getting up. One could rest three or four hours, then walk on the quay and feel as fresh as ever for the new effort of the evening to follow.

But the season was short—only a few weeks—and most of the year one led a very simple life in the bosom of one's family, or with only a circle of intimate friends gathered about one's hearth.

Of course the greatest functions were at court, and I am glad the three or four early years of my married life were during a time when the Russian court was arrayed in all its glory. About eight such functions were given by Their Majesties each season at the Winter Palace or the Hermitage. The court ball which opened the season occurred soon after the New Year. People came from all over the vast empire, wearing the quaintest clothes. At least once in a lifetime the effort was made to go to court by provincials, and, doubtless, patriots who travelled so far, after many years of service, to gaze on their "Little Father" and his beautiful consort, put an almost religious spirit into their pilgrimages. But I think they must have felt repaid for their effort and expense, as they looked on the most magnificent party in Europe. They carried memories back to Caucasian mountainside or Siberian plains, which were akin probably to fairy-land. They had walked through kilometres of great halls, filled with art treasures; they had seen three thousand people assembled, the women's gowns and jewels or men's uniforms of gold and furs of such richness as no other empire could boast. The frame was worthy of the picture and the picture of its frame. Surely Solomon in all his glory could not have equalled this great sight.

Nicolas II, alone of all European sovereigns, could give his three thousand guests dancing space enough in a single ballroom; he alone had room to seat them all at

A BIRTHDAY PARTY AT THE GRAND DUKE VLADIMIR'S, ELDEST UNCLE OF NICHOLAS II.

a well-served hot supper, with plate and rare china, napery and food from his own kitchens and storerooms. At these feasts and in all his gorgeous surroundings the Emperor always seemed most simple. His uniform was generally that of a colonel in one of the infantry regiments of which he was fond, or that of his own Hussars. Small of stature, with a painfully shy manner, His Majesty showed constantly how difficult was his rôle as the centre of these celebrations. I always thought as I saw him watch longingly some gay guardsman pass with a pretty partner hanging on his arm, how the Ruler of all the Russias must envy an ordinary young chap's freedom.

I dressed for these parties with feelings of elation, donning my best clothes and knowing it was all pleasure for me. We drove through the freezing night, toward a magnificent feast for eyes and ears, as well as a joy to light and frivolous feet like mine. On arriving I could not throw off my cloak quickly enough, and already before the staircase the excitement of the hours to come made my blood tingle. We climbed a long flight, lined with guardsmen picked for their beauty and size, and if it was the night when the Emperor's "own horse-guards" were on duty, they were surely all brunettes. Should one man be less black of hair he was dyed for the occasion to match his fellows. They wore helmets of gold, with metal imperial eagles spreading silver wings over them; their uniforms, red and gold and blue, were the best cut and fitted I have seen. The three or four palace entrances were guarded by different regiments, each lending a bright note of color to the scene. One door was for the military and naval guests; another received the diplomats; a third the imperial family; a fourth civilians. The crowds moved forward from each through hall after hall, greeting friends until they reached the grand ball-

room. There we stood about in groups, more or less
marshalled into the right space by the head master of
ceremonies, Count Hendrikoff, and some fifty of his
aides, all in much gilded but ugly heavy uniforms; each
of these men carried a long cane with ivory handle.

Rapidly guests gathered; then three taps were heard
on the floor, and silence fell. A last quick arrangement
of one's train or one's sleeves was possible before the
double doors opened. In the frame stood His Majesty,
looking as shy as possible, as if dreadfully sorry to interrupt. Behind him his adjutant-general, the general
of his suite, and His Majesty's aide-de-camp; one man
of each rank was on duty daily for the twenty-four hours.
Count Frédéricksz, in those days a baron still, extraordinary for good looks, with Count Benkendorff, grand
marshal of the court, also stood there. These two large
men accentuated the Emperor's shortness, though the
sovereign was of fairly heavy build and had broad
shoulders, which he held quite straight. Usually he
bowed quickly, and then stood quietly gazing at the
great crowd with very patient eyes—a look of something
like deep sadness in them. His face was typically Russian—broad, with an effect of flat surfaces. He had
deep, earnest, handsome eyes, dark gray-blue, with a
charm all their own; a rather short, heavy nose and high
cheek-bones; a mustache and beard covered what seemed
to be a rather large mouth, but was perhaps only thick-
lipped. A short neck and very short hands were his
other marked traits. His Majesty was altogether a sympathetic figure, had one met him casually as a private
person, and I always found myself feeling sorry for him.
To his right stood—when she came at all—the Empress-
Mother, graceful and gracious, smiling, glancing about
at people, with a nod to those she knew, or turning to

speak in friendly fashion with her own gentlemen and
ladies in waiting. The Empress-Mother wore black, and
her perfect neck and shoulders could well bear the trying
full court décolleté. Nearing sixty, she was still able to
hold her own in the eyes of her subjects. She did not
stand long in the doorway, but moved off somewhere and
settled down almost at once, having those with whom
she wished to converse brought to her. Her chosen corner was usually the gayest of the ball.

Going through the room she had a pleasant intimate
word for many a person. "What a pretty gown!" or
"Is that the new diadem I heard about? It is lovely,"
and so on.

Some old man, receiving a gentle, winning glance,
would bow low, then straightening he would preen himself and say to his neighbors: "It is twenty years since
Her Majesty saw me last, yet did you see how she remembered my face? And how young she looks! As graceful, too, as ever." A great gift this in the sovereign who
still reigned in Russian hearts by her womanly softness.

When the Empress-Mother did not come to court the
opened doors disclosed the young Empress Alexandra
standing on her husband's right. The elder woman was
given first place, and if both were there the Emperor's
consort stood at his left. Doubtless this was hard for
her pride. There were many difficulties in her life besides. She had no son to follow Nicolas II, and it was
said at court this preyed on the young Empress's mind
and heart continuously, and drove her to cultivating
charlatan doctors and saints. She found in the constant presence of Michael, her husband's brother and
heir, a reminder that her children were all girls. Whenever she received a woman in audience she asked: "Have
you children?"

"Yes, Your Majesty."

"Girls or boys?"

"A boy, madam."

Instantly Her Majesty's face was strained, and there came a pause in the conversation. This happened to me every year, so I know; and I never was so happy as when in 1904 my elder daughter was born in the spring, and that same summer brought our Empress the little lad whose life and early death were to be such a tragedy.

That next winter the empress's first words were: "I hear you have another child."

"A girl, Your Majesty—while we all congratulate you on the birth of the heir!"

After that year the manner of the Empress was quite different to me, and we had a long and very pleasant chat each time I was received by her in audience.

The young Empress was exceptionally well-read and could talk on a number of subjects. Seemingly also with her own circle she could laugh and be gay, and she was devoted to her husband, her children, and her few intimate friends. She was full of compassion for those who were in trouble, but apparently she hated her surroundings and the people whom she should have found congenial. She hated, also, the ways of court life and every tradition of the old palaces. She drove away those who wanted to help her, drove away, little by little, the Emperor's few trusted and tried comrades, reduced the palace life almost to a tête-à-tête, the fakers who captured her imagination being the only people outside the family circle Her Majesty tolerated. Even in early days, instead of leaving all court housekeeping arrangements to various officials who had previously attended to such matters, she wanted parlor-maids introduced into the Winter Palace, instead of the old men servants. This hurt the servitors' feelings. and Her Majesty's newly formed corps of maids could not or would not do the work. Everything had to be changed back, while it was said the Empress tried to introduce the "ways of the German and English bourgeois houses" to Russia's court!

I heard this story from my mother-in-law, and it was typical of the kind of thing constantly being told. Always some unfortunate little remark or act, attitude or expression, marred the effect of what one was anxious to believe—that our Empress wished to do right by her subjects and to please them, just as they were anxious to act nicely toward her and love her, as they did the Dowager Empress. Everything miscarried, though, and left disappointments. Explanations were not possible, because of her rank and her rather forbidding attitude. Often I have thought this sad woman was the victim of a huge misunderstanding, yet undoubtedly her own words and acts built it up.

I had several personal experiences of this. First, at the very beginning, her unnecessary criticism of a pretty and correct enough gown on a stranger who was anxious to please, roused the animosity of a large group of young women. Then her attitude of sitting in judgment on society and its gay ways, which was sure to offend the court circle, was unwarranted, since the Russian aristocracy was as well behaved as any in Europe, and many a diplomat exclaimed over our virtue as compared with society at other posts. Later came the gradual estrangement of herself and the Emperor from the warm, loyal men and women, who had been ready to give the young sovereign the same devotion they had dedicated to his father. It was curious how differently the Empress acted from others trained to the same rôle.

I have seen the Empress-Mother or the Grand Duchess

Marie thank some woman or even some child with touching words and smiles for a little gift brought to their war
charities.   This effort of smiling was made often when
they were weary physically and mentally, or worn down
with responsibility.   Whether my baby girl brought a
knitted scarf for a sick soldier, or some rich man gave a
thousand pairs of boots, or I carried to them a donation
in money from sympathetic Americans, their pleasure at
least seemed hearty and genuine.   But the young Empress received a check one day for six thousand roubles to
help her sewing-circle for the wounded, at the beginning
of the Russo-Japanese War, and Her Majesty only said:
"Thank you, every little bit helps somewhat!"   The
donor explained this money came from a group of foreign
women who had raised the gift by their own work, and
afterward a lady in waiting was begged to see if she
could not obtain a few words of thanks, signed by the
Empress, to send to the far-away sympathizers, so they
would not imagine the fund had been lost, or was not
appreciated.   After a whole year a typewritten note of
stiff thanks was sent, bearing the signature of Her Majesty's secretary!   It was reported the sovereign had
said: "It will be quite sufficient if A—— signs!"

In spite of this strange way of doing and of her manner with nearly every one who came near her, one could
not look at the beautiful apparition in the palace ballroom doorway without feeling sorry for an evidently
unhappy woman.   Much taller than the Emperor, she
was of heavy build, especially when I first knew her.
The head with its proud pose was classic and stood out
splendidly in the throng about her at court.   The Empress had a wonderful cameo-like profile, made for sculp-
tors to copy on coins.   Her features were regular, her
blond hair abundant, though drawn back tightly and

rolled into a bun with the utmost simplicity. The court hair-dresser, Delcroix, was in despair. "Her Majesty does not wear a coiffure—it is merely a hard lump and everything must be only tight. Yet she is so beautiful!" he would exclaim. Nearly always dressed in white, her complexion was soft and pretty. The eyes were deep and tragic or desperately bored, or very cold and severe; one felt held at a distance and as if one were clumsy or lacked understanding. The Empress loved jewels, and wore a great many large and magnificent stones. In her diadems or small round crowns, with row after row of pearls and diamonds from throat to waist, hanging and flashing, she looked her best. Also, in Russian court dress she was magnificent, and I admired her extremely during the last war years in the Sister of Mercy costume she invented for herself.

In 1900 already there was much discussion about the Empress, especially as to her complaints of Russian society, which were rather resented. Her criticism of this or that custom or person, her strange tastes and ways, like Her Majesty's attitude at a court ball, seemed to fit into the tales which were spread about. A very small bow, without a smile, was vouchsafed her curtseying subjects; then she stood or sat wherever etiquette put her, looking straight to the front; painfully intimidated, militantly on the defensive, doing whatever was her official duty, but under protest, as it were, she spent much of the evening standing or sitting alone, while those near her felt rather uneasy, fearing her critical eye or comment. I believe she thought she was disliked and that she suffered an agony of shyness. Meantime, between sorrow and resentment, most of St. Petersburg society vacillated, while the breach widened. Those on one side made an occasional advance, only to be rebuffed—

she, on the other, wanted the sympathy which her pride prevented her accepting, and she brooded on her troubles always.   The whole situation was encouraged, of course, by the least desirable people at court, since they hoped to fish in troubled waters.

At a court ball, after some time of dancing, our long, sweeping trains on the floor were a good deal damaged usually by the officers' spurs.   The latter could not be left off, and we might not hold our trains up—etiquette forbid!   I managed never to care if I was torn and ragged, because I was so keen about dancing.   I loved the space, music, and. order of these functions.   The scene as we moved in to supper was even more perfect than in the ballroom.   Often, when the Grand Duke Michael was my partner, we went in to supper the second couple, following Their Majesties directly, and the great stretch of the hall filled with enormous palm-trees, a bed of hyacinths or roses at their bases, with each palm the centre of a supper-table for ten, created a sylvan picture of the South in the Palace of the Czars.   This with a thermometer fifteen to thirty-five below zero outside!   Every stranger gasped when he saw that room for the first time, and even Russians—of all people the least given to bragging!—felt rather proud of this fairy-land of flowers and tropical trees.

The Empress presided at her table, lovely but saying little to those who occupied places of honor on her left and right.   Following supper, after a further wait, she and the Emperor (and, when there, the Empress-Mother) moved toward their door and gave the final signal.   The music stopped; Their Majesties smiled and bowed; we bowed and curtseyed low in return and then they disappeared.   The ball was over and we all wandered off to our distant carriages.

On Carnival Sunday a small party of two or three hundred guests was always given. It was the prettiest and smallest court affair of the year. There was a dinner in the art galleries of the Hermitage first, and dancing in the small ballroom of the most ancient part of the palace. The conservatory, full of singing birds, was thrown open. There was a very elegant cotillion, with flowers in quantities from the imperial greenhouses, and no one but the young dancing group (and only Russians of that) were guests. Twice only exceptions were made in my time: once, on the eve of their departure, Prince Kinsky, of the Austrian Embassy, and his lovely wife were asked; and another time the two daughters of the British Ambassador, Sir Charles Scott, were invited as a last compliment to their father before he retired from diplomatic life.

CHAPTER XII

THE JAPANESE WAR AND THE REVOLUTION
OF 1906

DURING these early years I spent my time exclusively between the duties of our attractive home, with its nursery, and the gay functions which made up my round of society life, intimate or official. I began to feel I was making many friends, both men and women, and I was growing Russian in my ways. I loved all I was doing and was anxious to make those whom I admired realize my sympathy and enthusiasm. They answered my expressions of understanding as if sure of my sincerity, and adopted me completely within a short time.

My youth and high spirits did not prevent my seeing much that was sad in Russia. Both in the country and the city there was a yearning spirit among the people which made its appeal and a restless striving toward progress which promised trouble in time. This deep agitation came to the surface occasionally, in the anxious words of some older man of public affairs, or even in conversations I had with many of our officers or the more serious women. There was food for thought and anxiety in various things said, and I caught myself wondering if it were possible that what they talked of might be true. This was especially so toward the end of 1903.

Through our holiday-making in the early years of my married life there were small domestic problems, too, some of them a little difficult to solve. I had inherited a few of the old servants who had been with my mother-in-law for years and they objected to moving from her large establishments to our less important home. One old fellow, a Pole, Lavrenti, had been my father-in-law's valet, and now was given us as butler and general manager of our household. He treated us as children, and to give him orders meant nothing in the way of results. He was always running up-stairs to the Princess, either to complain of our unreasonable ways or to report what we were doing if he thought it harmful.

One day he told the Princess my husband "made great disorder and noise working with his tools"; another day he carried her the news that I had said there was a spot too slippery on the overpolished floor of my salon, but that "in reality the fault was with my American shoes, whose heels were too high." The old man was always borrowing plate or glass or kitchen tins from my mother-in-law's pantry and kitchen, either to save us money or himself the trouble of going out to buy such things. We were being accused of appropriating her property, as her old Auguste said everything which disappeared up-stairs was found in our quarters!

We were thoroughly annoyed. Finally the break with our tyrant came one day, when, after ringing for him several times, Cantacuzène went to see why the bell was not answered. He discovered the metal ringer had been carefully wrapped in cotton, so Lavrenti, slumbering peacefully in an armchair beneath it, should not be disturbed! After this experience we passed the old chap to my sailor brother-in-law, and immediately our relations with Auguste and the Princess became smoothed, besides which our own comfort was much greater.

I had all sorts of quaint trials getting our household started. I fortunately began with few theories, and such as I had were soon left behind. The family servants had traditions they considered much more important than the ideas of any newcomer, and I learned their ways more easily than they did mine. Also I found it very agreeable to be cared for by the devoted, gentle, intelligent crowd; and when they realized I had no desire to change their life, but was happy among them, they were quick to adopt my suggestions, and very pleased if I noticed any small innovation and complimented them on it.

They always called everything "ours," and took vast pride and pains to make our small entertainments a success. Innocent snobbishness was one of their most amusing weaknesses, and nothing gave Andrew, our next butler, keener pleasure than to have a party with some of the imperial family, or to announce that "Grand Duchess So-and-so asks Your Highness to the telephone," when I had visitors, and he could interrupt conversation with this bit of ceremony.

All the servants were "our children" and as much members of the family as we ourselves. They expected us to take care of them and be interested in their personal affairs, and they were sure of our help and forgiveness when in trouble or at fault.

In all the years I was in Russia no servant ever left us of his own accord, and only a few were dismissed—those few being some picked up accidentally, who had not the patriarchal ideas. In the house, silver, jewels, money, and other valuables were kept in drawers and cupboards which no one ever locked. It would have been an insult to do so, for never to my knowledge did anything, however unimportant, disappear.

The baby, young Mike, was common property. Old Auguste, his great-grandfather's valet, and his father's nurse, Grandmother Anna-Wladimir, would gossip endlessly with his own nurse as to what resemblances they thought most prominent. When the boy was born, Auguste made me a gift of several jars of some strawberry preserves which I had once declared excellent when I had tasted them at the Princess's. Incidentally she prized these too much to serve them often, as the stuff was made of fruit exceptionally large and fine from Bouromka's hotbeds. At the moment I thanked Auguste without noticing more than that he had shown me a nice little attention in offering me a dainty I liked. But when preserves were served one day I made inquiries, only to find the old fellow had simply taken his gift from the storerooms in his charge. "The Princess won't mind; she will never know; and even if she does, I will tell her it is much better to tempt your appetite in illness, and when you have given us a young prince, than to feed these preserves to visitors." This was his only explanation, and there was no sign of regret or consciousness of having given what was not his. On the contrary, he and the Princess were one, and I a sick child who had deserved the best. One might as well be converted and accept this code of morals, which had its charm.

I remember the drama each week, when my mother-in-law paid her bills and scolded Auguste for a crime he never admitted till after their accounts were settled to his satisfaction. He was called thief in the process, for invariably his supply bills were enlarged, to cover extra sums which he gave to my young brother-in-law, thus augmenting the boy's allowance for goodies and fun at the Page Corps School.

Regularly my mother-in-law, when the last book was gone over and settled, would say: "Now admit you have stolen at least twenty roubles for Guy."

And Auguste would tuck the money in his pocket and the books under his arm and reply, "Well, Your Highness, boys are only young a little while, and they need always a little more than they have," and would go away contentedly, while the Princess, with tears in her eyes, would tell us how touching the old fellow was, and how he loved Guy. Bad policies theoretically, but in practice they worked out well.

This young brother belonged to us all, and had his special place always in our small home. In fact, both my brothers-in-law spent much of their free time near my tea-table. Our baby was always sprawling or creeping, and later walking and playing, about the open fire in my salon at five o'clock. It became the pleasantest hour of the day—one for quiet talk and restful discussions, from which I learned more of Russia and my new compatriots than in any other way. With freezing weather outside, inside the open blaze, singing kettle and cosey armchairs helped any caller, who dropped in, to thaw his ideas. People stayed long enough to go into the chance subject of interest. Pleasant regimental comrades, a few agreeable foreign diplomats, gradually, also, some older men whom I met at dinners, came, and began the intimate circle which later through the years was to grow considerably. I liked these people, and though at first my husband fought rather shy of "tea-parties," after a time he fell into the habit of coming home from his club to smoke his last afternoon pipe in his own easy-chair and join in the informal talk. I heard a lot about certain regimental interests and grew to know the ideals and ways of the men who composed our organization. I was told much of Russian life and thought by degrees also. I scarcely had to study or even to ask questions. My education progressed rapidly.

In listening to my visitors each day I began to catch their attitude and atmosphere, to realize what remarkable culture they had, and how the literature, art, and music of the country, its history and great past, made them, as well as the peasantry, what they were. It was absorbingly interesting, and I grew to love my Russians more and more. It was their theories about themselves they were unconsciously spreading out before me, and which I was just as unconsciously taking in.

Strangely enough, in the apparent quiet which reigned, these men showed signs of anxiety as to what was ahead of us. Often they spoke of the peasant, of his backwardness in education, yet of his cleverness—and they spoke of their own efforts to develop these dark millions. They would almost always talk of the bureaucracy with impatience and annoyance, sometimes criticising Peter the Great for installing it, with all the general clumsiness of our governmental machinery. They complained of the difficulty each man had in obtaining action in cases when it would be an advantage all round. Of the injustice and favoritism being practised or allowed, there was also much said. The party which wished reforms or improvements was large, and their blame of the Empress's policy in isolating herself—of the undesirability of the shut-in and exclusively family life of the sovereigns, of the protection given to cover various scandalous exploitations by a group in our Far Eastern Siberian country—was extremely marked. The names of Abaza, Alexéef, and Bézobrazoff were at the time constantly circulating and were anathema, and when I asked what these men had done, "Stolen and exploited; everything!" would be the impatient rejoinder. Witte's figure was looming large on the horizon. He promised to be a giant in history, while Pobiédonostseff was another name bandied about in all conversations. Generally considered too ultraconservative, though respected for his honesty, his influence was supposed to be great on our imperial rulers, and was thrown entirely into the scales on the side of retrograde actions.

Especially Witte was discussed more with each succeeding month. Of comparatively no fortune, he was a man self-made and proud of that fact. I even wondered, when I met him, if he did not put on some of his uncouth ways to underscore his personality and make it more striking. He had been a railroad employee—station agent, it was said—and he had by degrees climbed to the eminence of being the Minister of Finance. He had a large group of warm admirers, who cited his talents on all occasions and told of the way money was being drawn into the government coffers by the monopoly of the sale of vodka, while at the same time the people were being served with a brand purer than before. Also, we were told of his successful efforts in the establishment of the new currency and the fixing of better measures of exchange. I did not know what all this meant, but it sounded well, and even those most against him admitted that Witte was a big man. But they thought him too ambitious and domineering and a danger in many ways, since he was supposed to be trying from his position in the finance ministry to command the cabinet and rule the empire—replacing private by government ownership of railroads and other services, sending his various agents abroad to sit beside the Russian ambassadors and report direct to him, and making himself responsible for many a move which tended to his keeping the reins of government in his own powerful hands.

As time passed, both those who praised and those who blamed Witte found material to prove their theories. The first group gave him great credit for the Portsmouth Treaty, negotiated in spite of the ever-changing orders and the constant antagonism toward him at home. His friends gave him equal admiration for the manifesto he dragged from the sovereign during the revolution, that of the 17th of October. The opponents of Witte through those years howled him down for these very things, saying the peace treaty was made just when Russia might have won the war, as Japan was worn out, and that the manifesto was a matter of cowardice on Witte's part, though he was always a liberal.

Long before these events he had made a trip across Siberia, and was received everywhere with honors, which, we were told by gossips, were so great as to make the sovereign jealous. The Trans-Siberian Railroad was largely a creation of Witte's, who was for economic development on the eastern outskirts of the empire, I heard. But Germany's action and certain political influences at home brought about a situation which roused Japanese suspicions. This in turn produced an atmosphere requiring but a small spark to light the war fires. His worst enemies never denied that Witte's talent kept Russia from financial disaster during the war and the revolution of 1905, or that he developed our industries as no one had till then. But it was always added that this was not Slav, nor for the good of a country so essentially agricultural as ours, and that though Witte might know about foreign affairs he did not know our own people well.

I listened and my curiosity grew, till one day I met his wife, of whom also gossip had much to say. She was a lady of vague antecedents, and I decided they were vague only because so many excited people told such extraordinary stories about her. She stood easily on her own merits—a woman of forty-five or so, of dark beauty and dignified manner, with a most intelligent expression and a luminous smile. Her clothes, of simple cut, per-

fectly fitted her still fine figure. She wore few trimmings
and few jewels, but those she did wear were admirable.
She held herself proudly, never made an advance con-
versationally. Her response was warm enough to seem
grateful, however, and her talk was both intelligent and
cultured. She was Jewish by origin, though belonging
to the Russian Church and attending it. She had married Witte rather late in life and he had adopted her
daughter and given the latter his name.

Madame Witte was never received at court. Little by
little, however, she formed a group of friends whom she
held firmly to her. I thought her magnetic when we
met, and afterward watched her career and her husband's with curiosity. He overshadowed all other figures between the time I first realized how great was the
drama being played in Russia and the moment when the
first Duma was dissolved—and she in her way was acting as brilliant a rôle as her husband's.

Witte, I think, cared socially for only a few persons,
but with these his vivid conversation was very interesting. I had the opportunity of enjoying the treat of
hearing him on two or three occasions—once at a dinner
where some one tempted him to contradict a statement,
and he had plunged into graphic descriptions; twice
when he came to me and in a quiet hour of tête-à-tête
talked of his American impressions and his desire for a
future understanding between his people and mine. He
had greatly liked the Americans during his short stay in
the United States. He had met my parents and remembered a long chat with my father, while he admired my
mother's beauty.

Usually at a dinner-table, however, he was taciturn to
a degree. Many women who were his partners thought
he meant to insult them, and they said that to hear him
eat his soup was agony. One person told me he had

watched him pick a chicken leg and throw the bone under the table! The great man was ugly, but with deep, fine eyes and capable hands. He was huge and looked strong, though he was not compactly built. I found him rather attractive in looks as well as in what he said. He seemed to care in society only to see his wife surrounded and his adopted child enjoying herself. A crowd looking for benefits as his power increased gathered about them. The daughter married a Narishkine, son of one of the empire's greatest families, and a fragile little boy was born to this young couple. To see Witte at his best one had to see the great man with that grandson on his lap—the great bear then knew how to be as tender as any old nurse might have been.

Through the period of revolution the concessions made to popular demands and the meeting and disillusions of the first Duma, I became convinced in spite of hot attacks on his motives that Witte sincerely meant well and wanted to see Russia move forward. I think he wanted to inaugurate many liberal reforms and to co-operate with the most patriotic elements the country could produce. Somehow most of these did not trust him, and whether this distrust was deserved or not, it was fatal to the success of the work undertaken by Witte. As the best were not with him, he joined up with the most extreme and less understanding to get his majorities; then, disillusioned, or from a desire to establish a better balance, he swung back toward the reactionaries and tried to save the situation by seemingly tying up with them. This see-sawing was disastrous to him, as to the prestige both of the government and the Emperor. The latter forced Witte to drop out of public life, a sad and deeply disappointed man, while Stolypin took over the government.

Witte during the final epoch of his power seemed to

lose courage. He apparently feared to make decisions
or to face physical danger. He lived in the Winter Palace by his own demand, surrounded with guards, and
one had to pass several pairs of sentinels to reach Madame Witte's salon. Of course his enemies made capital
of these signs. Those who supported him still vowed he
was sincere, far-seeing and patriotic, loyally devoted to
the sovereign's best interests, fighting the vacillations of
the Emperor, the intrigues of would-be rivals, and never
supported by His Majesty in critical moments. That it
was this memory which made his retirement so bitter
seemed certain in spite of his new title and his great
fortune. Those who hated him told us it was his own
fault he was not trusted and was put out.

I never knew the truth, but it seems certain he was
not a man who inspired faith in his integrity of purpose.
After he had been dead some time I was listening to a
woman talk, who for years had been an intimate friend
of the great man, and she said: "He was the greatest
genius of the times. He had a man's big body and
brain, but his weakness was to have with these a woman's
nature and its fluctuations. It was because he wasn't
quite perfectly balanced as between brain and character,
I think, that he had so many failures and disillusions."

Perhaps that was the secret.

In 1902 I found myself one evening at an official dinner, next to a large man with a strong, handsome face
and rather long gray hair, which was thin on the top of
his head. His noble poise and fearless, keen eyes particularly struck me. The dinner was at an embassy, and
the newly arrived chief of mission, or his secretaries, had
been sufficiently vague about Russian etiquette to place
people according to their rank of birth instead of their
official bureaucratic rights.

Several of the older men were consequently furious, and criticised their host, but my neighbor, turning to me, said with a smile: "They are amusing, are they not, to fuss so about where they should sit? For my part I admit I think it is a great improvement to sit at the end of the table between two young and pretty women instead of being always up at the head with old people like myself. I'm grateful to Providence, and think this system should be encouraged."

I was equally delighted personally, for I rarely had such an interesting partner as this. Plehve—for it was the Minister of the Interior—and I began a friendship that evening which lasted till his assassination. I knew little of his policies. Afterward I heard he stood for all that was retrograde and severe, and I heard him blamed, too, for much which others did that was wrong. I am inclined to think if we had talked of politics we should have disagreed often, but in the two or three seasons during which the busy man came frequently to my tea-table direct from his chancellery or cabinet meetings, he never talked of his work in any instance I can recall.

Occasionally he looked dreadfully weary, would take his tea, sink into a chair, and say: "Tell me what you have been doing—have you been gay?"

Always a chatterbox, I would plunge into details of my latest ball or my baby's last achievement, while he would slowly sip his tea, and listen as if to the story of a child's game, with his big, shaggy head leaning on the hand which shaded his eyes. After an hour he would get up, and with a "Thank you for a very pleasant rest," he would depart. If others came in he joined in the talk enough never to seem a weight—but no more. When we were alone, or when he was less tired, he would stretch back deep into his chair, his head straight, one hand holding the other, or both at ease on the chair-arms, and he would tell me quantities of intensely interesting things from Russia's history, or about the psychology of the people and their art, music, and literature. An ideal companion, full of life and color, he gave me much of his splendid fund of knowledge in these fitful conversations.

My curiosity was intense. He knew it and was never trite. It was a strange friendship, for Plehve was older than my father. Except that I knew he had a delightfully typical old lady for a wife (since I had met her at official functions and we had exchanged calls), and that he once mentioned he had a daughter much my senior, I heard nothing of his home life or his work. His patriotism seemed great, and he carried his heavy responsibilities with a superb strength, which made no complaint, while he lived unflinchingly up to what he thought was his duty, with no fear or care for himself.

Our last conversation proved this mentality. It was late in the spring and I was leaving for the country in a few days. Plehve had come to say good-by, and remained until one or two other callers had departed. After a little silence he rose to make his adieux.

"I am sorry you are going away," he said seriously. "I have enjoyed coming here sometimes for a quiet hour very much, and I'm afraid I won't see you again."

"But I shall be back in town in the autumn, and, on the contrary, I hope you will again take up this nice habit of dropping in on me often."

"If I am still alive I will surely be among your frequent callers, but these people who think I am doing everything wrong, and who have been trying to assassinate me for some time back, are more than ever trailing me now. Probably they will get me soon."

"You are Minister of the Interior with the police in your department. Why don't you protect yourself?" I asked.

"It wouldn't look well, nor be well, for me to surround myself with police and show fear, would it? When I have things to do I go out like other men, whatever the consequences. I'm afraid there is only one way—to perform one's duty and take what comes. If I disappear there will be some one to replace me. A pleasant summer to you, and thanks again!"

He kissed my hand, and departed with his shaggy lion's head thrown well back and his step as tranquil as ever.

Within a few weeks—I think in July—one morning Plehve was starting for Peterhof to make his weekly report to the Emperor, when on his way to the railroad-station a bomb was thrown at his carriage. The vehicle, coachman, horses, and the Minister of the Interior were blown to bits—beyond recognition. I mourned his tragic end very much, for I knew that whatever his policies he was honest and faithful, devoted to his Emperor and his country, and that few had his courage and energy, as well as the unselfish spirit, which readily sacrificed his private tastes for constant thankless service and threatening dangers always so perfectly realized. He was the first older man I saw much of after my marriage, and he seemed to me typical of the best in that mistaken group of the ultra-retrograde officials of old Russia.

One felt great changes with each succeeding season. The Japanese war came unexpectedly upon us. Shortly before it the great Ito passed through St. Petersburg, hoping for a friendly reception and to make a loan. He was badly received by our government, and pushed

on to England, where he effected both a loan and soon
afterward a treaty, I think.

I heard from the American Ambassador that Ito had
spoken to him of my grandfather; said he had heard I
was married and living in St. Petersburg and had asked
could the Ambassador not arrange a meeting with me?
Instead of telling me about it, the diplomat had taken
on himself to reply that he could not do so, as he felt
sure no meeting could be brought about, since I was
now a Russian, and Russians were showing great preju-
dice against the Japanese.

I was much annoyed when my ex-compatriot told me
of this speech of his to the statesman from Japan. It
would have been most interesting to meet Ito, and my
personal action would have neither shocked nor incon-
venienced any one, for Russians are thoroughly broad-
minded. Besides, if there was a strain, perhaps un-
avoidable in government circles, it seemed unnecessarily
underscoring it to have a diplomat draw it into personal
relations. I was disappointed and indignant over the
matter, but it was too late to counteract a most unfortunate impression.

Soon afterward, at the first court ball of the season,
my young brother-in-law was on duty as the Emperor's
page. Standing just behind the sovereign, he made the
tour of the diplomatic circle and heard the Emperor's
remarks and questions to each chief of mission; also the
latter's replies. To the Japanese Ambassador His Majesty took great pains to be especially gracious that evening, giving him more time than to any one else, and
there was a feeling created in the minds of all as they
listened, that a responsive attitude was noticeable. With
their last words the Emperor and Japan's representative
each expressed pleasure that certain difficulties were

overcome and their two empires were good friends. When he came home my brother-in-law told us of the incident, and several other people corroborated his statement.

But the following day, to our horror, bad news spread. The *Variag* was sunk, and the declaration of war followed almost instantly. My husband's regiment was not ordered to Manchuria, so I knew of the war only by hearsay. I could not yet read enough Russian to follow in the newspapers our progress at the front. I was quite ill; our eldest little girl was born a few days before the *Petropavlovsk* went down in the fleet's battle at Port Arthur. As time progressed, however, I became more and more absorbed by events in the East—Port Arthur's siege and splendid defense; the heroic fighting of our troops, always insufficiently supplied by a single-track and newly built railroad; the noble efforts of Prince Hilkoff, Minister of Communications, to keep the provision and troop trains moving, his going out and living at the point most difficult to arrange for, and his death out there from exhaustion toward the end of the work he carried through with such genius. I was also interested in Kuropatkin's early prestige. When he left he had so many icons given him, it was said he had to add an extra car to his special train. He had been chief of staff to Skobeleff, the brilliant figure of the Turkish War, and few doubted his capacity to carry everything before him as our generalissimo.

For many months no one in St. Petersburg talked of anything but the Manchurian news, but little by little changes occurred in the tenor of our conversations. There were tales of disappointments and disillusions; there was bitterness, pity, the desire for rest and peace, and an ever-increasing anxiety; tales of battles and ships lost;

tales of the incompetency of the commander-in-chief and
some of the other favorites; tales of confusion and suffer-
ings among our troops; tales of officers and men under
fire doing heroic work, all circumstances against them.
On the other hand, the entertainments were criticised
which were being given on the special train of the commander-in-chief, and on that of the Grand Duke Boris,
who with a gay party had volunteered for service, only
to gather a golden sword of St. George and to treat his
blasé tastes to a new sensation. A few others were also
blamed, but very generally the army was admired. The
inefficiency of the war ministry was being proved. Also
one heard constantly of the weight of political power in
the army; how the commanders were hampered from St.
Petersburg; how there was jealousy, or fear of letting the
head men out at the front handle the situation and perhaps gain more power and glory than was good for them.

The second fleet was being built and was to go to Far
Eastern waters. My sailor brother-in-law was leaving
with it on the *Alexander III*, one of its biggest ships.
He was all impatience to be off, yet he said—and others
of his comrades constantly repeated the same thing—
that from the work being done by incompetent hands
through favoritism, and the stealing going on among
contractors and those who handled the contract-making,
everything about the new fleet was wrong and of secon-
dary quality. These splendid-looking sea-monsters of our
new unit were doomed to go to the bottom as soon as
they were touched in battle. No one seemed to be considered punishable for these thefts or the criminal care-
lessness, and no inquiry was possible. The Grand Duke
Alexis was among those most seriously accused. We
heard that the admiral who was to take this fleet to sea
came and begged the Emperor on his knees not to give

him the responsibility of this command, as he knew the
ships were not seaworthy nor properly armed and armored.
Then gossip told how our Emperor had explained that
the fleet as it was must go. It could not be rebuilt, and
the admiral must prove his devotion and save the imperial honor.

The Emperor wanted to move out to the front himself, and had many a long argument with those about him
on this subject, but was persuaded not to go, since his being so far away from the capital in such grave times would
strain the home situation. It was already serious and
needed careful nursing. Once there was talk of the
Grand Duke Nicolas-Nicolaiovitch taking over the entire command of our armies, as Kuropatkin made retreat
after retreat and no advances. I heard the Emperor
sent for him and offered him the first place at the front.
Nicolas-Nicolaiovitch was reported to have replied he
would accept in the emergency, but on one condition:
he would carry all the responsibility, but he insisted on
giving military commands without advice or hampering
from the capital. The Emperor and his advisers could
not make up their minds to such a decision, so the Grand
Duke refused to take over the campaign. Things consequently stayed as they were, and Russia drifted to the
final defeats at sea and on land. Disorders and talk of
revolution meanwhile grew and the pessimism in the
capital became more and more noticeable, with constant
shilly-shallying on the part of the government.

The death of my sailor brother-in-law from tropical
fever, contracted on the long trip to the Orient, threw us
all into personal mourning, but one's soul was weighted
anyhow with the general misery and danger. We women
worked with one or another of the sewing groups, preparing bandages and underclothes or warm woollen garments

for the soldiers.   A lot of my women friends went out to
Siberia with various hospital trains or Red Cross units.
I personally, though I managed to be half of each day at
the large workrooms organized by the Grand Duchess
Marie-Pavlovna, found time for nothing more, because
of my two babies; one was but newly born.

All parties took the form of bazaars or concerts and
theatricals for the benefit of war sufferers, and even the
few informal gatherings, where one dined and rolled bandages or counted and folded finished sewing, were subdued with the thought of much suffering and discontent
just beyond our protected circle.

In the early years of my married life I had spent
nearly all my time in St. Petersburg; even during the
summer months the cool northern climate seemed more
pleasant than did the intense dry heat of the steppe-
lands.   After my typhoid we had moved into our new
apartment on the beautiful quay of the Neva, and it was
there when we were settled that little Mike was born.
The summer of 1901 I spent with my mother-in-law at
Bouromka, taking the boy there while my husband was
in camp and at the manœuvres.   Both the baby and I
felt the heat, though otherwise I liked the quiet of our
days, while the light French wit of the Princess as well
as my young brother-in-law's bubbling joy in life and
warm affection for me prevented dulness or lonesomeness.
It was amusing to see baby develop, and during that
summer I had also the happiness of a visit from my
parents.

My father had arranged to get a leave from his duties
in the Philippines at the same time my brother's furlough
from West Point was due, and with my mother they had
taken the long journey to join me in Russia.   I left
young Mike with his paternal grandmother, while with

my brother-in-law Guy and my maid I travelled north
to meet my own home people. It was a delightful re-
union, and we spent ten days in St. Petersburg sightseeing together.

I had had no time or occasion since my wedding for
anything like this before, and I felt carried back to my
girlhood days as we wandered through the Russian palaces, museums, and galleries, filled with marvellous treasures generations of Romanoffs had had offered them by
vassals or had bought with singular good judgment and
good luck. We visited Tsarskoe, Peterhof, and Gatchina, and drove about the environs. In the beautiful
white nights of summer we were very loath to go to bed.
The sunset left a world of delicate mother-of-pearl tints,
and the park drive, out over the islands, flanked with
magnificent trees of the northern forests, was full of
nightingales who thrilled one by their love-songs, while
the soft atmosphere made river and land, gulf and sky,
seem of fairy texture. We were tempted to expect Cath-
arine the Great, with her courtiers, to step from the terraces of Erlagen palace. I loved those islands as I have
loved few spots in the world. In those early days they
hypnotized me by their special charm of form, color, and
atmosphere; later they became associated with my life
by the habit I formed of wandering in their beautiful
paths or driveways with the children or with some friend,
when I needed fresh air and exercise or opportunity to
talk or think. During the Great War and the revolution they were a refuge from the signs of misery which
invaded every part of our capital except their sheltered
dignity, and one went to them for a rest to eyes, nerves,
and mind.

My father had not been in Russia since his youth, and
he found much to interest him besides mere sightseeing.

In the politics, the countryside, the capital, and the mode of life there were changes—a move forward. He kept repeating that my adopted people would become the greatest in all the eastern hemisphere when they had lived a little more. He thought there was much room for reform in the government's method, but he loved the patriarchal life of landowners and peasants, while their artistic taste, quick, soft charm, and talents did not escape his observing eyes. He liked very much our frame and occupations, grew quickly attached to my husband, whom he had not met before, and with whom he was soon on excellent terms. Also he very much liked my family-in-law, whom he met at Bouromka, and he adored the chubby, creeping grandson, who regarded him with serious brown eyes, and then stretched out his arms and took possession of a willing conquest. It was nice to see the two together and to mark the mutual love of the great, strong grandfather and the wee boy.

From St. Petersburg to Bouromka we went by Moscow and Kieff, which I had never visited till then, and which I vastly enjoyed in such company.

Everything was made simple and easy for us by the excellent ability to organize which the fifteen-year-old Guy displayed in piloting our big party. Restaurants, museums, excursions, or train accommodations were apparently all equally easy problems for this young cicerone to handle, and, without a single word or sign of agitation, he carried our party of six through two weeks of varied experiences, travelling and sightseeing. He finished up by landing his charges at Bouromka one morning at early dawn.

It was very amusing to show my family the life of the great agricultural district of Russia, with its waving fields of wheat, its myriad workers, and all the machinery

CHILDREN OF PRINCE AND PRINCESS CANTACUZÈNE:
MICHAEL, BERTHA, AND IDA.

we used. That we were so far from a railroad and so dependent on ourselves for everything, yet so able, by organized effort, to supply ourselves and be comfortable, even luxurious, surprised them. The enormous space outside and in the house, the number of servants and work-hands in the château and on the estate, the beauty of the park and lake, the rolling land and forests, the richness of soil and crops, the size of our herds and the variety of our production dazed their American mentality, used to ringing a telephone or buying things ready-made, without previous planning. That we made the bricks, cut the timber, forged the metal, had our own plumbers, our doctors for man and beast, produced our own food, whether it was the butcher's meat, the smoked hams and game, the fish, vegetables, bread, sweets, and so on; made our own linen and kitchen pottery largely, did the panelling, inlaying, or carving, making rugs and laces; also that what few things came from outside, whether books, pianos, macaroni, rice, and tea, or a few other luxuries to eat or to wear, had to be dragged by carts seventy-two versts in the good season—were facts difficult to grasp. That a telegram came fifty miles in a rider's pocket, and the mail and newspapers the same distance three or four times a week, struck them as funny. These primitive ways were doubly strange as compared with the excellent cooking and hand laundry, with the smartly dressed party at dinner, the admirable works of art, the family portraits, the twenty thousand volumes of famous rare editions in the great library, and the collections of cameos, jewels, engravings, bronzes, old silver and china; not to mention our cellar's treasures, some vintages going back to early days of the nineteenth century.

Our life seemed very attractive to my father and brother, with business and the work of gathering a yearly income mingled with drives through the forests or cross-country to points where harvesting hands were grouped, as if for their ornamental qualities. The forge, the mill, the stable, the stud, and the machine, carpenter, upholstery, carriage, and other shops amused and interested my American sightseers visibly. Our little world and Bouromka's activities fascinated them, and we were busy each day examining all parts of the thirty thousand acres of intense and model productivity.

My mother liked the house and baby best, but the men enjoyed the out-of-door life and delighted my husband and brother-in-law, who took them hither and thither over the estate. What hypnotized them was the size of the place, and when they realized that Bouromka was one of four, and that half of its land had been taken from us and given to the peasants at the emancipation of the serfs, it rather took away their breath. My father liked the old servitors and their picturesque ways, and he had occult means of communicating his good feeling to them, for during years afterward the dear creatures were always talking of the visit of the "American general" and what he did. My mother they had seen before and saw again, but my father's one visit sank deep into their simple minds.

CHAPTER XIII

THE 1906 REVOLUTION

IN the summer of 1903 I went abroad to the wedding of my eldest Palmer cousin in London, then spent the season on the Normandy coast with our boy, and that autumn·joined my dear aunt for a motor trip through northern Italy and southern France, with the châteaux of the Loire thrown in to make our programme perfect. My husband had been able to join us for this journey. Later, in Paris, we were in grave anxiety over a serious case of typhoid which laid my aunt low after we returned from our wanderings. I remained with the invalid till the holidays, and reached St. Petersburg only at the beginning of the season, a few weeks before war broke out.

We had taken another motor trip in the delightful country of the north of France and into Belgium the year before, and I realized with joy how well my aunt and my husband understood each other. Uncle Palmer had died, and we had been so fond of him it made an added bond by· our sympathy with my aunt's mourning.

The summer of 1904 I spent in St. Petersburg and at Bouromka between war work and family cares. The peasants were being drawn on for mobilization, and their attitude toward the war was most curious. They were not in the least aware of what it was all about, and were not especially interested. Japan was an empty name— so was Siberia, for that matter, it was so far away—and to be fighting out there did not mean to them a defense of their land. Yet they were perfectly docile. The Little Father needed them; they were called, and went, unmurmuring, asking no questions. I stood on the porch

of our village town hall and heard the proclamation read
to a group of dignified, serious men who had bathed and
put on their holiday clothes ready for departure. Round
them clung their women, in gay kerchiefs and embroidered national costumes, while curly-headed children held
to the hands of the protectors they were to lose so soon.

Silent and respectful, they listened to the imperial
orders, then to the voice of their priest, as he chanted a
service and blessing, while the women wept and the children hid their heads against the latter's skirts, frightened. We had come down from the château to bid our
village contingent Godspeed and to bring each soldier a
little medal of St. George to protect him in battle. For
the first time I admired as well as liked our peasants !

A splendid lot of fellows they were who went out to
fight, and their spirit was the braver since their ignorance
offered them no arguments for sacrifice. They went into
danger just because they were called for by their Great
White Czar. With heads held high, they sang one of the
sad strains of Little Russia as they marched away; but
the parting had been hard, and the women's arms and
children's nestling heads had been difficult to give up.
Round two or three babies' necks I saw the red silk cords
on which our little medals had been hung. These had
changed places with last kisses and were to protect the
wee ones instead of the strong men themselves, it seemed.
Our village women were very helpless at first, but soon a
committee was formed by the elders among the peasantry. Men left at home organized the general labor of
all the commune lands, so the families remaining without
breadwinners should be cared for still.

The war had an excellent effect on our people. They
learned to handle questions of provisioning the extra
women and children, in this showing both ability and

good sense. The soldiers who travelled across the empire brought back new light, with ideas of Russia's size that were not mythical; in certain cases an enthusiasm for our great Far East which led to the emigration of a lot of fine people to the Siberian plains. . The era of the war and the miserable management of everything brought out a new spirit in many classes of Russians. The liberals—and most of the nobility I saw were in this group —felt it was high time the country should be put in order and helped forward, with education given and land reforms made, as well as various other necessary measures to be taken for the general good. The army officials were keen to see a saner policy pursued by the government and wished the sovereign would make reforms of his own accord. These might be gifts now. We were beginning to feel that otherwise they would become concessions torn from him in the near future.

I do not think the young Empress had at that time any special political influence or ambition, but her personal weight with the Emperor was very great, for he was deeply in love with her. From taste, or because she was beginning to feel her unpopularity, she influenced him always more and more toward a mystical, religious, retired life, and by degrees, with one excuse or another, she got rid of all those who thought the Emperor's duty was to show himself oftener and take more part in the nation's life.

The court was reduced to a small number of attendants, among whom Mademoiselle Tanéeff—soon to become by her marriage Madame Wiroboff—was beginning to appear constantly with her mistress. The Empress's poor health was a good reason for seeing almost no one, and this and the fragile heir's extreme youth were the excuses for long sojourns at Tsarskoe Selo or at Peterhof.   The distance from the capital made refusing to receive everyone appropriate.   Previous to this time the lady in waiting and the aide-de-camp on duty each day had invariably eaten at the imperial table. Now, by the Empress's desire, they were no longer invited, and many rebelled at being held at arm's length. The intrigues Madame Wiroboff was always carrying on against one or another of her colleagues, who were gradually being banished, made us all angry.

Charlatan doctors followed one another in an occult situation at court.   Meantime the Emperor was influenced into leaning toward the most reactionary of the ministers, supposedly very largely by his wife's advice. This was not a settled policy, however, and he swerved away from time to time by some word, gesture, or act which made his faithful subjects who were anxious for his success breathe again, with renewed hope.

Once a great deputation came to him, and was received with all due pomp in the Winter Palace.   It came to petition humbly that an assembly of the people's representatives might be convened, asking only consultative rights.   These men were thoroughly snubbed, and with a few cold sentences were sent about their business. Events jostled one another.   One could scarcely get one's breath, with the new anxieties and excitements of the winter of 1905.   There were disorders in the factory districts in Poland.   At Moscow and in several other cities real revolution was occurring.   The murder of several ministers and of the Grand Duke Serge, also attempts on the lives of many prominent men, added bloodshed. Finally the crowd from the outskirts of the capital came to the Winter Palace one January Sunday to see the Emperor and call to him for bread.   His flight to Tsarskoe—against his will, it was said—and the orders given to fire on the crowd were bad signs. The imperial guards were all sent out for this work of calming and patrolling the city, and I know there was a meeting of some officers (of one regiment, at least), who questioned whether these orders were not to be disobeyed. They fell into line, however, and followed the road of military discipline. But with many the temptation to rebellion was very strong, as they realized everything had been done to make the situation acute, and that the nation had been long-suffering in the hands of a blind bureaucratic machine which, however good its intentions, was terribly out of date. Every reasonable man and woman felt reforms were in order.

For months the pendulum swung backward and forward. The Emperor resisted the upheaval, but the war disasters occurred, peace was signed, every one suffered, and at last the situation in the capital became critical. Post and railroad service stopped, there was a question of water and electricity doing likewise, and no one dared prophesy what each day might bring forth. Through the Bloody Sunday period in early 1905 my husband with his comrades was on duty in the streets. He had been called to the regimental barracks on the Saturday evening, and had said, if he could, he would give me news by phone, but I was not to try to reach him. Sunday one of the officer's wives who lived in an apartment in the barracks rang me up to say our commanding general had asked her to notify all the women that our troops were ordered out on duty against the rioters. She could not say where they were going, but were there further news she would let us hear. After talking it over, we wives decided the trouble must be out in the factory districts.

Sunday night there was to be an informal dinner at the

Orloffs', who lived some twenty minutes' drive from us. To get there I had to pass up the quay, across the palace square, and down the Grand Morskaia. I telephoned to Princess Orloff, who told me she did not know who would come, but that all was quiet in her neighborhood and she was alone and anxious to have me there for company's sake. Her husband had been on duty with the sovereign for forty-eight hours past, and had accompanied the imperial family to Tsarskoe the night before. Of course she had not heard from him. Wouldn't I come and dine even if we were to be but two? I said I was at home with my babies, had been cut off from all rumors for twenty-four hours. Also that the streets in my quarter seemed normal and I would make the attempt to get to her, reserving the right to turn back in case I encountered obstacles.

I ordered out my small open sleigh, with a single fast trotter and faithful, strong Dimenti, my favorite coachman, thinking this unpretentious vehicle would not attract attention, and the big man and rapid horse would make for safety. On the quay, when I started, there was no sign of life. Then suddenly as we glided onward we saw small fires burning, cavalry horses picketed about them, while the riders sat on the ground warming themselves. Sentinels marched up and down in the biting cold, and here and there in porters' lodges of some palace or ministry buildings hot coffee or soup was being served to half-frozen officers. The soldiers were more comfortable, for their arrangements were made as if at manœuvres and their portable kitchens were at work. No provision was made for the officers. Some sent home, as did my husband, for a fur robe and sandwiches with a bottle of wine, while others took turns enjoying the hospitality of friendly neighboring houses to snatch

sleep. They spent their waking hours seated on the
curbstone by the camp-fires. The thermometer was far
below freezing, the air like crystal, and the river and the
town deadly silent, as I crossed them. Gold domes and
spires of our churches shimmered, and the palaces looked
as proud and splendid as in ordinary times, though a pall
of fear and threat haunted the picture, and it seemed
horribly lonesome to be the only person about. I reached
my destination safely, after being stopped as I passed
the cordon of troops going into the palace's protected
zone and getting out of it again. We sat alone at dinner, Princess Orloff and I, and first one message, then
another, came to us. It was said that a riot was taking
place at the other end of the Grand Morskaia with machine guns trained on the mob. It was then reported
the mob was marching out to Tsarskoe Selo, to attack
the imperial family in their refuge. We were told about
ten other wild rumors which the frightened servants
brought in from their expeditions to the tea-houses in
the neighborhood, or which were telephoned us by friends
shut up alone and as panic-stricken as ourselves.

There was to have been a gala ballet at the Imperial
Opera House that night, and the Orloffs had arranged
their dinner as a prelude to the performance. Of course
we did not think of going, but to see how the public
temper was a footman telephoned to the box-office, and
was told, of course, the performance was off, and the
place was surrounded by sentinels, like most other public buildings. Three times that evening we got authen-
tic news. Once my husband telephoned to me, mainly
to say that I was crazy to be out, but incidentally he
announced the quarter where he was stationed with his
squadron was quiet and that they had not fired a shot
nor seen any rioters in the twelve hours they had been

there near the Marble Palace. I was not to be anxious, though they were ordered to spend the night. He had sent an orderly home for his fur robe and long fur coat and had thus heard of my escapade. I told him I had moved easily, was in plain tailor clothes, and using our small sleigh, and I reassured him as to the wisdom of my expedition; regaled him, also, with the sensational gossip which had reached me.

Then we had a telephone from Prince Orloff, long distance from his apartment in the Imperial Palace at Tsarskoe. He said to his wife the trip out had been easily accomplished; they were well protected by some of the guard regiments stationed at Tsarskoe; that many of the Emperor's suite had rushed there to show their loyalty; several of the court group showed great nervousness when every little while the rumor was served to them that the mob was on the highroad; that the Emperor himself was entirely calm and had shown courage; had not wished to leave the city, but was persuaded "in order to save bloodshed." He said the Empress was very anxious and nervous for the Emperor's safety and that of the Czarévitch and her other children. She had been tranquillized, however, by General Orloff (no relation to Prince Orloff). The general at that time was the dashing young commander of the "Empress's Own Regiment of Lancers of the Guard," and was supposed to have been in love with Her Majesty. He assured her no one should approach the imperial family save over his own dead bódy and those of her twelve hundred devoted lancers! Prince Orloff gave us but an outline of all this over the wire and filled in the blank spaces when I saw him a few days later.

Finally, Prince and Princess Bélosselsky telephoned to their daughter (Princess Orloff was born Bélosselsky) to

say there was serious rioting in their quarter of the sub-
urbs, on the islands, and that if she could put them up
they purposed to move into town, bringing some of their
household, their two daughters-in-law and three grandchildren, abandoning temporarily their Krestovsky palace. Happily the Orloffs' home was large, for the house
party lasted several days, and became a gay picnic, the
danger once over.

I went home that night as I had come, and remained
indoors all day Monday with the children. In the afternoon I had a prolonged visit from Mr. McCormick, the
American Ambassador, accompanied by two or three of
his secretaries. Mr. McCormick had received a cable
from my father, telling him to take care of the children
and me at the embassy, and he had therefore come to
fetch us. I felt sure news had been greatly exaggerated
in transmission to America, and as the danger, if there
had been any for us, was over, I refused to take refuge
as planned. I found Mr. McCormick appreciated the
reason in my argument, and on my promise to let him
know and to change my mind if anything occurred to
make me apprehensive, he said he would cable my family
I was safe and comfortable, and give them the real conditions.

Afterward I heard my parents had been seriously
worried, as the New York papers had talked of Bloody
Sunday in large print and announced the Neva was running red with blood and fifty thousand people had been
butchered! As a matter of fact I have never heard it
said there had been more than two hundred and eighty-
five killed in those days of disorder.

The spring was much quieter in town, but on various
estates grave disorders occurred. Some châteaux were
burned or looted, and all landowners felt anxious. How-

ever, I think in all the cases where looting and burning occurred, there had been landlords absent for years, no longer in touch with their peasants, and frequently a German superintendent had managed the estates and had squeezed the people and exploited them. At one place, that of old Prince K——, there was really a personal hatred of him for his oppressions. His own class greatly blamed him. Most estates in our rich and beautiful province of Poltava had about our experience.

In the early spring there had been some 'threats made against our superintendent, and the latter, feeling rather small, alone against the three villages, had promptly abandoned his post and taken the first train for St. Petersburg "to report." My mother-in-law and husband did not receive the faint-hearted gentleman at all well, and he was dismissed at once from our service.

Naturally the regimental commander would not give my husband leave of absence with the city under martial law, and my brother-in-law was but a boy and at school, so old Auguste started with his own ready consent to go down to Bouromka, talk to the peasants, find out the trouble, and report by telegraph. He went, sent back word everything was all right, and stayed on juggling with the situation till another man was engaged and installed and my husband could go to settle the new superintendent. This was after St. Petersburg was perfectly quiet

When we first reached Bouromka in early summer it looked and seemed about as usual. We enjoyed our stay extremely. I heard from some one of the servants the way our peasants were being won to revolution was by propaganda sheets which announced His Majesty had been captured and thrown into prison by the bureaucrats and landowners, and that he called on his peasants to come to his rescue. This seemed a most eloquent tribute to our humble peasants' loyalty to their ruler!

Late that summer I went abroad with my two children to see my aunt. I was glad of the rest and a change following what had been a most exciting year. Cantacuzène had his autumn leave after the manœuvres, and he joined us. We were motoring in England when he received a telegram ordering him back at once to his regiment in St. Petersburg. From Oxford, where the wire found us, he started within an hour by direct train for the Dover boat, and I was to follow as soon as I could gather up our children and baggage and get accommodations on the North Express. A week later I made the crossing from Dover to Ostend with the two children and their old nurse. My French maid had refused to come along, saying it "was madness to go to a country in revolution," so I abandoned her in London. We found comfortable compartments in our *wagon de luxe*, and with nothing, as I supposed, to disturb us till the changing of trains at the Russian frontier, we settled ourselves, unpacked our bags, had dinner, and the youngsters—aged four-and-a-half and one-and-a-half years—were tucked into their berths.

After passing Liège I was just beginning to undress when a conductor came through the car and stopped at my compartment door. He knocked and I opened.

"Are you the lady going to St. Petersburg whose tickets I verified a little while ago?"

"I am."

"We have just had news at Liège that the Compagnie Intérnationale cannot take passengers through, beyond the Russian frontier, as all trains are stopped there by a strike. The telegram is from Königsberg, ordering us to warn all passengers. Madam can go through to Königs-

berg and wait there, or get off at Berlin. I am sure as
soon as possible service will be continued."

I felt rather dazed by the possibilities. This news
meant probable danger in St. Petersburg—certainly pri-
vations of various kinds; supply of fresh milk cut off.
Little Mike and Baby Bertha were young to face all
that. Yet I wanted to reach home as soon as possible,
for it seemed it was there I had a first duty. If I took
the children to Berlin or Königsberg I would be tied
down by them to a foreign city till life at home became
entirely settled, and I neither wanted to linger in Germany nor did I feel I ought to abandon them anywhere
on the road and push on alone.

Suddenly I had a brilliant idea. I would take our
whole party back to London, pack the children off to
America with my aunt, and then, being foot-loose and
free, I would return to the frontier of Russia and see
what could be arranged about getting through to the
capital. I asked the conductor if I could get off at Aix-
la-Chapelle and get my baggage from the baggage-car?

"That will be in a half-hour, madam, and I don't
know; such a thing was never done before, to get off a
North Express in the middle of the night and desire to
open the baggage-car, which is sealed, and take out baggage which has been checked through to St. Petersburg."

I asked if he could take those trunks through to their
destination.

"No, madam, but Aix is so soon."

I persuaded him that Aix was as good as Berlin to
take off trunks, and that since the train's stopping completely at the Russian frontier made an unusual circum-
stance, the mere fact of another exception to rule was
but a detail.

He went off to get the train-master and bring him to

discuss our situation and my unreasonable ideas. Meanwhile I roused the tired babies and nurse and put them back into their clothes. I was convinced that to return to London was my right programme. The train-master or conductor-in-chief was easy to convert, and soon we were scrambling down into the dark night from our well-warmed, cosey compartments, with our trunks and bags thrown out beside us and the North Express disappearing in the distance.

After a little I began to think I had made a grave mistake. The station was dark and deserted, the night cold, and I had not planned my next steps. I found a man to carry our hand-baggage and asked him about the nearest hotel. He showed me one across the road, said it was not good, but he thought I could get two or three rooms there. I started him, the children, the nurse, and the small baggage over. Then I went to the station-master, who arranged for our tickets to London, gave me the time of departure early next morning, and reversed my trunk-checks so our things would return to London with us. I also sent a telegram to my aunt. I was able to rejoin my little people then with everything prepared for the morrow's trip.

I did not like the looks of the hotel people, still less the rooms' aspect; but the children were too weary from their long day and our trip from London to go farther. I put them in the inside room with nurse, who assured me the sheets of the beds had been used and the wash-stand not cleaned. I was unsympathetic, said as it was after midnight and we must rise at five she could let the children sleep outside the bed-covers on her own travelling-shawls with their little pillows, and that they need not wash till we were on the London Express next morning.

They were all much too sleepy to care long about discomfort, so my advice was taken and quiet soon reigned
in the temporary nursery. I had the sitting-room to
myself, and was very much frightened by the noise and
looks of the place we were in. It had gilt, shoddy furniture and mirrors; dirt everywhere; a door that though
locked, looked as if it would shake down easily under
pressure. Everything in the room was cracked or broken
as if fights were the natural ending of the days' entertainments, and from somewhere in the house came
shouts, oaths, and shuffling, which to my frightened ears
seemed very threatening.

About daylight things quieted down, and though a
few guests started off singing in the street, while others
tumbled up-stairs past my door, banging against it by
accident, no harm came to us. I had spent most of the
night awake, resting on a sofa, with my revolver on the
table by me. It was the only thing I had unpacked.

When the hour to depart came the town was still
asleep, but a push-cart was found and our bags piled on
it and taken to the station. There the head man was
most attentive and put us into our right train, politely
arranging all our baggage, out of pity for our forlorn
state, I think.

Years before I had been with my father at Aix-la-
Chapelle and had kept a charming memory of the pretty
town and its beautiful old church so closely associated
with Charlemagne. Now I was glad to shake its dust
from my feet, and feel I was going back to England.

Once in London everything worked out for the best.
My aunt said, with her sweetness of old days, she was
delighted to have us back for a little, and that she would
take the children safely to my parents in America. The
latter cabled they would gladly keep their grandchildren

for me. My husband wired his consent to my proposed plan. So one morning early I parted from the little people. My aunt and the babies started for a steamer at Southampton, I for the Dover-Ostend boat to attempt again the trip home—alone this time, with baggage much reduced, and one small trunk so packed that in case trains were not running in Russia, I could arrange to travel by troika sleigh from Germany to St. Petersburg, leaving my heavier trunks at our frontier station.

At Liège I was told again no trains were going through. At Berlin the news was still unchanged, but I felt encouraged, anyhow, for the American Ambassador, Mr. George Meyer, and his secretary, Mr. Miles, going to St. Petersburg, got on my car. I knew I would have protection and company, whatever happened. As we neared Russia the train emptied rapidly. Finally I think there were no travellers but Mr. Meyer's party, myself, a nice young man I had met casually in society in St. Petersburg, and one other stranger. At the frontier the embassy chasseur in uniform met the Ambassador.

I had been asked by my husband to bring him back a new revolver, also one for a friend of his; this besides my own. I was in grave doubt as to how to pass my purchases into a country where both arms and ammunition were recently forbidden. Mr. Meyer solved the problem.

"What have you in that case?" he asked, pointing, and I answered that case held my jewels.

"Well, suppose you confide your finery to me. I can pass it by the customs, since it isn't dutiable, with a good conscience. Before handing it over, if you want to pack cartridges in your jewel-case, I don't see who can prevent it."

I did this on his hint, and when we got out to change

trains Mr. Miles politely helped carry my valuables, choosing that particular box, so my dangerous weapons actually entered Russia in another's hands.

Once the frontier was crossed our advance was mere chance. One train had started ahead of us and had reached Gatchina without mishap, from which place the travellers had gone to St. Petersburg by sleigh. We expected to be stopped at any station and to take this same means for the final stages of our journey—so we had our rugs and bags strapped and ready. At each station, however, some official would come through the train and announce that since we were still safe, we would push on to the next town. We would thank our good angels for their protection and would take up our cards or books again, postponing anxiety.

The dining-car, of which we had taken possession, was cheerful, and on the whole the journey passed easily, with just enough of the unexpected to make it constantly interesting. Triumphantly we rolled into the big station at the capital, and felt we were the first to open traffic again on the full length of the route.

My husband came to meet me, glad to think the children were in safety and that I had returned home for the winter in spite of the troubles, which still kept the city's inhabitants on the alert. There had been a general strike on and off for two or three weeks. Amateur volunteers had been sorting and delivering mails, and even the telegraph had not functioned for a time. Now things were quieter, but no one professed to know what the morrow might bring forth. The winter promised to be interesting.

When disorder had been calmed in St. Petersburg and elsewhere, and the iron discipline of Trepoff as dictator was relaxed, a new government established itself. It brought a notable change on the landowners' estates and to the peasants' homes; at least this was so in our province, south of Kieff, where I saw events develop. The Grand Duke Nicolas was put in command of the troops in and around St. Petersburg; and though he stood for discipline, and maintained it in the city, he was also just and generous, a Russian among Russians, and understood his charge and responsibility. He lived up to his duties with the same calm, intelligent grasp of the subject which he showed later as commander-in-chief during the World War. He expressed confidence and showed it always.

Unused to his ways, the secret police suffered a long-drawn-out agony in their efforts to guard his person. They annoyed him extremely by their ceremony, and finally, I was told, the Grand Duke made a bargain with them. He offered on his side to give up all pleasures—not go to the theatres, or operas, or his club—but whenever his duties took him on inspection tours, or to Tsarskoe to report to the sovereign, or elsewhere for his work, they—the police—on their side should not pester him with their warnings, advice, care, and attention. If they could guard him without his knowing it, they might have this pleasure. I fancy after that the secret police were led a life of it by the fearless and energetic Grand Duke, though he did give up his club and his evening engagements for a time; but he worked all day, and they were always tracing or trying to trace his movements.

I know once he had come to pay me a call at tea-time, and about half an hour after his departure police headquarters rang me up.

"Has the Grand Duke left your house since long, Your Highness?"

"About half an hour ago," I replied.

"And he did not mention where he was going?"

"No."

"We heard from some one at the palace he was going to you, and we had your street and home guarded, but now he has again escaped our care, and yet we are responsible for his safety, and don't know where to find him."

The voice sounded desperate. I inferred the grand personage—for the chief was that in every sense—probably was not momentarily as popular with this harassed official as he was with his troops and the people on the streets.

His splendid figure and eagle face were becoming a well-known and welcome sight as he moved about the city unostentatiously in an equipage from the club cab-stand, or his own unpretentious sleigh with a beautiful single fast trotter drawing it.

Another figure growing popular in St. Petersburg at this time was that of Stolypin. He had been made "President of the Council of Ministers" and had been allowed to form a cabinet largely of men who were liberal.

After himself, the most noticeable personality in this group was Krivaschène. Newly named Minister of Agriculture, he possessed intellect and character, knew his duties to perfection, and the peasants' psychology as well. Speaking no language but Russian, even in society, this man of rugged and brusque ways made a great hit, and was soon a much-invited and highly honored guest at many a great dinner, where on serious subjects he led the conversation, and in frivolous ones looked on and listened in silent study of society's queer ways. He was a very powerful person, this Krivaschène, with many natural gifts of brain, but little culture. A self-made man, reliable, loyal, and patriotic, he rapidly won general confidence. He had none of Witte's affectations and was much better liked, I think.

Stolypin also had a nature and a physique which were impressive; tall and well-bred-looking, he did not, however, seem cosmopolitan. Somehow I thought him a little queer in full dress, though never clumsy, undignified, or shy. He was of noble birth and great culture, and knew his nation well. He was extremely interesting on many subjects, especially concerning Russia, and if one could sit and converse quietly with him at the dinner-table or elsewhere he had immense charm and magnetism. I do not know of any one in the Duma or the government who had his reputation for eloquence. Somehow his type made me think of Lincoln, or what my conception of Lincoln was, and I was always delighted to be at a party with him, because it generally meant a pleasant half-hour of his company in some corner where he and one or two others would sit apart from the crowd. He loved music, and when a function was being arranged in his honor, usually a good programme of music was a part of it.

He had a wife and children, to whom he was devoted, but they were not comparable to him in personality. Every day one heard of this modest man's real accomplishment in work. He linked up the Duma with the government, drawing out the best each held, and though parliament at times. gave him disillusions, he attributed the mistakes of that body to its inexperience, and was never ruffled by opposition or lack of support.

With Krivaschène's co-operation Stolypin thought out and introduced the land reforms, which were to be tried in a few of our Little Russian provinces, and, if found satisfactory, were to be carried out all over the Russian Empire. Each peasant individually was to own and keep his land, do with it as he pleased, and get the full benefit of the work and care he put into it. The old system of land being held in common by the villagers, with the portions transferred year by year to different hands for cultivation, had produced discouragement, laziness, run-down crops—for the good-for-nothing man did as little as possible, while the sober, hard worker, if he fertilized and ploughed his share deeply, saw the square he had improved given away in a season, his good grain sold, mixed with the other's bad, and no result to him but his own weariness. The sense of proprietorship, however, brought energy, ambition, and pride. In turn these put the people forward so rapidly, that within a few years we saw our peasant farmers owning three hundred and more acres bought from their own group or from us; soon good machinery and animals were purchased, they grew grain as fine as ours and sold at the same prices.

Stolypin never had the Emperor's friendship. I think it was represented to His Majesty that much which was being done, though conducive to law and order and an increase of prosperity in the realm, was not exactly in line with old autocratic ideals. Therefore the sovereign was told he should not too much encourage this man's enthusiasms. Apparently, however, Stolypin took such difficulties calmly. He faced in the same way the various attacks of which he was a victim now and then in the parliament, and sometimes even from his collaborators. Danger lurked for him at every turn from the assassin. Sipiaguin, Plehve, and the Grand Duke Serge had been killed, and unsuccessful attempts had been made on several others. Stolypin's house was blown up and one of his daughters severely wounded, and a second effort was made without the man's temper or nerves being ruffled or his calm service to Emperor and country changed.

In Kieff finally he met his end, through a revolver-shot fired into his stomach by a young degenerate, paid for the task. Stolypin remained tranquil and serene during several long days of agony, when no hope of recovery could be held out. He sent for his family and quietly prepared for death. The conduct of the sovereigns at that time was looked on with surprise, for beyond a first formal message of sympathy and another final written word of condolence no notice was taken by them of his death. It was said by some the Empress feared to have her husband either see Stolypin after the shooting or to have His Majesty attend the great man's funeral; others said it was by request of the secret police that the Emperor avoided all this. No one knew, but a bad impression of weakness or lack of appreciation was rather general.

Politically, through the ebb and flow of opinion, we felt Russia was moving forward, and that in a few short years the Emperor would give a constitution, for it would be demanded of him by healthy elements in the nation. They sanely waited, worked for progress, and were not mere degenerates or hasty visionaries. Parties were forming of some substance in the second and third "Duma," and were learning to handle themselves. Russia was growing fast. The occasional step backward or to the side was resented, though many such occurred, for a strong retrograde group was always ready to stem the tide. Of this party the Empress was supposed generally to be the protectress, and her influence with the Emperor was used always in that direction. Old Gorymékin was her protégé, and there were others than he behind the scenes, who used Her Majesty's prestige to cover

their machinations, I believe largely without her knowledge. She chose her companions, unfortunately, from
the worst people within reach, and deliberately began—
by Madame Wiroboff's advice—to get rid of all the
decent, self-respecting, loyal people who had been about
her at first. The Emperor by degrees lived more and
more strictly in his family circle, with only two or three
attendants with whom the Empress liked to talk. Even
his aides, his secretary, and Prince Orloff, who for years
had been his friend, comrade, and confidant, were being
attacked. The struggle was on, and was growing more
and more marked at court each month.

There was criticism, rivalry, and much personal bitterness, yet evolution or even revolution (a "palace revolution") was often spoken of by those from whom I
should never have expected it. It was a new atmosphere altogether which we lived in.

CHAPTER XIV

CALM BEFORE THE STORM

O UR own life had been changing somewhat. We had made two delightful trips to America, visits long to be remembered for their happy reunions and crowding pleasures. We went in 1906, and made a beautiful trip with my lovely aunt and my favorite cousins through the American Far West. We visited Chicago and Washington, and stayed on quaint Governor's Island, where my father was in command, saw all the old friends in New York or elsewhere, and enjoyed many a country house party. When we returned to Russia we took the children with us. "The Revolution" was over by the beginning of 1907.

Just then Cantacuzène was named to the staff of the Grand Duke Nicolas, and a companionship of service began which during seven or eight years was a constant happiness to my husband. Born of perfect understanding on both sides; a paternal loyal affection on the part of the splendid chief which never wavered, and an absolute devotion and enthusiastic admiration on my husband's part, relations were always reliable and appreciative. All these qualities on both sides during times of stress were required, for the Grand Duke was sincere, and though ready to lay down his life for his kinsman, the sovereign, he was very anxious, naturally, that the influences around the Empress should not do her husband harm, either in fact or in public judgment.

The Grand Duke, suspicious of the Germans, feared the Kaiser's caresses for our ruler and country. He was anxious to get fortresses and cannon established on our western frontier, and he pressed preparation, but with little or no effect. He threw his influence into breaking up the compact which Wilhelm had engineered during the latter's visit to our Emperor's yacht in Finnish waters. I do not think our chief ever trusted or liked Count Witte. He never said this that I know of, but it was considered a fact, and Mr. E. J. Dillon's description of these years when he was Count Witte's confidential aid would seem to prove this theory of mine.

However, at the time of the "Willy-Nicky correspondence" the Grand Duke loyally worked with Witte, and helped the latter straighten out the political tangle, and our sovereign to regain his foothold. I believe my husband's chief never took part in politics after that. He studiously avoided them, and demanded the same attitude from his court; but every one knew he stood for law, order, and liberality, and that he was pro-Russian first and, after that, pro-Ally—never pro-German. Also it was known the Grand Duchess Anastasia, his wife, was a Slav princess by birth—a Montenegrin—educated in St. Petersburg and thoroughly anti-German. She had been one of the Empress's intimates, only to be suddenly and rather roughly dropped—no one quite found out why, though every one spent much time guessing.

It required some tact and discretion to live in our court atmosphere with its various currents, but this was less difficult with Russians than it would have been elsewhere, as society was simpler among them than among most other peoples, and unless one were particularly clumsy in criticising, one was allowed to live in peace and think what one pleased.

Through those years I began to feel a great interest in politics and see a good deal of the diplomats and cabinet members. Mr. Izvolsky, the Minister of Foreign Affairs, and his wife were very sympathetic, and their salon, where I went often, always seemed full of interesting people.

Orloff's palace was growing more and more a political centre, too, and every one went there to get some message to or from the Emperor, knowing Orloff's unassailable honesty, as well as his heart of gold and excellent judgment. Both he and his attractive wife were intimate friends of ours, and I have them to thank for much of my pleasure in my Russian life.

There were a number of other houses with hospitable rooms, where conversation was a delight. Every one was gay at gatherings, whatever his anxieties outside might be. So living in our group was very agreeable during those years. There were a number of diplomats who took part in our pastimes. Hardinge, the British Ambassador, with his winning wife, had a host of friends. He was followed by Sir Arthur Nicolson, most popular and astute of suave diplomatists. A really great American, Mr. Rockhill, before whom the world stood at attention, was admittedly the most important foreigner in St. Petersburg during his stay there. Another American who made an admirable position for himself was Mr. Meyer. Both men had extremely attractive wives.

The capable and brilliant O'Beirne, one of Russia's best and ablest friends, was part of our inside circle, winning every one's affection incidentally to doing his work well. When years later he was again coming out on a war-time mission with Lord Kitchener and was drowned, all St. Petersburg society sincerely mourned the man, who had served his own country, yet had been a loyal and firm friend of Russia, too. There were a number of others we saw often, but in more formal manner, for our path lay among the ultra-Russian groups, and my husband's service was altogether military. My tastes also inclined me most toward the people of my adopted country, whom I loved more and more the longer I lived among them. We spent nearly all our time within our home country, largely because of my husband's duties and interests, and because of our growing family. In November, 1908, our third child was born, a golden-haired baby, the first Cantacuzène to have blue eyes.

That same year a new note was introduced into our lives by our buying a pretty cottage at the great military camp of Krasnoe Selo, within an hour's driving distance of the capital. We rebuilt this home, and made it very attractive with furniture and ornaments of generations ago, keeping it all in one period. Arranging the buildings and the little garden which surrounded them was our greatest joy during the next six years. It grew to be the most delicious corner in all the country around, we thought, and it drew our friends from the environs. The grounds especially were very pretty. Planned with infinite care, we had given them a simple character, with flowers from the woods and fields, established and made welcome. I took particular pride in my roses and sweet peas, and our production of these was wonderful for so small a place. An old-fashioned summer-house formed by the branches of living, graceful beech-trees, inter-laced, held my tea-table, and each day a pleasant group gathered there for a restful hour after drilling. The peace of the sweeping, soft-green background, the witch-ery of perfume and the splendor of our view out over the plains toward the proud capital of Russia, with its gilded domes and spires, closing in with our horizon of the forests and the blue Gulf of Finland was ideal. Our visitors asked how this gem of calm prosperity could be kept up in a military camp. They came often to see us from Peterhof, where the court sojourned in summer, or from Tsarskoe and St. Petersburg itself. We grew to love this home best of any we owned, and our life was always happy there.

In the mornings the children and I rode, and my young companions were as expert at this sport as they were at various others. I felt very proud to show them off, and to have them with us riding through woods and over fields. My afternoon was spent pottering about the garden, while in the evenings, if we did not go out, we generally received in most informal fashion such of our friends or comrades as dropped in on us. My husband's duties with the Grand Duke kept him extremely occupied, and to us the five or six years previous to the World War represented the best part of our lives.

In 1910 we made another trip to the United States, which was delightful, when we spent four months with the family and old friends, filling our time with delightful excursions again. We journeyed down to Florida and fell in love with that part of America because of its sunny, turquoise sky and sea, and smiling landscapes. For Christmas in Chicago, twenty-odd of his descendants gathered round the ninety-year-old patriarch, my Grandfather Honoré.

It was pleasant to find my father in the full flush of his career, settled at Governor's Island and, having made a fine fighting record, still active and doing good in his patriotic way. Since the Spanish-American War he had not left the army, and was thoroughly satisfied in 1910 at the head of his profession, holding the confidence and love of all who worked with him or watched his activities. The final fruition was worthy of the fine promise of earlier days, and at sixty he was hale, hearty, able, and still keen.

My mother also felt her life to be most enjoyable, and had hosts of friends who surrounded her. She apparently took as much pleasure as ever in life.

After this visit home I never again saw my father alive. Within a year he showed the first signs of the illness that was to claim him as its victim, and through the winter of 1911–12 he went on with his duties, knowing he was doomed. No realization of his danger came to my mother apparently until it was too late to let me hear, so it chanced that returning home from an official party in St. Petersburg one night I found a cable asking me to go across the sea because my father asked for me, and during the preparations for that distressing journey another wire followed, saying that my father had died suddenly. One has to know the misery of such a departure and trip to realize what it means to be too late, and to miss the last words or last smile of one who was deeply loved. Never can I forget my journey: the hideous travelling through Russian snow and over the bleak plains of East Prussia. Only semiconscious of what I did, I felt the kind acts of my family and friends who helped me to get off and the kind hands that did what they could to ease pain or smooth difficulties away before me.

I realized little by little through my numbness their presence, their silent, gentle sympathy and efforts, and how much I had grown to belong to my adopted countrymen, and they to me. All through the voyage my devoted old maid was producing new books or papers, or a new dainty with which to tempt my appetite, and it was always by the wish and the generous attention of some friend left in St. Petersburg that she was acting. They had supplied and instructed her in advance.

The landing in New York and the heart-break of the

funeral, the touching demonstrations of admiration and love for my father by his comrades and his soldiers, by the old policemen who had served under him, and by the city of New York, won our gratitude and moved us deeply. His body was taken through the city's thoroughfares, lined with vast crowds; the latter stood with heads bared, and bowed, wiping their eyes as the gun-carriage passed, draped with the flag he had served since his thirteenth year in one capacity or another. We went up the Hudson, taking this devoted son past the place where his father lay, to another above it and equally beautiful, on the great river.

At West Point our pilgrimage ended. There, amid his comrades of old school and army life we deposited this son of the academy, who had been so devoted to his school and had lived by its high traditions. After taps sounded we left my father to his long rest from the great suffering he had borne without complaint, the worthy follower of his sire in that as in all else.

It was hard to accept the situation. That the post at the head of our family was empty and the strong man gone, seemed unbelievable. My mother was broken up, her life changed in every way, and a little relaxation from the shock and strain of the preceding weeks seemed desirable. She was prevailed upon to accompany me abroad, and within a few days after the funeral we sailed for Russia, where I had many duties claiming my early return.

For two years I led a life of complete retirement. The children, growing older, needed my attention, and I stayed much at home, with enough to fill my days in the round of home duties and such quiet pleasures as music at concert or opera gave me. The ever-increasing circle around my tea-table, where friends gathered to talk informally on all sorts of subjects, still retained its interest in my eyes, and the conversation never lagged, nor was it dull, for in that varied group many of our strongest men and most attractive women figured.

Time passed and I felt that not only was I studying Russia and its people, but that through these clever minds, even at play, as they were, I was learning much of the world at large with its political questions. Always it seemed to me the Russian mentality and attitude were generous, large, and strong. I grew also to love our peasants and the patriots who strove to lead them forward and to place our nation higher for its ideals and ambitions than any other one in Europe, were splendid. It seemed to me we had a great future, and that at last the liberals more and more were moving toward an evolution of the right sort; that it would be but a short span of years until parliament would have strong legislative rights, and a responsible ministry would answer for mistakes or be acclaimed for its creative efforts.

Many men talked of a constitution. It was well known that when certain of the ministers who most insistently advocated reform went to the Emperor with reports and suggestions His Majesty listened with sighs of deep sympathy; and also that in spite of Madame Wiroboff's efforts certain honest courtiers held their influence. The Empress was constantly ill, and she kept around her a strange crowd, who spent their time flattering her and feeding her with gossip and charlatanism. She was drifting away, living solely for her children and for her occult group of friends.

There was no doubt in any one's mind as to Madame Wiroboff's relations with Rasputin, or of the fact that she had invented him and declared him to be a miracle-worker, thus installing him as a sort of back-stairs prophet.

His prayers were said to do the Empress good, and also
the young heir to the throne, who was an invalid. Madame Wiroboff had persuaded Her Majesty that she herself could not survive being separated a day from the
mistress she adored. Also she was convincing about
Rasputin. He was devoted, and a simple peasant; it
would please the people of Russia to know a representative of theirs stood high at court; without knowledge, but
by the pure, real faith which moved him, Rasputin had
power from on high to prophesy and heal, and his inter-
vention averted the nervous pains from which the Empress had suffered since so long.   The latter was brought
firmly to believe all this, and the fact, continuously re-
told, that her son was stronger and would eventually
recover perfect health by their private saint's constant
intercession and watchful care, made the distraught Empress a victim, yielding more and more to the foul
influence of the plotters.

As she gained power and dared to show it, Madame
Wiroboff made a few allies in court circles, all among the
worst elements, who either feared her or hoped to share
the spoils she gained.   Many of us realized the wretch
was doing harm, but how much no one could calculate.
We saw her creeping into the intimacy of the sovereigns,
but she played the fool extremely well and was never
suspected of political ambitions.   We discovered early in
the game that she wanted to seem a figure in the court.
Many people shrugged their shoulders and decided to
accept punishment for ignoring the favorite's pretensions
if necessary.   Many would not call on her.   She and I
spoke when we met, but the acquaintance went no further, for to me, as to many others, Madame Wiroboff
was a repulsive creature.

As for Rasputin, I never met or saw him. Coarse,

vicious, hideous, he was known to be, yet he exerted an unholy fascination on a number of women, who crowded about him and composed his clientèle. He drank and in general lived brutally, though without other plans than to be materially enriched, or to have warmth and finery and food.

Those who had known the Empress enough to realize her culture, were much distressed to see her so badly advised, but there seemed nothing to prevent her being exploited. Several devoted subjects tried to warn her. It was no use, for she had chosen her path, and remained unmoved by any pleadings. She put aside all loyal friends of her best interests, who showed their courage at the price of her favor, and she held more firmly to her occult group, while her influence over her husband grew and grew, till by degrees he lost familiar contact with those who might have given him real enlightenment and truth. Still she held to Prince Orloff, and believed rightly in his honor and devotion. The latter's tact and power were constantly used to stem the intrigues at our court.

Early in 1913 was celebrated the three hundredth anniversary of the Romanoffs' accession to the throne, and in the pageants connected with all this the court lived over again the acclamations and enthusiasm of the dynasty's early days, when for his virtue, intelligence, and grace young Michael Romanoff had been chosen by his people for their sovereign, and was fetched out from the retirement of the convent in which he was being brought up by his good mother. The great deeds of our imperial family through three centuries of history were recalled in tableaux, song, and ceremony. An official reception occurred at the Winter Palace, when each guest in national costume was given a golden insignia to mark

THE PERSIAN COSTUME DANCE IN ST. PETERSBURG DURING THE 1914 CARNIVAL.

his or her attendance that day at court. Deputations came from every province, and from vassal states, with gifts for the sovereigns, and these received with all due pomp, surrounded by the imperial family and their attendants.

Never had the palace looked more magnificent, nor had the power of the ruler seemed more assured. The city of St. Petersburg was officially dressed in gayest bunting, while at night the imperial crowns or monograms, with emblems of state designed in colored lamps, made vast decorations which lighted up the streets. Two special gala fêtes were given. One, offered by the nobles of the capital to their Emperor, was a ball in the "Council Hall of the Nobility." The magnificent white marble ballroom dated back a century at least, and was wonderful that night. All of us had put on our best clothes and jewels, to do honor to the imperial guests of the evening.

The entrance of the sovereigns was very impressive. They were met by the "Grand Marshal of the Nobility of the Province of St. Petersburg" at the outside entrance. He offered his arm to the Empress-Mother, who on this occasion had graciously accepted the invitation. Prince Soltykoff, who had the dignity and manner as well as the blood of the boyars—aristocrats—of ancient Muscovy, handed Her Majesty, always graceful, through the "polonaise" which ceremoniously opened the ball. They were the most stared at and admired couple in the room, and the old Empress's popular figure, still slim and elegant, was at its best in walking. She smiled at her subjects, and they became her captives anew and swore renewed allegiance under their breath to this ever-attractive woman.

The Emperor in full uniform looked uncomfortable

and intimidated. He walked as rapidly as possible, in military fashion, as if anxious to get the ceremony over and hating to be stared at. It was somewhat of an effort for the beautiful young Countess Koutousoff in her long robes to keep up with His Majesty's quick stride, which was not in time with the music. She spoke to him, and her partner replied timidly to the wife of the "Marshal of the Capital City's Nobility"; then he smiled, made a determined effort to slow down, and did his duty. When he saw the bows and curtseys on each side as he passed down the lines of nobles with this radiant partner at his side, he distributed various shy, small nods. It was evident the whole thing was an effort to his nature, for in the earnest, deep-gray eyes there was an eloquent appeal; and as the marching neared its end he seemed relieved; then, as the trial ended, he bowed and relinquished the hand of his fair lady partner with a grateful sigh.

As for the younger Empress, she had had one of her habitual attacks some days before and was still suffering, it was said; but she did her part in the procession. The "Vice-Marshal of the Nobility of the Province" gave her his arm. She towered above the little man in her splendor. Diamonds and pearls glittered on her head and neck and dress, making her, as always, a gorgeous statue. Her eyes were stern and sad, her mouth made a straight, hard line, drawn in physical distress and mental rebellion at the necessity of carrying through a ceremony she disliked, amid a court and nobility she did not care for. Not once did she smile nor look to right or left, though at intervals, quite regularly, she inclined her head to the throng which pressed forward. Every one said, coldly enough, that Her Majesty was looking very handsome. When she finished her turn she settled on a chair at once and remained silent and forbidding, with a tragic face, all through the entertainment.

It was a scene well worth even her admiration that we gazed out on. The room, three stories high and spacious in proportion, the myriad crowd that filled it with their color as they moved in rhythm to the lovely waltz music, was perfect. The vast columns of cream marble, wound with garlands, the rich red velvet of draperies, the golden woodwork, the bronze and crystal of chandeliers or high candelabra, made a picture difficult to rival, and one felt the proud nobles of the empire had done their best and might well be proud of their success.

A few nights later there was a gala performance at the opera-house. This time the sovereigns were hosts to their court and to the government officials. And again all those present wore their best, a different best from the ball splendor of the earlier function. In the orchestra seats sat venerable senators and members of the Council of the Empire in court uniforms of green and red and black, much trimmed with gold embroidery. Here and there some gorgeous ex-commander of an imperial guard regiment stood in military uniform of equal brilliancy, carried with elegance and ease. In the loges, tier on tier, sat cabinet officials and their wives, glistening with decorations, all the ladies of the court in their fine jewels, and men whose rank or service brought them there by right. The imperial family filled the large boxes. In the centre box of the house sat Their Majesties. When they entered they were acclaimed with long cheers, echoing to the roof, and with the national anthem, and again, as on the previous occasion, each responded as prompted by his or her nature.

Around the sovereigns sat the members of the imperial family, according to his or her rank. To every Grand

Duchess in the imperial circle was attached a page that night, brought out by ancient etiquette from the page corps to do his service. Chosen for their fine physique and handsome features, these youngsters, in high boots and tight trousers, their uniform coats bedecked with gay gold lace, stood at attention, and held the fur scarf or delicate lace fan of the various Romanoff ladies. To the background they added rich notes of color. The house had never had a grander evening. The composition of the audience and the performance on the stage rivalled one another in their perfection. Parts were given of several patriotic operas. "A Life for the Czar" was played and sung, and, if I remember rightly, Chaliapin gave the first act of "Boris Goudanoff." The national anthem and the wild applause and cheers were oft repeated before the sovereigns retired and the party broke up. This performance was followed by a supper and ball at the palace of the Grand Duchess Xénia, the Emperor's sister.

After assisting at the week's rejoicings, the Emperor, his wife, and children retired again to Tsarskoe, and we were left with the impression of a fairy dream, which had lasted a few days and had renewed our historical loyalty for the throne and its occupants. It was whispered about, however, that the Emperor and Empress had not shown themselves sufficiently to the simple people of their capital and had made no effort to capture the love and admiration of their humbler subjects; and as a reason for this neglect, it was added that since the demonstrations of 1905 and 1906 the sovereigns hated the populace and had no desire to win the love of St. Petersburg's citizens, but wished, on the contrary, to keep as far as possible from dangerous crowds. It seemed an unfortunate attitude to many of us, and regret was expressed on all sides they had been so badly advised.

A GROUP OF WAR WORKERS IN PETROGRAD, INCLUDING THE MOTHER OF THE CZAR.

The next winter, 1913-14, I had laid aside my mourning finally, but expected to take little part in what promised to be a gay season. Fate decreed otherwise, however, and that last winter before the war I passed in dancing. It was a last fling before the breaking down of all that had made the frame of our brilliant youth and life, and it seems as if we all instinctively felt we must eat, drink, and be merry, in fear of the destruction due with the morrow's dawn.

I had meant to continue in the quiet habits of life which I had formed during my two years of mourning, but St. Petersburg's celebrations for our set continued for some time around Prince Alexander of Battenberg, who came out to stay with the Grand Duke and Grand Duchess Kyril. Perforce entertainments given to amuse this guest, whom we had all known and liked during a previous visit, drew us back to the ways of youth again. Fête followed fête, and the season culminated in a carnival week such as St. Petersburg had not seen since before the Japanese War. We enjoyed it and forgot to be old.

Among other things, a beautiful Persian dance was organized, was practised and danced under the orders of a ballet-master, as the central performance at a costume ball. A few nights later this was repeated, after dinner, at the home of the Grand Duchess Marie. It was to amuse the Empress-Mother, who wanted to see her nieces and nephews, with their friends, masquerade. The clothes and jewels in the Oriental forms and colors were very striking and becoming, and the men and women who took part wore all their finery. Our spirits were high, both at the rehearsals and on the evening of the gay show, and the dance's general effect was really beautiful, near enough the gorgeous East to be quite satisfactory.

Possibly Persians would not have realized we aimed to look like them, however!

That year, as usual, the sovereigns and their court spent the spring in pleasant comfort at Livadia, on the coast of the Black Sea. Both the Emperor and the Empress were fond of this their personal home, and, with the excuse of Her Majesty's health and that of the Czarévitch, they lengthened their sojourn in the south each year. Many government functionaries rushed back and forth from the capital to Yalta, complaining of the long journey, but very glad, really, of the possibility of visiting, as part of their service, the pretty city lying at the foot of the hill with its white palace and magic gardens.

That year the Crimea had attracted many members of the imperial family, who—each with his suite—were housed in their villas along the shore. The Emperor worked part of each day with his government officials, walked with the gentlemen of his suite over many miles of pathway planned for his enjoyment across the hills, and lived otherwise a quiet life.

The Empress, save for her hours in her family circle, gave herself up to the companionship of Madame Wiroboff and the latter's friends, who were her intimates. Daily Her Majesty drove through the imperial park in her victoria, with Madame Wiroboff beside her, and Rasputin a third in the party. At last some one at court told the Emperor of these expeditions, and persuaded him to influence his wife, as gossip was busy with her name. After various discussions the Empress consented to modify her programme, after which she started out on her drive with only Madame Wiroboff in attendance. But Rasputin was waiting at some point in the route chosen, was picked up, and had his drive till they dropped him again only at the last moment, before the palace door was reached. Guards' and courtiers' tongues wagged as much as ever.

Both Madame Wiroboff and her occult partner were growing arrogant in 1914 toward the members of the court, whenever their imperial protectress was not watching; but in her presence they always played modest rôles and represented themselves to be a pair of humble saints who spent their time in prayer. Officials were approached by them for favors, however, and in their petitions covert threats were felt.

This scandal was an underlying note of warning in those weeks of the imperial family's last residence in their Crimean palace. On the surface everything went smoothly, and many a gay beauty held her small court in the colored villas or in the salons and loggias of the old Hotel de Russie. No one had an anxious thought for the future, though the clouds were gathering rapidly overhead!

At the end of the spring the sovereigns and their followers returned north, and they scarcely had time to settle for the summer at Peterhof, make preparations and receive the President of the French Republic, who was scheduled for an official visit of about a week's duration, when the murder at Sarajévo suddenly startled all Europe. The menace of its touching us was not sufficiently felt, however, to cause any change of programme, so the feasting and receptions, the reviews and gala theatres to honor our ally and our guest were continued, in full security that all was well. At last the visit ended and Poincaré sailed away. Then we realized quite suddenly that we had war to face and at short notice.

Someone recalled to everyone else's notice how during the week's festivities the face of Admiral Heinze had been hideous and his behavior strained.   The truth was realized too late about this representative of the Kaiser attached to our Emperor's person.   War came, and in the history of Russia a chapter full of the picturesque was closed and a new one begun, in glory and in pain, which was to lead to crucifixion and martyrdom for our whole nation.

CPSIA information can be obtained
at www.ICGtesting.com
Printed in the USA
BVHW081236300919
559784BV00001B/40/P